AUTHENTIC INDIVIDUALISM

*A Guide for Reclaiming the Best of
America's Heritage*

R. Philip Brown

University Press of America, Inc.
Lanham • New York • London

Copyright © 1996 by
University Press of America,® Inc.
4720 Boston Way
Lanham, Maryland 20706

3 Henrietta Street
London, WC2E 8LU England

Library of Congress Cataloging-in-Publication Data

Brown, R. Philip
Authentic individualism : a guide for reclaiming the best of America's
heritage / R. Philip Brown.
p.   cm.
Includes bibliographical references and index.
1. Individualism. 2. United States--Civilization--Philosophy. I.
Title.
B824.B76   1995   141'.4'0973--dc20   95-39964 CIP

ISBN 0-7618-0151-0 (cloth: alk. ppr.)
ISBN 0-7618-0152-9 (pbk: alk. ppr.)

Dedication

To Ruth, Nancy, Patricia, Arick, Stephanie, and all of the other teachers in my life.

Contents

Foreword

Does liberty and equality include fraternity? Even if it did in other times and places, is modern America a place where communal values should take precedence over individual ones? What is individualism anyway? Am I my brother's keeper or just my brother's brother? To what extent do I bear moral responsibility for my brother's well being? What did Gouvener Morris mean when he wrote "promote the general Welfare" into the preamble of the Constitution? Could the founders possibly have anticipated what general welfare legislation means today in terms of funds expended and the difficulties of administering them efficiently?

Such questions as these are high on the political agenda of Americans today. Elections are won and lost in reference to them. Propagandists on all sides appeal to visceral understandings of what individualism means and the extent to which I ought to share what I have with you. Do I have a moral obligation to share? If it were not for my individual achievements--the money I earn from the sweat of my brow--there would be no largess to share with the socially and economically disinherited. Some individual goose must lay the golden eggs of capitalism or there would be nothing for the government to tax and redistribute in the name of social justice. I think I am a goose. In one of the oldest doctrines of American jurisprudence, a corporation is also an individual, which makes American business a goose. We geese are also entitled to social justice.

The emotional power of this debate demands a closer look at what individualism is and what its limits are. The book before us renders such a service. Its particular value is that it starts at the beginning, in history and thought, and thoroughly and suggestively explores not only the boundaries of authentic individualism but the implications of the book's encyclopedic learning for new paradigms of organization theory and administrative leadership. The author acts as an intellectual guide who touches and pays respect to every major theory of individualism, and in the end develops his own model of authenticity. He earns the right to do so.

Readers not conversant with the place of individualism in American political theory might be reminded that American theorists have always seen the individual as a rational, self-interested person, entitled by nature to certain rights such as life, liberty, and property. Governments are created by contracts among such individuals to secure their rights and maintain order. Otherwise governments are limited in their powers. Rights, contracts, and limits to government are all concepts that suggest a major role for law in organizing social institutions. Indeed, the nature and extent of individual rights are determined and redetermined in each term of the Supreme Court of the United States. Do my rights include the right to privacy? Do I have a constitutional right to bear arms? Do I have the right to insist on politically correct speech? We live in a rights oriented society.

Inherent in the American view of individualism is the assumption that private striving to fulfill needs is the best means of distributing the rewards of economic and social life. Our Puritan forebears made it plain that striving itself was both a public and a private good. Let us sail across the North Atlantic into the teeth of a west wind, they said in the great Puritan migration of 1630. Sailing south to the Canaries and across on the trades can only make us weaker. We must strive. The Holy Commonwealth will be built on hard work and courage and perseverance so that the grace of God may abound. Though the theological origins of blessed work have been forgotten in secular America, the motive force of earn-what-you-get has not.

There has never been a serious challenge to individualism as the dominant interpretation of the written and unwritten American Constitution. The Bill of Rights saw to that. In terms of the classification systems of political theory in the West, the individualism that Americans prize is but one aspect of liberalism. So ingrained is liberalism in our national life that such tensions as exist within its consensus are mostly over the priorities of the natural rights of individuals. Are property rights paramount, with emphasis on participation, justice, and change? Even though all liberals agree that property rights are important, some are willing to reduce the priority assigned to property in favor of human rights. Despite the bitter conflict that such a debate sometimes engenders, the actual differences between liberals and conservatives in American politics have proven to be quite narrow. We argue in the middle. We elect presidents who move toward the middle, as Barry Goldwater will testify.

Readers can further prepare themselves to appreciate this book by realizing that the centrist liberal tradition of America generally has little place for conservatism as defined by its modern source, Edmund Burke, and as described by Clinton Rossiter in his definitive *Conservatism in America* (New York: Random House, 1955, 1962). The reason is the sacred myth, metaphor, symbol, and legend that revolve around individualism.

Conservatism posits that society comes first. It has an existence apart from the individuals who make it up. It is a continuing organism with a life of its own. It progresses through centuries borne by the individuals who happen to make up a society's population at any given time, but they themselves are transients, changing from day to day in the great cycles of birth and death. People have no claims prior to those of society and no rights except those that society gives them in furthering its own needs. Because people are emotional and frequently irrational, they need order. Liberty is the product of an ordered society in which people are able to do what is right and desirable for them to do.

Classical conservatism does not deny the inevitability of change. It simply does not believe that change is meritorious for its own sake. The change that is appropriate--more social justice for the individual, let us say--is the change that society is ready for and that fits the established traditions of society at a given time. Society is a long line moving from the past through the present and to the future, a partnership of generations, not of individuals. In such a design, government cannot be either the creature or the servant of the people. It is an agent of the society.

Because of the inherent inequalities in the distribution of talent in society, some people are better qualified than others to decide what government policies should be. Either the franchise should be limited, therefore, or other means should be devised to insure that people of talent predominate. In ancient China it was the elaborate civil service examination system that produced and sustained the administrative, or Mandarin, class. In the Iroquois Confederation of early modern North America it was the demonstrated power of any tribal member to persuade in council. In all conservative cultures political equality and majority rule have been considered illusory and undesirable. Only those with the requisite talent should decide what government must do on behalf of the society, and individuals' lives are directed accordingly.

It would appear, therefore, that there have been few classical conservatives in the American political tradition. What American conservatives wish to conserve are elements of liberalism. Those are the elements not contaminated by yet another stream of political thought commonly called radicalism. Liberalism was not initially democratic. American democracy is a special version of liberalism forged out of radical claims for wider participation and rights made by the poor, blacks, labor, immigrants, women, and a dozen other categories of people without pedigree or registered talent. Throughout American history radicals have forced economic redistribution from the haves to the have nots, always mounting their challenges in the name of democracy against the established economic, social, and political order.

Radicalism is responsible for equating liberalism first with democracy and then with individualism. Radical thinkers emphasize the good qualities in human nature and the potential inherent in all people. Solely by the fact of their existence people are entitled to a variety of human rights and opportunities. This enables them to transcend selfish acquisitiveness and develop both a fraternal sense of community and satisfying interpersonal relations. Radicals also believe that drastic reconstruction of society is sometimes necessary in order to achieve their goals. Government should be employed to create the conditions for specific improvements in public policy--the enlargements of the franchise, for example--and then be reduced to minimal functions consistent with the policy's operation. Obviously the clash of the American brand of conservative and radical constructs leaves liberalism somewhere in between, occupying the ground common to both ideologies, individualism.

Pragmatic and property-conscious Americans have often impatiently rejected or devastatingly ignored radicalism's "unrealistic" arguments. Yet claims for greater equality, participation, and respect keep rising decade after decade, normally as a version of democracy. The claims have a continuing effect on liberalism, particularly when the conflict with the inequality fostered by liberalism's commitments to individual liberty on the one hand and property rights on the other becomes clear. Liberalism has evolved over time, giving newer interpretations of individualism in the direction of the communal *we*, which this book recognizes and provocatively discusses.

Liberalism has come to have two parts. One is a central core of unchanging basic values and purposes. The other is a penumbra of specific positions on issues and tactically flexible orientations toward what government ought to be doing about this matter of public policy. In the central core of unchanging values are individualism, limited government, natural rights (especially property rights), and legal procedures. Individualism is by far the most fundamental value. The individual is more important than government. Government exists for the purpose of permitting the individual to serve his or her own needs and attain personal fulfillment. This commitment has remained essentially unchanged from the founding of the republic until now.

But the political environment has changed. The conditions of social life are different. Early liberals believed that the chief threat to individualism lay in government actions, so they bound government with prohibitions on the one hand and practiced laissez-faire as a basic policy on the other. This position was stoutly defended for the first hundred years of our history. Toward the end of the nineteenth century, however, two related developments led some liberals to question the desirability of following a nearly absolute policy of laissez-faire. One was the rise of corporate and economic power to the point where it became clear to many that government was no longer the chief threat to individual success. The other was the awakening of concern for human rights and social welfare as opposed to an extensive emphasis on property rights.

In the first instance the accumulation of private power and the leverage it gave to some to direct and affect the lives of others led some liberals to feel government must be used to redress the balance and restore for the cause of individualism some semblance of equal opportunity. Granger laws, rate regulations, and trust busting are examples of such uses of government. They appear to be entirely consistent with liberalism's core value of seeking to promote the individual's capacity to serve his or her own ends and reach personal fulfillment.

In the second instance all liberals acknowledged the importance of property and economic rights, including the right of individuals to maximize the profits attainable from use of their property and the propriety of economic motivation. It was a telling accident of history that the American Declaration of Independence and Adam Smith's *The Wealth of Nations* were published in the same year. Likewise the Puritan divines of Massachusetts had openly declared that individual profit seeking was the best way to advance the economy and ultimately to raise the standard of living for all. The China of Deng Xiopeng reached the same conclusion in the 1990s. The ownership of private property, quite disparate elements have agreed, is the basis of individual and state productivity. Sufficient property gives individuals a stake in the society and leads them away from revolution toward moderate and stable political behavior.

But modern life is more complicated than this. Yet another element of individualism must come into play, what our author calls authentic individualism. Authentic individualism must be mindful of the other. Suppose my sufficient property deprives you of *any* property. Suppose my economic well being drives you to the margin of existence. In fact the conditions of existence for many people are so marginal that individual action is necessary merely to preserve another's existence. The by-products of industrialization, urbanization, and monopoly control include impoverishment, unemployment, and severe practical limitations on economic opportunities. The pre-Civil War agitation over the plight of blacks and women's rights contributed to a continuing focus by some liberals on the conditions of the less successful people in their society. A split developed between liberals who saw natural rights in terms of civil and human rights and social welfare and those who continued with a more exclusive commitment to property rights.

The first group now sees government as a necessary tool for freeing individuals from the external forces that limit them from attaining their ends. It has used government more and more for this purpose in the twentieth century. The second group continues to place its priorities on economic rights--frequently because of the conviction that this remains the best way to advance the standard of living for all in the long run, not just to advance personal self-interest. They have steadily resisted "government interference." Aside from the acknowledged difference in the relative priority of human rights, however, all remain steadfast in holding the core value of individualism. Issue-positions have shifted among the majority of liberals to produce an almost complete reversal of their views of the propriety of the use of government, but there has been little or no change in their basic commitment to the individual and the attempt to make self-development possible. This is indicative of the flexibility inherent in liberal thought and part of the explanation of the confusion present in the use of the term *liberal*.

Individualism is so pervasive an American value that it often subsumes the popular usage of the terms *liberal* and *conservative*. Most conservatives today are fundamental devotees of the property-rights variant of liberalism. Most liberals are proponents of the social-welfare brand of liberalism. Specific issues in public policy making are frequently too narrowly defined to engage the *basic* differences that divide liberals and conservatives. Ironically, liberals who historically have been much attached to individualism and laissez-faire increasingly talk in terms of the conscious use of government on behalf of the totality of individuals, a *collective* notion. Conservatives, who once talked about a collectivity under the label of *society*, and who readily subscribed to the conscious use of government as a necessary aspect of society, increasingly employ the language of individualism and limited government in an attempt to prevent what they consider the unwise and manipulative use of government. Labeling can be so misleading that we are all well advised to use as much precision as possible in describing the value choices and specific events that color our lives.

On November 4, 1995, a 25-year-old Jewish militant named Yigal Amir shot and killed the Israeli Prime Minister, Yitzhak Rabin. It was an act of individualism, the first political assassination in the short history of Israel. Amir thought that if he could kill the one man who was driving the nation toward peace with the Palestinians, he could stop the entire process. The one killed the one. But Jews did not kill Jews. The entire point of the founding of the Jewish state was the presumption that Jews were safe among one another. All the conservative ideology about the covenant among those of the past, the living, and the yet unborn was in place in the quintessential example of the collective society. Now Jews began to ask themselves, "What kind of people have we become? What rot has infected our national soul?"

A thoughtful answer for the Jews and for all analysts of modern individualism, both authentic and inauthentic, is provided by James A. Michener in his novel, *The Source* (New York; Random House, 1965). Deep in the book (pages 684-85), Michener draws a conversation between the American archeologist, John Cullinane, and his Israeli Assistant Ilan Eliav. It begins with Cullinane's question:

"So let me ask it again. What does an average, non-orthodox Jew like you think of the parallel development of Judaism and Christianity?"

Eliav let go his knees and leaned backward on his pillow, thought for some time, then drew himself forward and said, "I've always thought that classical Judaism was about ready for a new infusion sometime around the year 100 C.E. The old patterns were ready to be enlarged. For proof, look at the concepts we get from the Dead Sea Scrolls. Or the development of the Talmud. So I've never resented the eruption of Christianity. The world was ready for it."

"Why?"

"Possibly because Judaism was a hard, tough old religion that didn't give the individual enough free play. It could never have appealed to the world at large. The bright, quixotic religion of Christianity was ideally suited for such a proselytizing need."

"Is brightness the difference between the two?" Cullinane pressed.

"Partly. Because, you see, when Judaism did reform by means of the Talmud it went backward toward its own nature. It became harder and more irresponsive to modern change, whereas the Christian church moved forward psychologically, and in a time of wild change an organism that is retracting has less chance than one which is expanding."

"Seems to me it was unfortunate for Judaism that in the years of decision you had the inward-looking rabbis, whereas Christians had outward-looking church fathers."

"Right there you beg the question," Eliav said slowly. "You say you were lucky that in the critical years between 100 and 800 C.E. Christianity went forward, and we were unlucky that during the same years Judaism went backward. Don't you see that the real question is forward to what, backward to what?"

Cullinane reflected for a moment and said, "By God, I do! That's what's been bugging me without my knowing it, because I hadn't even formulated the question."

"My thought is that in those critical years Judaism went back to the basic religious precepts by which men can live together in a society, whereas Christianity rushed forward to a magnificent personal religion which never in ten thousand years will teach men how to live together. You Christians will have beauty, passionate intercourse with God, magnificent buildings, frenzied worship and exaltation of the spirit. But you will never have that close organization of society, family life and the little community that is possible under Judaism. Cullinane, let me ask you this: Could a group of rabbis, founding their decisions on Torah and Talmud, possibly have come up with an invention like the Inquisition--an essentially anti-social concept?"

Eliav went on to say that the primary difference between the Old Testament and the New was that under the influence of the latter, Christians discovered the priesthood of all believers--read individualism--and the reality was so blinding that for centuries they came together and built another new church--sometimes a cathedral--and killed another million people who did not believe as the spirit of the God commanded. The Jews, he said, avoided intimacy with God and lived year after year in their ghettos and grubby little synagogues working out the principles whereby men and women could live together. Michener offers a telling indictment in *The Source*, for Yigal Amir moved out of his ghetto of thought long enough to murder in the name of right belief.

If Western Christendom did indeed move forward, as Eliav suggested, but moved forward merely to "a magnificent personal religion," leaving unanswered the question how can men and women live together in society, that question remains the burning intellectual, moral, and practical question of our or any day. No serious discussions of professional or personal ethics can proceed without dealing with it. As grand as the claim may appear, this book addresses that fundamental problem in a thoughtful way. How to live together in community is not solved conclusively or even approximately in some ways, but the polemic carries us along in the right conversation raising the right issues at the right time.

R. Philip Brown is a lawyer working as an Assistant Attorney General of the State of Michigan. This book was his dissertation for the Doctor of Public Administration degree at Western Michigan University in 1994. I served as chairman of his dissertation committee and helped him think through some of the critical issues presented here. He quoted me just enough times to earn my enthusiastic support of his work. If the truth be told, however, he moved well beyond my mentoring into what I consider a comprehensive view of authentic individualism all his own. Dr. Brown's work deserves to be read and pondered. It is a major contribution to scholarship and the process of moral reasoning.

Ralph Clark Chandler
November 27, 1995
Kalamazoo, Michigan

Preface

Overview

This book examines American Individualism; what it seems to have become, whether it needs to be changed, what direction it ought to be guided, and how to inspire the necessary message for the 21st Century. It concludes that the modern brand of American Individualism has come to embrace rapacious self-interest as its prime meridian. This radical individualism rejects or ignores our Founders' early recognition of self-interest as a part of human character that demands conscious countervailing action to contain it.

Self-interest was intended by the Founders to play the role of virtue in American government and society. However, the Constitution-makers fully understood that self-interest must be continually reigned-in by a virtuous and enlightened state of mind, as well as by the structure of government. Misunderstanding this realistic but negative perception of human nature and limited concept of individualism held by the Founders, modern America abandoned any effort to contain it. Self-interest climbed from playing the role of virtue to being a virtue in American life. Individualism in the U.S. came to mean personal particularity rather than singularity of thought, and human prerogatives were elevated above the integrity of the human soul.

Organizational life and social culture now compel individuals toward more radical manifestations of individualism as bureaucracy and society increasingly define personal relationships by rules, regulations and rights. Otherwise incompatible with individualism, this actually contributes to individual and group differentiation when individuals function simply as technicians without the opportunity to gain fulfillment, and they experience existential isolation, becoming detached from their moral and spiritual side. For identity in and control over their own lives, people engage in even more individualistic behavior: working, planning, attaining, or rebelling.

The true meanings of freedom and individual rights are perverted and trivialized by this radical individualism as a way of fighting back, but it too has corrosive effects that diminish individual autonomy. Accordingly, what we are and what we pursue needs redefining and we need to take being human as seriously as we take our personal rights. We need a new brand of individualism that lifts up the ethical and human dimensions of life over the excessive differentiation and particularistic manifestations of individualism practiced in America today.

As a result, scholars, citizens, managers, and organizational leaders should strive to inspire a search for alternatives to a Lockean self-interest gone wrong that has become the foundation for American Individualism. One such alternative is a journeyman philosophy called authentic individualism, which recognizes and nurtures the developmental nature of ethical conscience, teaches human dignity as the moral norm, and takes a moral sense of becoming human as seriously as personal rights.

Method

Individual rights have been the driving force behind the laws, social framework, and collective psyche of the people of this country for two centuries. In the United States, freedom is embodied in the concept of individualism, and the U.S. Constitution, particularly the Bill of Rights. Through a history of individualism culled from U.S. history and the history of Western philosophy, this book describes what role the individual played in philosophical and political thought from the early Greek and Western religious influences up to and including modern times. First, it examines various concepts of individualism that arose in Western philosophy and United States history. The same kind of examination is made of history in this country. Thereafter, because history seems to be governed by a certain kind of dialectic--

thesis, antithesis, synthesis--the work attempts a synthesis (although not in the Hegelian sense) of individualism from Western philosophy and U.S. history toward a normative theory of authentic individualism. Finally, the practical effects of authentic individualism on public administration will be explored, including leadership theory, organizational theory and ethical considerations.

The purpose of this research is to (a) develop a theoretical, normative model of authentic individualism--a journeyman philosophy-- that can be adopted by the individual citizen and public administrator as a basis for action; and (b) consider the ramifications of that model for organizational theory, leadership theory, and ethics in government. The prime goal of the book is to articulate a perspective from which individuals, including American organizational leaders and professionals in business and government, can more clearly understand and effectively work in an increasingly complex environment of which we have imperfect knowledge and over which we have little control. The model of Authentic Individualism developed in this book attempts to make human commonalty the starting point for all organizational principles and decision-making by embracing a philosophy for governing personal actions and public policy that honors human dignity and prizes social responsibility.

Structure

The Introduction in Chapter One discusses some of the literature defining and examining individualism. Parts One and Two examine the political and social ideas related to individualism as they appear in Western philosophy and U.S. history. Chapter Two traces development of the concept of the individual from the Ancients through the Greeks. From there, Chapter Three carries the inquiry from St. Thomas Aquinas through the Renaissance and Reformation to the scientific revolution. Then Chapter Four brings the study of individualism in philosophy up to modern times. Chapter Five examines individualism in the developing United States, and Chapter Six continues the analysis through revolutionary times, ending in Chapter Seven with its evolution during modernity.

Chapters Two through Seven are not the author's original creation, but constitute facts culled from histories and historical documents written by others. Therefore, aside from the synopses of Parts One and

Two, Chapters Two through Seven are derived entirely from research of outside sources, subject of course to winnowing and organizational processes imposed by the author. A model of the individual for each period discussed in Parts One and Two is derived from the information reviewed in Chapters Two through Seven.

Part Three develops a model for more socially responsible action of the individualist in the Third Millennium. Chapter Eight is devoted to a description of the need for this new world view for public life, called authentic individualism. Chapter Nine describes the conceptual framework for, and the concept of, authentic individualism. A discussion of the implications that authentic individualism holds for public administration and consideration of its implications for group theory, leadership theory and ethics are all discussed in Chapter Ten.

Each Part begins with a Synopsis and ends with a Conclusion of the information contained in that Part. Accordingly, the book can be read or reviewed in summary fashion by simply reading Chapter One plus the three Synopses and Conclusions.

Acknowledgments

During the nearly four years it took to prepare the manuscript for this book, I have benefited greatly from the efforts of teachers, colleagues, and family. Their contributions to this endeavor range from substantive criticisms and suggestions for improving the book, to careful proofreading of the manuscript, to moral support when the burdens of completing the project seemed too great. For their generous assistance, I thank them all; without their help I would not have finished. A special thank you is needed for Dr. Ralph Clark Chandler, Professor of Public Administration and Political Science at Western Michigan University for the *locus* he gave the book in the excellent Foreword he contributed. My greatest appreciation, however, is for Nancy, my wife. Her example served as my guiding inspiration and her endless support, love and patience sustained me.

CHAPTER ONE

Introduction to Individualism

The professional literature written for government and other organizational leaders focuses little attention on individualism. To the extent it is explicitly discussed, it usually appears briefly, undefined and abstract, as something against which other theories, such as community, are proposed. It may also appear as an unstated methodology behind other proposals, such as a plea for personal autonomy in new organizational theories, but it received little detailed attention in the theories of leadership, management, organization, or administration. However, it generates considerable attention in the literature of social science, political science, philosophy, and also anthropology, where individualism is ascribed varied and sometimes conflicting descriptions.[1]

Destructive Rationalism

According to Arieli (1964), the term individualism was coined by the Saint-Simonians to characterize the condition of humanity in nineteenth-century society. The concept was part of a comprehensive social criticism and was used to describe the negative and destructive character of the society. Based upon an ideal of organic and unitary social order held together by traditions, common purpose, and functional interdependence, the doctrine of Saint-Simon created a new synthesis from the revolutionary elements of the Enlightenment and conservative reaction to it. Saint-Simon introduced the term individualism to describe a doctrine based on individual reason, rights, and interests. The Saint-Simonians drew from the turbulent period through which the world passed with the French Revolution. In this context, the Saint-Simonians introduced the term individualism as a generic principle from modern times manifested in liberalism, laissez-faire attitudes, atheism, materialism, skepticism, Protestantism, and utilitarianism. To them the term individualism stood for spiritual rootlessness, destructive rationalism, utilitarianism, hedonism, and exploitation under the disguise of laissez-faire. This doctrine presumed to build society into "an agglomeration of selfish individuals without past and without future, without piety and without dignity, without faith and without loyalty" (Arieli 1964, 221). Individuality, on the other hand, stood for human dignity, the capacity of humans to grow in reason and morality, for liberty, equality, and fraternity.

Primacy of Conscience

The concept of individualism in American society seems to have first been discussed by Alexis de Tocqueville over 150 years ago. This French visitor of the 1830s, defined individualism as "a calm and considered feeling which disposes each citizen to withdraw into the circle of family and friends" and "threatens to grow as conditions get more equal" (Bellah et al. 1985, 414). As wealth spreads, he continued, such individuals "owe no man anything and hardly expect anything from anybody" (Ibid., 11). According to Arieli, Tocqueville also distinguished between individualism and individuality. Tocqueville called the latter enlightened self-interest, or self-interest rightly understood, which inspired the individual to shape personal destiny, capacities, and faculties as an active member of a society identified with liberty and jealously maintained. The former involved a withdrawal from society, a loss of strength and character, an apathy toward the public weal and enjoyment of the pleasures of privacy. To Tocqueville, individualism destroyed the individual with its indifference toward society.

American thinkers picked up the term individualism to describe the Jeffersonian ideals of self-government, free society, and the "rights of man", and its value content changed completely with transplantation to the U.S. The term was synonymous in the old world with selfishness, social anarchy, and individual self-assertion, but here it came to denote self-determination and moral freedom. Instead of the European negative value, individualism was closely connected with the Puritan tradition, and came to describe the primacy of conscience and reason which gave sovereignty to the individual over oneself and the abrogation of all authority. Individual dignity and the spiritual value of the perfectible individual human soul became the founding concept of the American nation and the central doctrine of American social and political culture.[2]

Human Dignity and Autonomy

In defining individualism today, some writers invest it with the attributes of a discrete and describable theory. Lukes (1974) sums up individualism's prescriptions in three ideas: (a) a view of government based on consent of the citizens, which may but need not be in the form of a social contract; (b) a view of politics representing individual interests, rather than estates, social function, or social class; and (c) a view of government as confined to enabling, satisfying and protecting individuals' wants, interests, and rights with a clear bias toward laissez-faire and against influence, alteration, interpretation, invasion, or abrogation of such wants, interests, and rights.[3] These principles stand on the bedrock of liberty and equality, but do not include fraternity, or community, according to Lukes. This latter value is not a cardinal ideal of individualist thought.[4]

For Hiskes (1982) individualism is a collection of disparate ideas with five fundamental threads of individualist thought that do not always coalesce. First, there is belief in a prime moral value of individual human beings. Hiskes notes:

> The paramount dictum of individualist thought is 'ultimate moral principle of the supreme and intrinsic value, or dignity of the individual human being.' Individuals have moral worth qua individuals, according to this doctrine, regardless of their special

characteristics or their relationship to other people, to God, or to any social or political entity. (Hiskes 1982, 12)

A second important element of individualism is the notion of autonomy, or self-direction, according to which an individual's thought and action is one's own and not outside one's control. This self-directed individualism, rejects conformity and outside control, and places much emphasis upon the idea of individual responsibility and accountability for action.

A third important individualist concept is that of privacy, or private existence in a public world; an area within which the individual should be left alone by others and be able to do and think whatever one chooses in order to achieve one's own view of the good life. Fourth is faith in the efficacy and value of self-development, or growth, which assumes uniqueness of each individual, progressive development of human beings, and moral progress.[5] The purpose of government is confined to enabling individuals' wants to be satisfied, individuals' interests to be pursued, and individuals' rights to be protected. Lastly, individualism casts the individual as existing with invariant human psychological features which determine behavior and specify interests, rights, and needs.[6]

Hiskes disputes the exclusion of community from individualism and attempts to demonstrate that individualism is communitarian as well as libertarian. He does this to overcome what he believes are legitimate criticisms that individualist political theory over-emphasizes rights, freedom, and the pursuit of narrow self-interest. Once the individualist concept of community is embraced, he believes a concern for others inherent in it will ensure no abuses of freedom, rights, or self-interest. For Hiskes, the ability of individualist theory to accept community will largely determine its acceptability as a philosophy for organizing the contemporary political world.[7]

Mutual Recognition

Gilbert (1990) sees individuality, not in some atomistic vein, but emerging as a part of social and political relationships. He rejects moral relativism and attempts to establish an objective political theory called democratic individuality based on mutual recognition of persons. Using as a springboard the universal judgments that slavery and genocide are monstrous and abhorrent and not merely matters of opinion, Gilbert makes a claim of empirical proof that moral discovery occurs, and that humans have sufficient rationality, empathy, and sympathy to participate in political life and to have rights and duties. This claim of empirical ethical discovery serves as the central justification for his theory of limited moral objectivity which he describes as a version of moral realism. Gilbert's theory rejects any notion of individuality that supposes human isolation and self-subsistence in conflict with either communitarianism or the simple notion that all social, political, and moral life is relational. Instead, his theory holds that notions of mutual recognition, capacity for moral personality, and self-respect underpin individuality and support reasonable theories of the self.[8]

Gilbert's theory is based upon (a) Aristotelian eudaemonist ethics, in which acting for the good of others is seen not as an abnegation of self but as a choice to be a certain kind of person, and (b) a full conception of autonomy, individuality, and self-respect, which he draws from Hegel and Rawls. The former, according to Gilbert, sought to revive an ancient understanding of the common good in the midst of a seeming chaos of individual pursuits that characterized civil society and to articulate the invisible spirit of commonalty that reconciles individuals. Democratic individuality rejects the kind of social theory that values natural characteristics of isolated individuals--preferences that are instinctively or genetically driven--which then determine social interaction. Instead, it uses a eudaemonist theory to flesh out the basic Rawlsian claim of creativity in all-talented, universal individuals by stressing the commonalty and mutuality of respectful persons.

Absence of Restraint

Gans (1988) speculates that individualism may be as old as human history. He defines individualism as "the pursuit of personal freedom and personal control over the social and natural environment. It is an ideology--a set of beliefs, values, and goals--and probably the most widely shared ideology in the U.S." (Gans 1988, 1). Gans sees multiple individualisms, e.g., corporate, narcissistic, and popular. His explication of popular individualism coincides with what is often conceived of as radical individualism. Practitioners of Gans' popular ideology "support the welfare state--as long as it keeps their welfare in

mind" (Ibid., x). The adherents to popular individualism hold jobs
rather than pursue careers, hope to be free to choose goods, services, and
ideas relevant to self-development, desire something for nothing, as in
more government services and lower taxes, and want public services
because they are free and leave more earnings to be used in pursuit of
user values. These popular individualists want government to guard
their pay and savings against inflation, help with college expenses,
clean up the environment, and make sure that they can work and enjoy
the fruits of their labor. At the same time, they would like government
to cut spending in general. For them, citizen participation in
government is too strenuous. An increase in anti-social behavior, such
as bullying, racism, and greed is associated with this brand of
individualism.

The popular individualists, as Gans describes them, have almost all
the qualities of radical individualists. To the values Gans notes, only
two should be added to round out the radical individualist's personality.
One, is the belief that he or she, or their group, is special among the
human population. Bellah et al. (1987) say a belief that we are all
unique is a basic tenant of American individualism, and they observe
that we imagine ourselves as special creations, set apart from other
humans. Perhaps that accounts for the second new value of the radical
individualist; the assumption in the national belief system that the
appellation American applies only to citizens of the United States
whose ancestors arrived after the Pilgrims.

Community

To Bellah et al. (1987), individualism is a very complex system of
ideas about the nature of social life and the foundations of morality.
They believe "the great irony of modern individualism is the belief that
individualists should find themselves independent of social institutions
. . . against a backdrop of ever expanding systems of social control"
(Bellah et al. 1987, 11). They label the attitudes described by Gans
above as the first language of American individualism.[9] At various
times they call it radical individualism, expressive individualism, or
utilitarian individualism. Whatever its name, this first language "feeds
an 'illusory quest for private fulfillment' that 'often ends in emptiness'"
(Ibid., 198). Jobs and careers have replaced callings, the family teaches
self-reliance as the cardinal virtue of individuals, a feeling develops that

"you got to try everything at least once," and modernity--a culture of separation--arises. In it the rational, self-interested individual emerged as *economic man*, and he made trade, exchange, and competition the "coordinating mechanism[s] of social life" (Bellah et al. 1985, 20). Because this radical, American individualism undermines the conditions of existence, Bellah and his associates see the most important tasks today as that of recovering "insights of the older biblical and republican traditions" (Ibid., 35-36).

Avineri and De-Shalit (1992) pit community in opposition to individualism. They state that beginning in the 1980s the most crucial and substantive challenge to Neo-Kantian theories emerged from scholars called communitarians where debates with individualists have become one of the most important and fascinating issues of political philosophy. They describe the debate between communitarians and individualists as both methodological and normative. The communitarians argue that the premises of individualism--such as the rational individual who chooses freely--are wrong, and the only way to understand human behavior is in reference to social, cultural, and historical contexts. Communitarians assert that the premises of individualism give rise to morally unsatisfactory consequences, among them unjust distribution of good.

Both communitarian and individualist theories begin with the image of the individual. However, communitarians claim social attachments determine the self and require that behavior be analyzed in view of people's aims and values, rather than tending to distinguish, as individualists do, between who one is and the values one has. The communitarian community is more than a mere association; it is unity in which the members are individuals. It contrasts with the individualist conception of community, where a person is freed from the dictates of nature and the sanction of social roles, which communitarians argue makes no sense of our pervasive social life.

Individualists see the non-communitarian community as based on cooperation for mutual advantage, where theoretical and instrumental character of social relationships is emphasized. Individualists criticize communal morality as being relative to the community itself and argue that when moral relativism is embraced it makes no sense to complain about the abuse of human rights in other societies. They argue that moral principles are universal and capable of being discovered by the detached philosopher. Normatively speaking, communitarians argue that personal autonomy is better achieved within the community than outside. The individual can only maintain identity within a society or culture of a certain kind, and community is, therefore, a need of the individual, who has intrinsic value to the community itself and to relations with other members of the community.

On the other hand, some individualists adamantly reject any attempt to derogate the priority of liberties. They claim rights should not be pushed aside for the sake of any idea of a general good and that the role of government is to insure basic rights and not promote or sustain any idea of the good life. Other individualists agree that the concept of community as a good is not alien to individualism, but that this does not necessarily contradict the priority of the right. Still others go so far as to concede that community is a human need in the sense that a value of one's own life is only a reflection of and derivative from the value of the life of the community as a whole. Most individualist theories subscribe to the proposition that the right is prior to the good and, the individual is prior to the collective.[10]

Hiskes (1982) describes five forms of community. The first is organic unity, or Gemeinschaft, as a naturally existing being. This community is founded upon common or united interests and results in a perfect unity of human wills. Community members in the aggregate or individually do not contain all elements manifested by the community and the community itself is greater than the sum of its parts. In this type of community, the organic whole can manifest a will as a singular and unitary whole, and it is permissible to say that the community acts as a singularity, that such actions are willful, and that the community as a whole has rights. According to Hiskes, the organic community wields a significant degree of control by the communal center, an a idea which he says is rejected by all proponents of individualism.

The second type is the community of public interest. It is not organic with a single center of consciousness, but consists of myriad of centers of life and consciousness, of true autonomous individuals who are merged in no corporate unity and whose purposes are lost in no corporate purpose. Unity in this sense is best defined as some aspect of the individuals themselves or as some characteristic they possess. Social relationships constitute the community and do not exist between, among, or around individuals, but within them as a part of their very being. Every individual possesses the relationships of the community as a part of one's own physiological constitution.

The third type of community is one of private interests in which the interests of private persons bind them together as they seek their own advantage. This type of community is primarily concerned with preserving individual freedom and relative autonomy in a communal setting. The existence of authority, or governance, is the key to the community of private interests, and it is obsessed with preserving individual autonomy in the face of any communal threat. As a result, this type of community is vulnerable to the criticism that such a concept of a community renders that term virtually meaningless.

The fourth type of community described by Hiskes is the anarchist community of respect, which exists because the intellectual diversity of persons not only motivates but forces individuals into reciprocal opening of their souls. No person is complete or self-sufficient intellectually, but needs others, their knowledge, and special abilities to complete one's own. The anarchist community is one marked by a mutual sharing or reciprocity; not only one's intellect, but of one's feelings and very self. Full development of individual gifts--individuation--cannot be attained by the individual in isolation. The community of self-respect rejects an institutionalized system of authority in favor of interpersonal, face-to-face confronting of deviant behavior that covers the entire spectrum from rational argument to intense pressure, including public censure. It, therefore, becomes questionable whether such solutions impinge upon personal freedom to any lesser degree than would an institutionalized form of authority.

In conclusion, Hiskes outlines a fifth type of community called community as caring. This community involves three distinctive normative considerations: First, it is valued as the object of a particular attitude. Second, it is a relationship between persons characterized by the sharing of moral values. Third, it is itself a particular moral value or sentiment. Community as caring construes the social fact of community as a special quality of individuals, not the group, which exists within individuals, not between them. Lastly, community as caring is by nature non-ideological in its approach to the role of authority since its consensus upon ethical norms insures an equal amenability towards decentralized and disbursed authority structures as towards centralized ones. According to Hiskes, in order to find a road from self-interest to community, individualism must promote a transformation in the perception off the individual by demanding that the actions and interests of others be considered and objectively evaluated at all times. Without such a transformation, individualism cannot accept community and cannot escape denunciation for narrow pursuit of self-interest.

Radical Individualism

Tucker (1980) classifies individualism as three types--radical, utilitarian, and possessive. He notes that there is little to be said in favor of an individualism that conceives of the individual as essentially the proprietor of one's own person for which one owes nothing to society. Such a possessive individualism is founded in a special conception of natural rights that holds freedom from coercion as the fundamental political value. This brand of individualism supports the claim that individuals owe nothing to society for the skills which they acquire when they are trained to accomplish sophisticated tasks. It also rejects any attempt on the part of government to act in the name of distributive principles of justice, the leveling of wealth, the establishment of equality of opportunity, or the elimination of poverty, which it holds necessarily involve exploitation of the individual.

Tucker also describes utilitarian individualism as one of the traditional theories hostile to the notion that there are natural rights. In place of the assumption of natural rights, utilitarian individualism places concern with maximization of the general good by promoting efficient policies for it. Radical individualism is the third kind described by Tucker who associates it with Dworkin's and Rawls' two theories in which the right is prior to the good. This brand of individualism subscribes to the proposition that individuals have a natural right to mutual concern and respect, and it takes an intermediate position between utilitarianism and possessive individualism.

Tucker claims that individualists aim at establishing a science of society which is universal, which they believe is possible because human responses and ways of adapting are general, not specific to particular cultural periods, and may be known. These individualists are therefore skeptical of all explanations which attribute purposes to social entities apart from the concerns of the persons who function within them. Thus, such individualists do not suppose that people are not changed by their values, but only that sociologists should not dispose of the individual entirely when providing social explanations. Although they are cautious in their judgment of the extent to which individuals can be said to be shaped and molded by life in community with others, they would admit that individuals acquire social dispositions. They, however, resist the temptation to see social life in organic terms and argue that socialization does not produce such extreme changes in people that no general characteristics of human nature remain.

Valuational Points of View

Bettelheim's (1960) formula for achieving autonomy in a mass age is that human heart must know the world of reason, and reason must be guided by an informed heart. Bettelheim sees the achicvement of self-realization, the preservation of freedom, and the adaptation of society to both as the overwhelming problem of the modern age. In order to manage such a feat, heart and reason can no longer be kept in their separate places. This requires a subtle balance between individual aspiration, society's right for demands, and human nature; an absolute submission to any one of them will never do. Bettelheim believes that the solution is not found in the simple beliefs of our forefathers where intellectuals now look for comfort, but lies in finding ways to make this an age where humanity dominates. When this is done, autonomy no longer implies that the individual has or should have free reign. Instead, Bettelheim believes that if human instincts were unchecked society could not exist. Therefore, order requires a consciousness of freedom based on the continuous balancing and resolving of opposing tendencies within one's self and between self and society. Such inner controls are built only upon the basis of direct personal relations and not by obeying society's demands. They are only internalized by identifying one's self with people, love, and respect. When either the individual's idiosyncrasies or the power of society reign supreme both eventually cease to exist.[11]

Perry (1944) sees the individual as the seat of value. He recognizes that the nature of the individual is penetrated and conditioned a thousand different ways by society; that the minimum human entity is the triad of mother, father and child; that human experience and development are inseparable from familial and tribal relationship; and that human beings are economically interdependent. In recognizing what Perry calls undeniable facts, he rejects individualistic doctrines that (a) place the individual prior to society on the basis that the latter is an artificial construction, or (b) assume individuals can live without society and can achieve their highest possibilities in isolation.

Nevertheless, the final values of life begin and end with the individual. The good life cannot be imputed to society, but resides in the individual:

> Only the individual can fit the conclusion to the evidence, within the circumference of his own experience and thought. Only the individual can store up the experience of the past and use it for the interpretation of the future. Only the individual can establish an order of preference, and choose from a range of alternatives. Only the individual can by understanding the inference govern his actions by a general principle. Only the individual can subordinate means to ends, and create an hierarchy of interests under the regulation of a dominant purpose. These functions of the human individual are the attributes of personality, and elevate the good life to a personal plane. (Perry 1944, 451)

All of these considerations, Perry believes argue against imposing any uniform creed upon all members of society and argue in favor of allowing the individual to act according to one's own conscience and reason.

While the individual is the seat of all value, Perry accepts humanity as the universal recipient of good, because the meaning of individual is not one individual, but all individuals. An individual's happiness is good, but an individual has a duty toward all individuals, and all distinctions between individuals are irrelevant. Accordingly, while the individual is the moral finality, the principle of inclusiveness, or universalism, is the co-equal complement of individualism.

Identity

Erich Fromm ([1941]1969) approaches individuality from a social psychology perspective. He had been working on a character structure of the modern human and the problems of interaction between psychological and sociological factors. However, because of political developments of the time and the dangers he thought they implied for "individuality and uniqueness of personality" (Fromm 1969, vii), he interrupted that study to concentrate on "one aspect of it which is crucial for the cultural and social crisis of our day: the meaning of freedom for modern man" (Ibid.).

The emergence of the individual from original ties, Fromm calls individuation. Before individuation, individuals have primary ties to the outside world that restrict freedom but provide feelings of security, orientation, belonging and roots. One aspect of the process of individuation is "growing aloneness" (Ibid., 39-40, 44-47), a cutting-off of the ties that bind. When economic, social and political conditions do not allow realization of individuality, while at the same time the primary ties have been lost, the lag makes freedom an unbearable burden. "Powerful tendencies arise to escape from this freedom into submission, or some kind of relationship to man and the world that promises relief from uncertainty, even if it deprives the individual of freedom" (Ibid., 47, 52).

PART ONE

A Model of the Individual From
Western Philosophy

Synopsis

Homer and Hesiod, early Greek poets and philosophers, suggested a peculiarly indivisible synthesis of the individual and the universal. Capricious, vain, and individualistic Gods represented human desires within a cosmos rather than a chaos. This cosmic theme was taken up in the Milesian Monastic philosophical concept of process, or ordered change and was absorbed into the world process Heraclitus called *logos*. Later, the Sophists injected a new element of skeptical pragmatism into Greek thought and man soon became the measure of all things. These Sophistic scientific views mediated a transition from an age of myth to an age of practical reason and led to Pluralism in place of religion. Such views found a home in Pythagorean theory, but Pythagoreanism's atomistic flavor caused rebellion first by Socrates, then Plato and later Aristotle, who sought compassion, unity, moderation, and enlightened self-interest in place of discord and war. Plato's and Socrates' transcendent individual soul and Aristotle's social animal all sought universal permanence. This line of thought enticed Roman Stoics to stress the importance of positive social duties to replace self-interest. The wreck of the Roman empire laid the ground work for a deeper peace assured by religion and Augustine's *human predicament*. The Christian discovery of God overthrew Classical philosophy and gave the West an unchanging universe and a sinful, bespotted, corrupt, and ulcerous view of humanity that dominated attitudes for more than 1,000 years. The message of an all good and loving God from Jesus gave way to the message of obedience from Paul, and the synthesis of God and man from St. Thomas was replaced by the all-powerful and vengeful God of the universal priesthood from Luther and Calvin. The church dominated a descending, theocratic theme of government and law that soon rotted from corruption within to be pushed aside by individualism and science. Renaissance man and power politics, with the rise of the nation state and capitalism, released the individual from institutions and encouraged focus on this-worldly affairs. Scientific reason placed God, the human mind and human soul in an immaterial reality separate and apart from the material reality of the human body and rational brain.

First a contributor to, then a victim of, this energetic and unstable society, the Christian Church underwent cataclysmic changes that undermined central authority and orthodoxy. Arising out of the Papal corruption and ecclesiastical abuses, Luther baptized a universal priesthood of believers. Personal interpretation of the Bible and communication with God, and primacy of the individual conscience combined with and reinforced the process toward individuation, competition, and economic expansion already underway. Development of the scientific method propelled these forces forward as the church weakened, and a transformation of political and moral ideals revived learning and interest in the sounds, smells, and sights of nature. A quantitative, mechanistic view of nature displaced the theological at the same time nation states, capitalism, and self-improvement became the new model. The logic of science suggested a chasm between empirical, observable things-in-themselves, and the subjective human mind. This logic drove out values, which were mere appearances in a world of fact. Obviously, this Hobbesian, self-interested view fit very neatly with the individualist dedicated to self-improvement and the acquisition of wealth and power. Seeking to avoid this amoral view and still accept the new science, Descartes concluded that mind and body were completely separate substances so that the sciences of each could not contradict. This left a place for value in the universe as a part of the mind, but failed to stem the tide of egoism that spread throughout the Western world. Hume rebelled against this view and launched an attack on rationalism that aroused Kant and others to attempt a rational philosophy on a different basis. Kant saw Hume's attack as dangerous, contributing to the Romantic action against the mood of the Enlightenment. The Romantics saw the universe as richer, bigger, and more varied and exciting than thinkers of the Age of Reason. They believed reason imposed artificial structures on thought that failed to grasp the largeness of reality--an immensity that baffled science--and failed to recognize the continuous, living, dynamic nature of the universe. Kantianism and Hegelianism fought against these detractions and sought to rehabilitate rationalism by reuniting mind and body through ordered experience. Within this new view, self and objects were not distinct substances, nor mutually independent, but ordered elements in experience, where all knowledge contains elements drawn from experience yet supplied by the mind itself. These philosophies embodied a great shift from a static view of the universe to one of evolving through time.

The harsh effects of Industrialism and urbanization on the laboring class, and repression in Europe from institutional failure to adjust to change in values, expectations, and ways of living, led to much more practical, utilitarian, and pragmatic philosophies that emphasized social theory, alienation, existence, and being. These were intensely personal philosophies that focused laser-like attention on individual circumstances in the lifeworld of everyday experience. Emerging from them came the hard, courageous, creative Nietzschean *Overman,* who faced his anxiety, exploited it, suspended the ethical and prospered in the battle for meaning in an absurd world in which God was dead.

In an attempt to revive a universe with purpose, direction, and proportion, twentieth-century thinkers tried to break out of the Kantian framework. In that paradigm the objective world had been a construct of a synthesizing mind working on and organizing the senses. Modern theories conceive of the mind and self less mechanistically as creative, active, intuitive, continuous, unfolding, and evolving. Some are pragmatic, finding truth in what works. Others are scientific, searching for an objective pattern in a universe of loose and separate encapsulated entities. Still others are phenomenological, finding meaning in the interfusion, or interconnectedness, of all things and reconciled to living with uncertainty in a world requiring moral choices be made with incomplete knowledge.

CHAPTER TWO

The Individual of the Ancients

Because the history of philosophy has no definitive starting point, this study begins with what is known about the pre-Socratic philosophy of the Greeks.[1] Homer and Hesiod were early Greek writers and philosophers who influenced belief in various gods that controlled and often intermeddled in the affairs of humankind. In this view, individuals were seen as autonomous only insofar as the will of their vain and capricious gods permitted.

Ancient Mind--Age of Deities

The old religion of Homer and Hesiod was undermined by the views of Ionian scientists, Heraclitus and later Xenophanes and others, as a new science began to replace religious faith in much the same way that occurred in Europe and America during the second half of the last century, when old fundamentalism and a literal bible was undermined by Darwinism. Monism of the Milesian type was succeeded by Pluralism as the basic assumption of Greek thought, which conceived of the world process as a continuous cycle in which all of the basic elements were completely mixed up like a well tossed salad. In this mix of random combinations, a successful relationship sooner or later occurred. No

God planned it and the fact that humanity, with the faculties that existed therein, developed at all was a temporary and accidental result of this casual mixture of elements. As a result, religion declined and Pluralism arose in early Greek thought.

Milesian philosophers believed the concept of process, or ordered change, was important and somewhat later, Heraclitus--who was influenced by the Milesian thinker--called this "change according to the measures". To the Milesian Monastic philosophic view that reality resulted from the natural events rather than divine doings, Heraclitus added the belief that one's chief good was to listen, to become attuned, and even to become absorbed into the world process which he called *logos*. This term eventually came to denote a transcendent source of archetypes and providential principle of cosmic order that, through the archetypes, continuously permeated the created world. Whatever Heraclitus meant by the term *logos*, later Stoics and Christians placed a theological strain in his view of there being a universal order in the world.

On the other hand, Parmenides argued that everything was what it was, so that it could not become what it was not. Change was thus incompatible with being, and only the permanent aspects of the world could be considered truly real. Democritus proposed an ingenious escape from the dilemma of these competing views in the fifth century B.C. He hypothesized that all matter is made up of tiny indestructible units, which he called atoms. The atoms remained unchanging, having fixed size and shape, but they moved about in space and combined in various ways making the larger bodies which they constituted seem to alter. In this way change and order were reconciled, all change in the world was attributed simply to the rearrangement of atoms, and the doctrine of materialism was born.[2]

The next step in the development of Pluralistic philosophy occurred with the Pythagoreans, who reduced the cosmos to mathematical relationships between particles and entities. Not much is know about Pythagoras but it is guessed that his Pythagorean order was primarily a religious fraternity similar to a medieval monastery, where political power was joined with worship, and the pursuit of learning and science was cultivated as the means to spiritual redemption. Their most notable achievement was the concept of cosmos--the notion that the universe was not a chaotic hodgepodge, but a thoroughly ordered system in which every element harmoniously related to every other. However, this concept also appeared in Hesiod's thought and that of the Milesians. For them order was something imposed on basic chaos, whereas the universe was ordered for the Pythagoreans because all of its parts are related to one another mathematically. Pythagoras taught withdrawal from the world to engage in dispassionate contemplation of reason and mathematics.

The Pythagorean idea that the universe was well ordered and thus intelligible through pure reason was taken up by Plato and passed into Christian theology as one of the great heritages of the modern mind. Pluralists did not seem to reconcile the rational, thinking mind with the purely chance operation of the world process as they saw it. Not until Plato did philosophers fully recognize the problem of reconciling a purposive and valuational conception of the individual with a notion of a mechanistic universe.

Pythagoreanism and Atomism compliment each other remarkably. The former's emphasis on mathematics and the latter's view that reality consists of entities varying only in shape, size, and velocity, seem to have provided the conceptual basis from which modern physical theory began. Only the dominance of Platonism and Christianity and their emphasis on other-worldliness prevented the possibilities of the combination between Pythagoreanism and Atomism from being immediately seen. Consequently, the world waited until the seventeenth century for that combination to be completed.

Classical Mind--Age of Politics

Plato and his student, Aristotle, were the dominant philosophers of the Classical period, which can be described as the years between 450 B.C. and 450 A.D.[3] One cannot hope to fully understand their writings and political philosophy without also understanding something of the general mood of Athens during Plato's life. That mood was set by the Peloponnesian War, which was fought during the period 431-404 B.C. Athens' chief rival in the Peloponnesian War was Sparta, a City-State of disciplined and warlike people, who proposed a solution radically different from that of Athens to the disaffection of lower classes. Athens expanded the franchise to all adult male citizens present at any meeting of the Assembly as the final authority of the state. Sparta's elite ruled in constant fear that Athenian democracy would foment rebellion among Spartan serfs.

Athens was a vigorous, commercial democracy with a loose union of lesser independent agricultural states that were supplied with industrial goods from Athens and relied on protection by the Athenian fleet. Sparta had long regarded itself as the primary power in Greece, and Athens now challenged and even surpassed Sparta. Athens imposed embargoes on some of the lesser commercial states destroying their business and some of those, including Corinth, entreated the Spartans to join in a campaign against the Athenian expansionist policy. War began quietly in 431 B.C. with an attack on a minor ally of Athens.

For the next twenty-seven years it continued, while Athenian demagogues controlled policy. Throwing away several chances to reach an understanding with Sparta, they abandoned an earlier defensive strategy and were defeated in a foolhardy offensive expedition into Sicily. Though Athenian naval and military forces were decimated in the Sicilian expedition, the war continued for another ten years while bitterness over the hopeless struggle grew and the years passed. The war led to increasing criticism of Democratic institutions and political debate became less and less objective. Ideological struggle broke out in every city, and Athens itself divided into mutually distrustful groups, resulting in treasonable plots and corresponding purges.

Precious unity was lost in the partisan dissension of the Peloponnesian War as the old ideal of respect for law, religion, custom and patriotic duty to one's city lost force and gave way to the beliefs of a new type of individual developing under the pressure of decades of war. The new Athenian was a cynic who believed that might makes right and rejected old loyalties and virtues, unless they were expedient or helped accomplish private ends. Thucydides, a Greek historian in the fifth century B.C., gave this description of the prevailing attitude:

> The cause of all these evils was the love of power, originating in avarice and ambition, and the party-spirit which is engendered by them when men are fairly embarked on a contest. . . . Striving in every way to overcome each other, [party leaders] committed the most monstrous crimes: yet even these were surpassed by the magnitude of their revenges which they pursued to the utmost, neither party observing any definite limits either of justice or public expediency, but both alike making the caprice of the moment their law. (Jones 1970, 1:53-54)

Just when Greek intellectual achievement reached its climax during the fourth century B.C., Alexander the Great swept down from Macedonia through Greece. The qualities of Greek evolution--restless individualism, proud humanism, and critical rationalism--now precipitated its downfall, as the divisiveness, arrogance, and opportunism that shadowed their nobler qualities came to the fore. In this now tired culture, the ground work had been laid for that deeper peace to be found in a transcendent and other-worldly religion.

Plato was old enough to have fought through the last four or five years of the war with Sparta. He was born in 427 B.C. to a distinguished Athenian family and to a position of leadership and grew up in these years of defeat and of moral, social and economic dissolution. He could have been expected to play a leading political role as a matter of course in the overthrow the democratic government. However, reacting to his education-through-violence and cultural malaise produced by war, Plato learned from the excesses of the oligarchs and the savagery of the revived democracy that the will of the few was no better than the will of the many.

Socrates made more of an impression on Plato than anyone else. The former grew up at the time of Athens' greatest power and success, fought bravely in the war with Sparta, and performed all of the political duties that the democratic state had expected of its citizens. But he was not a politician, he differed from his fellows in knowing that he knew nothing, and he spent his days occupied in the task of proving to the Athenians their ignorance about things they had hitherto believed themselves well informed. Socrates' realistic and down-to-earth common sense was combined with cool skepticism about ordinary beliefs and opinions. He placed his own convictions in opposition to the public's and was inevitably disliked and misunderstood by the majority as a result. His indifference to public opinion and association with Oligarchs--enemies of democracy--led to persecution, from which he neither attempted to defend himself nor tried to escape. Ultimately, hatred and religious piety led to his imprisonment and trial. Thus, Socrates was the first individualist--an individualist's individual--succumbing to the tyranny of the majority for his beliefs; the great individualist who dared question popular belief.

Socrates built his own philosophy from and against the humanism and pragmatism of Sophistry, which was challenged by the impersonality of Ionian science. The natural philosophers attempted an intellectual foundation of nature by accounting for all diversity and change with the notion of alterations according to unchangeable laws in a common underlying substance. This naturalistic view of the world neglected morals and the human condition in the search for absolute first principles. Sophistry replaced this view with a practical concern for the here and now that exchanged speculation about the nature of the universe for attention to the world of human experience. They held that humans were the measure of all things and thus introduced a relativity that recalled humanity to itself. Nevertheless, because they believed achieving human excellence (their good) could not be accomplished outside society, the cultivation of the individual was viewed as necessarily political. In short, the Sophists, Thrasymachus among them, tried to present individuals as deserving of the respect of their contemporaries. In their return to the individual, Socrates followed them. However, they defined virtue as success in acquiring social, political, and economic status, with which Socrates disagreed.

Against this background, Socrates asked questions about the nature of a human self that science and Sophistry had ignored. His prime concern was not the political structure, but the relation of individual to society. He was an inner-directed, inward man who enjoined individuals to know themselves. The Sophists preferred probability to unobtainable truth and sought the uncritical consent of the many rather than the intelligent agreement of the few, but Socrates did the opposite. He insisted on the truth of one's own critical reflection by questioning the majority's accepted modes of thought and embodying human excellence, education, and virtue in one's life.

In Plato's dialogues, he skillfully dismantled Thrasymachus's view that justice is merely the interests of the strong and that social mores are protests of the weak. In its place, he introduced the concept of common good and defined it by what fulfills human nature rather than what people think they need. This fulfillment of one's nature, or the realization of one's proper potential, was given the Socratic name eudaemonia. A modern word for it is happiness, however, eudaemonistic theory is broader than simple fulfillment of one's desire. Its full meaning includes whatever is in accordance with humanity's real and essential nature. Consistent with this theory, Socrates' ethics held that wrong-doing and evil were not the result of weak will, sinful disposition, or bad faith, but of ignorance (lack of knowledge) to be remedied by education.

Accordingly, Socrates taught that virtue is any knowledge that makes the individual good. Such knowledge, truly practical knowledge --wisdom (phronesis)--is self-knowledge of one's nature, of what one needs, or lacks, or must have to fulfill one's human essence. The principles espoused by Socrates have come to be called Socratic Humanism, because he wedded the Sophistic return to the individual with the concern, caring, compassion, and empathy he found lacking in the majority's indifference to wisdom and virtue. He asked questions his contemporaries dared not answer.

When the citizens of Athens put Socrates on trial and executed him for impiety, or belief in human power, soon after his seventieth birthday, Plato was shocked into a philosophical career. He left the country to travel abroad, then returned to Athens and created the Academy as an intellectual center to which he dedicated himself until he died about 347 B.C. From this institution graduated Plato's most famous student, Aristotle. Though Plato was too young to have been of one of Socrates' closest friends, he set out to defend the latter's memory in a series of biographical dialogues. Plato's political philosophy is such a blending of his and Socrates' opinions that Plato's theory can be taken to mean the theory of Socrates-Plato.

Socrates' death confirmed Plato's aristocratic bias, convincing him that a state ruled by many is inevitably inefficient, indecisive, and irresponsible, because the many are ignorant, emotionally unstable, and narrowly self-centered. This belief that most people are egoistic heathenists led him to espouse rule by an elite few as the model for government. Not until philosophers (chosen from the elite guardians of the State) became kings or kings become philosophers--until supreme power and knowledge resided in the same person--could real improvement be possible.

According to Plato, the universe was constructed of ideal Forms, or ideas, that could not be observed, but were uncovered only by reason and contemplation of mathematical law. Plato carried over into his own philosophy Pythagoras's dualism between detached thought and action. Plato illustrated the relationship between the shadow world of direct experience and the world of Forms with a metaphor. Prisoners in a cave with their backs to the light could only observe objects (direct experience) by their shadows on the cave wall as those objects passed by the entrance. These imperfect projections constituted the world of observations. Only the world of immutable ideas (Forms) was illuminated and made intelligible by the sun.

Many describe Plato as genuinely interested in the individual and a few might even say he thought the individual in some sense prior to society. This view is supported by the elitist outlook apparent in his doctrine of selecting Philosopher Kings and Guardians upon individual merit. It also finds support in his analogy of the person as an animal. Both of these concepts are very individualistic in a modern sense. In the *Republic*, he wrote, "And where freedom is, the individual is clearly able to do as he pleases? Clearly" (Glendon 1991, 1).

On the other hand, it is said that Plato was not very heartily concerned and was even hostile toward the individual. This view is taken from the concern he expressed with types, classes, and professions rather than the conflict between individual and society. Severest of all are those who view Plato's teachings as totalitarian and hateful of the individual. These views do not seem to be supported, though it can be clearly stated that he was hostile to the raw individualist, might-is-right school represented by Thrasymachus. Indeed, Plato saw the self-seeking individual as hostile to society and characteristic of a diseased state of affairs within society.

One might say that Greek history in general and Plato's philosophy in particular showed traces of heroic individualism. Plato regarded the individual as a temporary union of soul and body, and his philosophy clearly placed development of the individual below that of the republic. This was perhaps consistent with his religiously oriented point of view. The profile of Plato is with his eyes on the heavens, but the point of view of his most famous student was distinctly more practical and earthly. Aristotle's philosophy which ascribed more importance to the individual, was less intensely metaphysical and relied on empirical observation and rationality.

Aristotle was born in 384 B.C. when Plato was forty-three years old and Socrates had been dead for fifteen years. He obtained his education at Plato's Academy, where he stayed for twenty years, not all of them as a student. He departed the Academy only after Plato's death in 347 B.C., when he disagreed with the head of the institution over emphasis on mathematics and mathematical knowledge. After tutoring Alexander, son of King Philip of Macedonia, he set up his own school in Athens, the Lyceum, in 335 B.C.

The similarities between Plato's work and Aristotle's is apparent, even though he departed from Plato's beliefs in many respects. While he sometimes criticized his mentor, Aristotle was fundamentally a Platonist and his work can only be understood as an effort to reformulate the insights of Plato. Plato was in favor of philosophical rulers properly trained for the work of government, but Aristotle's answer was balanced in favor of the rule of law.

> Rightly constituted laws should be the final sovereign; and personal rule, whether it be exercised by a single person or a body of persons, should be sovereign only in matters on which the law is unable, owing the difficulty in framing general rules for all contingencies to make an exact pronouncement. (Baker 1958, 127)

It follows that Aristotle adhered to a particular concept of justice and life in a political association--the state, or *polis*. A *polis* was an association of citizens in a *polity*, or constitution; an association of households and clans in a good life for the sake of obtaining a perfect and self-sufficing existence. According to Aristotle, the person was an animal impelled by nature to live in a *polis*. He suggested two ends for the state: (1) to satisfy a natural impulse to live a social life, and (2) to promote the common interest in the attainment of good. The latter required those institutions, such as a system of justice, which were necessary to such a life. The purpose of the *polis* was the good life and the institutions of social life were means to that end. This life was the chief end served by the state, both for the community as a whole and for each individual.

The *polis* belonged to the order of compounds, which meant it was like all of the things that formed a single whole; a whole composed, nonetheless, of a number of different parts. This was an important concept in Aristotle's philosophy, which defined the relationship between the rights of individual citizens and rights of the community. There were two sorts of compounds--the mechanical and the organic. Wholes were of the second, or organic, kind: they had a form (organic unity). A *polis* was a whole because it was an organic union of the *demos* (people) in the form of a political association for the attainment of a common end, the good of all. The rights of individuals were tempered by strivings of an organic whole for the common interest of all. What was right must be understood as what was equally right and the latter was for the benefit of the whole state and the common good of its citizens. Aristotle saw individuals as integral parts of the *polis* who, though separate and autonomous, shared the identity of the whole and bore a responsibility to it.

Aristotle held that the world was eternal and uncreated. Man and the world were in a process of development, not yet completely itself, waiting for further development beyond itself. The world presented itself not as collection of utterly separate and discrete things, but as a collection of multiple interrelated particulars. Every element in the universe could be known by transcending element, by seeing it in relation to other elements in the universe. Each individual was the fulfillment of purpose inherent in some other individual. Human behavior could only be explained in terms that the lower structures from which it developed and the higher structures towards which it was unfolding.

Aristotle rejected Plato's world of timeless forms for the world as a living, developing organism. The cosmos was interfused with purpose, and living things were ascribed immanent souls. This was an animistic universe that was ungenerated, imperishable and eternal--without beginning in time. It also laid stress on process through progressive goal oriented change, so it might be supposed that Aristotle gave primacy to becoming over being. Less dramatically affected by war than Plato, Aristotle accorded more respect to the choices afforded the individual in a social setting. Nevertheless, unity of the whole was still an overriding concern and individual will was governed by the common interest. An individual, defined as transcending self for the good of all, sought fulfillment by developing higher potentialities through knowledge and right reason.

These early Greeks expressed a view that the individual differed from nature, having an obligation to live in a characteristically human way, to carry out certain actions, and to abstain from others based on a feeling of pride in being human. This was a sense of noblesse oblige-- the individual must live up to responsibilities as a human--and was quite different from any feeling that the individual must obey a divine overlord's commands. These notions also connected with another key Greek concept of moderation, which was also thought to be a peculiarly human trait. Greeks believed people embodied inner-discipline and self-restraint and thought they ought to live by uniquely human law in their dealings with one another.

After Aristotle, Roman thinkers in the late classical period attempted to modify Stoicism to function usefully as a social philosophy in the Roman empire. These Roman Stoics gave elaborate descriptions of the various duties of humankind which replaced interest so that an aesthetic and altruistic tone continued to dominate their thought. One of these, Marcus Tullius Cicero, was a Roman lawyer whose talents brought him to the counselorship in 63 B.C. At this time the Roman Republic was in its last period and various contestants for supreme power fought in bloody civil wars.

Against the view that each individual's own pleasure was the sole good, Cicero affirmed the Stoic notion that the chief good consisted of choosing in accordance with nature and rejecting what was contrary to it. In other words, good for Cicero was to live in agreement and harmony with nature. In this regard, he believed no phase of life could be without a moral duty; all that is morally right depends on the discharge of such duties and all that is morally wrong on their neglect. For Cicero, reason, not divine will or enlightened self-interest, was the ultimate sanction for doing one's duty. Moreover, Cicero taught that the law of nature was applicable to all equally and, as citizens of one State were equal, all were subject to one law.

Another of the Roman Stoics, Epictetus, demonstrated the religious tendency of Stoicism by teaching that the individual should accept whatever God gives; that is, whatever life brings. Again, since all were equally God's creatures, they were all equally members of one community. One lost one's self-identity in this community and as a member of a greater union, sacrificed oneself willingly, if need be, for the sake of that larger whole of which he was a part. This line of thought could and did lead others to stress the importance of more positive social duties.

One of these others, Marcus Aurelius, lived from 121-188 A.D., was a member of a distinguished Roman family, oriented his thought around the central concept of nature, and believed everything disappeared from the cosmos by passing into something else, where change was orderly and regular. This orderliness was evidence to Aurelius that the universe was rational and intelligent and was, in fact, one living being, possessed of a single soul. Like Epictetus, Aurelius emphasized social duties such as an obligation to behave altruistically, to act scrupulously, to accept unaffected duty and love, to act unselfishly, to avoid the lie and to practice justice in thought.

In affirming obligations toward one's fellow, Aurelius looked back to the classical community based upon a sense of law and order and of balance and moderation which was one of the principal marks of the classical spirit. Aurelius's emphasis on duty abandoned the self-interest of Plato and Aristotle, reflecting a change in the culture that had become tired and discouraged.

About 200 A.D. Sextus Empiricus summarized the long and varied development of philosophical Skepticism. Like the Epicureans and the Stoics, the Skeptics sought peace of mind, but the Stoics held it was reached by recognizing individuals to be tiny fragments in an infinite whole. On one hand, the Epicureans believed peace of mind was reached by coming to know that the universe was a vast mechanism in which the gods did not and could not intervene. On the other hand, Skeptics thought it was reached by realizing that there was no conclusive evidence one way or the other for any of the beliefs by which people live. Skepticism supported a view that late classical culture was a tired and discouraged society in which peace of mind replaced social progress and self-development.

CHAPTER THREE

The Individual of the Dark Ages

Greek political thought emphasized independence, autonomy and self-realization in an interdependent social arrangement. This was irrelevant to those who survived the collapse of classical culture and the wreck of the Roman Empire. The fall of Rome around 200-450 A.D. was a devastating occurrence that profoundly impacted the course of Western philosophy. Augustine recorded the period as one of moral deterioration during which the Roman State descended from the "heights of excellence into the depths of depravity": The young were so corrupted by luxury and greed that "the degradation of traditional morality ceased to be a gradual decline and became a torrential downhill rush" (St. Augustine 1984, 69).

After the death of Marcus Aurelius in 180 A.D., Rome saw a succession of weak and incompetent rulers. For eighty years, not a single ruler died peacefully and between 235-249 A.D. there were no less than seven emperors. Near the end of the century a line of strong rulers appeared, but the Empire had already lost its vitality and been laid waste, commerce had been disrupted, and cities deserted. Because only the strongest measures could halt their ruin, Diocletian radically altered the character of the principate when he came to the throne in 284 A.D. Diocletian abandoned all traces of republican government and became a despot surrounded by ceremony. Called lord and master, even his subjects of highest rank were obliged to prostrate themselves before him. A sense of helplessness and defeat was produced in the populace, no doubt by the pressure of external events, the physical crumbling of the Empire, and civil strife, but also by Diocletian's internal reorganization of the Empire.

As their vast Empire went to pieces before their eyes, Roman subjects drew comfort from the belief in an omniscient, omnipotent, all good deity who was strong enough and wise enough to guide the affairs that human personalities could no longer control. Disappointment grew over the inability of the Empire to cope with economic crises and barbarian invasions. Mystery cults and other movements, contemporary with the rise of Christianity, all rejected the old humanistic-naturalistic ideal in favor of a supra-human excellence achieved only through some supra-natural agency that brought hope to the masses and reflected widespread uneasiness. To its contemporaries, Christianity was just another mystery cult; an obscure and inconsequential Jewish sect of very small significance. However, when Jesus repeatedly preached the imminent coming of the kingdom, the ordinary person in the street understood it in a political sense and took the promised kingdom to be a revival of an autonomous Hebrew monarchy that would throw the Romans out and establish peace, freedom, and prosperity. For the Romans themselves, this Messianic hope naturally created serious political problems, and since they had been so lenient with the Christians, they could not understand why the latter refused to conform.

Jesus began with God, not with the individual. For him the good life consisted in pleasing God, not in developing the individual to full form. Jesus also emphasized love and cooperation with one's neighbor, not for mutual profit and enjoyment, but because of the common fatherhood of God. This sense of common fatherhood emphasized the essential equality of all. Jesus' view was therefore genuinely altruistic, outgoing, and democratic. Because Jesus put aside Greek interest in egoism, courage, self-congratulation, and socially-oriented conduct, the questions became how to combine Greek insight into quality with the Christian emphasis on equality and how to create opportunity for all, rather than to select the fortunate few.

Paul's vision of the coming of the kingdom was less a final day of accounting or day of judgment than it was a spiritual state--the individual's union with the savior. To be saved was to be united with Christ. When one died, one became not only dead to sin, but alive to God through a union with Jesus Christ. Paul was unconcerned with the question about how the divinity came to reside in a particular human being, the man Jesus, son of Joseph, the carpenter of Nazareth. This

question of how divinity came to reside in humanity was addressed by
the unknown author of the gospel according to John:

> In the beginning the Word existed. The Word was with God, and the
> word was divine. It was he that was with God in the beginning.
> Everything came into existence through him, and apart from him,
> nothing came to be. . . . So the Word became flesh and blood and
> lived for a while among us, abounding in blessing and truth, and we
> saw the honor God had given him, such honor as only a Son receives
> from his Father. (Jones 1970, 2:50 51)

John, as this author has been named by tradition, moved in a
different world than Paul. The term translated as Word is the Greek
logos. Word, or *logos*, is a term drawn from Greek philosophy that
was foreign to the mystery cults and to ancient Judaism. To John,
Jesus Christ was not Paul's resurrected God; instead, he was more
exalted and more abstract--the *logos* of Hellenistic philosophy. As
noted earlier, the *logos* conception had faint beginnings in Heraclitus
and further development in Stoicism. The Stoics affirmed existence of
a creative and generative force which they called the *logos* and
conceived to be divine in some fashion. For John, Jesus was simply
the eternal and divine *logos*, the Word of God which took on human
shape and which acquired habitation at a particular point in space and
time.

John attempted to interpret the *logos* to the advantage of
Christianity, making the new religion philosophically respectable
among the learned of the day. It was an attempt to make God closer to
the people that sprang from the end of the old Classical culture's
emphasis on self-respect, autonomy and independence. The *logos*
represented primarily a sense of personal inadequacy, and a
corresponding need of external support that John shared with so many
of his time. God sent his only begotten Son (the *logos*), himself
divine but dependent on God, into the world so that through him the
world might be saved. Though John emphasized the tender mercy of
the Father, this personal interpretation of the *logos* doctrine with which
it was fused passed into the future of the church.

Developing Christianity was directed largely toward the uneducated
and the illiterate, but when Christianity became socially respectable
rational Platonism proved both a model and a threat. After Diocletian
abdicated in 305 A.D., Constantine established himself as emperor and
issued an edict of toleration under which Christianity obtained the status
of a State religion. The result of pressures of institutionalization,
movements within the church began to appeal to the magic of the

sacraments and a worship based on fear of God and of hellfire instead of love and identification with the divine. As institutionalism progressed, orthodoxy submerged responsibility and free will, and authority, inner-suffering, sincerity, and God-reality replaced reason, knowledge and social understanding. Pessimism and the human predicament became the predominant paradigms, from which arose a tension between the institution and that rare creature, the genuine individual. St. Augustine's work is understandable only as part of this Christian struggle for supremacy, orthodoxy, and a philosophical base. He formulated an ideology for the new alliance between the Church and state, reconciled Christians with imperial rule, and converted the Church into a powerful buttress of secular authority.

During the centuries it took for the collapse of classical culture, the idea of a human predicament gradually emerged. Reflecting a sense of insecurity and pessimism with which people had to come to look at this world, Augustine fully shared this mood. Classical philosophy, overthrown by the Christian discovery of God and modified through Augustine's writings, gave birth to a new kind of person, born out of the disorder and disillusion of the classical world, that was destined to dominate the West for centuries.[1] This person had an abnormal sense of sinfulness and guilt, which came from Augustine's estimate of the miserable predicament of mankind that was to dominate social attitudes for more than a thousand years. Augustine's influence and the feelings of guilt and sinfulness, passed to us through Calvin and the Puritans, is too pervasive to escape. Understanding one's self in America today means trying to understand Augustine.

Medieval Mind--Age Of Faith

In the Middle Ages the ultimate justification for all conduct was not reason, but the authority of divine scriptures and institutions. What distinguishes the modern mind from the Medieval is a secular point-of-view shared with the Greeks. For them and for today's society, life on earth is its own end, but for Medieval people life was beyond this world. During the middle ages, man's proper relation with the Creator became the primary concern of the Western world for some twelve centuries, including St. Augustine.

St. Augustine was born in North Africa in 354 A.D. After teaching Rhetoric in Rome, he became attracted to Neo-platonism. He suffered an agonizing conversion to Christianity in 386 A.D. and was baptized the next year. In 391 A.D. he was ordained a priest against his wishes and five years later was chosen Bishop of Hippo. He worked prodigiously, until he died in 430 A.D. as invading vandals besieged Hippo, fashioning the first philosophical explication of Christianity. As a result of his works, he came to be known as the great Doctor of the Latin Church.

Though his general philosophical view was Platonic, Augustine's outlook was theological not civic, and he approached worldly life from a vantage point totally distinct from the Classical thinkers. With the fall of the Roman Empire, Christianity transformed itself into a State religion, and a new kind of sovereignty emerged, in which the church eventually assumed control, replacing political principles with sacerdotal ones. In Christian philosophy, which differed radically from Classical, God was the primary and almost the exclusive object of concern. God replaced the Greek good, and man's relation to nature gave way to relation with an absolutely perfect being. Thus, Christians always felt a sense of failure; never being as good as one ought to be and never measuring up to that perfect being.

Unlike the Greeks, Augustine made no room for reason, teaching the divorce of body and mind, and advocating separation of the rational and spiritual. His authority was the Word of God, not rational Empiricism, and he believed the universe was moved by the love of God. He defined ultimate reality as perfection, and believed happiness, the chief desire of the State, was obtainable only through worship of the one true God. Unlike the Greeks--for whom morality was a social ethic with happiness as its aim, ethics were an optimistic look forward, and failure was ignorance that knowledge could cure--Christian morality was an element of religious practice, the Christian ethic was pessimistic, and falling away from the ideal was not ignorance but sin.

Sin was a special kind of evil connected with a self-conscious will; the willful rejection of the commands and wishes of an all-powerful Father. Instead of being cured by knowledge, bad conduct was insoluble by human means, and people required assistance to act virtuously. Perfection was never attainable--not because perfection is merely an ideal state towards which all strive and no one can ever fully attain--but because of man's inherent shortcomings, moral deficiencies and evil will. Citizenship in the City (community) of God was salvation through the worship and the rejection of all false Gods. Injustice was not inevitable in government, but justice could be found only in the commonwealth whose founder and ruler was Christ.

Augustine shared the Classical belief that people were social animals, and the individual was judged by participation in community. Community was not each and every association in the population, but an association united by a common sense of right in a community of interest:

> God chose to make a single individual the starting-point of all mankind, and that his purpose in this was that the human race should not merely be united for a society by natural likeness, but should also be bound together by a kind of tie of kinship to form a harmonious unity, linked together by the 'bond of peace.' (St. Augustine 1984, 547)

Friendship extended all the way from immediate family and City to the whole world, including nations with whom the individual was joined by membership of the human society and even to the whole universe.

Like Plato and Aristotle, the two dominant philosophers of the Classical period, Augustine and Thomas Aquinas were dominant figures during the Medieval period. A similar continuity of thought and feeling existed between them, because they shared a common core doctrine and faith as Christian thinkers, but these two figures were separated by eight centuries. This resulted in the development of new ideas, attitudes and values during the long period between Augustine's death and Thomas's birth. During this eight-century interval, sometimes referred to as the Medieval interval, the Dark Ages descended over the West.

Nearly anything that survived at all was chiefly the result of the church's existence, which passionately converted pagans to orthodoxy. By the end of the Dark Ages, Christianity was more widely spread, orthodoxy more firmly entrenched, and the church emerged stronger than it had ever been before the fall of Rome but, of course, profoundly changed. The early church had been episcopal and not papal, but now the bishops of Rome claimed primacy over all other bishops, Christian kings, and princes. The two-power doctrine between King and Church of Augustine's time had changed and a Christian king, *qua* Christian, was a subject of the pope.

By the eleventh century, the church--no longer an other-worldly society of brothers--had grown into a great secular institution. The popes became temporal monarchies with power greater than any of the secular sovereigns. By the thirteenth century, the church was so indispensable to Western society that any sudden abandonment of its secular role would have been disastrous. The average person--even when immersed in ordinary life and personal world--believed that earthly life derived whatever significance it had from a life beyond. This sense of dependency sharply distinguished the Medieval mind from the modern.

Feudalism developed concurrently with the this-worldly institution of the primitive church and emerged from the chaotic times before the dissolution of the Roman Empire with more and more responsibilities.[2] As the central government proved incapable of performing its proper functions, men of property in the various parts of the Empire collected taxes and, in the course of time, became responsible for the administration of justice on their estates. The life of the community came to depend on a complex set of personal relationships in which the Greek and Roman notion that every citizen stands in an identical relationship to the State and owes it individual loyalty was replaced by the notion of personal loyalty to the immediate overlord. Thus, the church and feudalism, the two great institutions of the Middle Ages, colored every phase of Medieval life.

For the greater part of the Middle Ages, ideas relating to the public sphere were shaped by Roman concepts and Christian doctrines concerning the structure of society as a corporation. They led without great effort to the thesis that the Christian was a member of the all-embracing, comprehensive corporation, the church. In Pauline language, the Christian became a new creature and underwent a metamorphosis during the sacramental act of baptism. As a result of the working of divine grace, the act of baptism divested the worshiper of one's natural humanity and one became a participant of the divine attributes. This had the important consequence that the individual no longer shaped one's own life in accordance with his natural, human insight and was no longer endowed with autonomous, indigenous functions. As a member of a corporation, the church, law was given to, not made by the individual. The individual became absorbed in the church which was itself governed by a monarchical, descending, theocratic theme of government and law according to which original power was located in one supreme authority.

These basic principles relative to the individual as subject to higher authority are contained in the Pauline letters. In his letter to the Romans, he stated the belief that every soul should be subjected to higher authorities, including princely power, because whatever power there was came from God. "What I am, I am by the grace of God."[3] What concerned and distinguished the Christian was faith and because one had faith one obeyed the law. Obedience was indubitably the message of Pauline doctrine.

Paul's message that the individual had no autonomous character made understandable Augustine's view that obedience to the command of superior authority was the hallmark of the Christian. This concept of superior and inferior, one above the other, summed up the status of the individual within a pure descending doctrine. It was this conception of inferior status which explained the prevailing Medieval view on and led to development of the concept of majority and its corollary of obedience.

This view of individuality was carried over into the body corporate of the kingdom as well. The individual was less in the position to assert autonomous rights under the body corporate of the kingdom, because the King's power itself was not derived from the people of the kingdom or any individuals, but from divinity. The fundamental presupposition of those with power in Medieval society was that the individual accepted one's standing, divested one's individuality, and followed direction from above. This subjugation of the individual was also contained in the concept of common father propounded by Classical Roman writers and Paul himself. Pursuant to this concept, the ruler was placed in a position with regard to his subjects as that of the father to his family and God was the father of all. These concepts resulted in the individual as subject having no rights whatsoever in the public field.

To the contrary, what mattered was the public weal, the public welfare, the public well-being, and the good of society itself at the expense of individual well-being if necessary. Society was one whole, indivisible, and the individual was such an infinitesimally small part that individual interests were easily sacrificed at the alter of public good. In this descending theme of government, property was considered an issue of divine grace, and the ruler was the full owner of all of the property of his subjects and could dispose of it as he saw fit. Disregard of the interests of the individual was not a disregard of rights because the individual did not have autonomy within this framework, but rather was a sign of complete absorption in society. Society was a large organism in which each member had been allotted special function which to be pursued for the common good. An individual did not exist for one's own sake, but for the sake of the whole society. Everything moved on an objective level of a divine plan which purposely disregarded the importance of an individual's contributions and initiative. The Medieval emphasis on the collectivist phenomenon successfully prevented emergence of individual rights.

Despite the descending theme of government just discussed, the lower reaches of the community took for granted that the individual had precisely the rights denied by those in authority. In the reality of transacting everyday business, the Medieval person participated in associations, unions, fraternities, guilds and communities, which considered the individual a full member. These were communities of equals, not initiated from above or legislated by a superior, but practiced as a natural way of conducting the business of the village. These expressions of communal will provided considerable assistance in the process of emancipating the individual.

Once the feudal system lost its military character, a practical system of government arose that accorded the individual considerable standing. Characterized by a strong personal bond between the feudal lord and the feudal vassal, rights and duties on both sides forged the first strong individual ties. A legal bond with mutual rights and duties created a kind of reciprocal equilibrium in which the obligations flowed one to another. Legal means for resisting a feudal lord and repudiating the feudal contract by the vassal existed under certain circumstances. Individual-personal relationships were created that did not exist in the descending form of government due to the institutionalization of faith. These relationships caused one great Medievalist, Sidney Painter, to say that the fundamental features of the feudal system passed into our political tradition, and individual liberty as part of the fundamental law was of feudal origin.[4] Within the feudal function of kingship, law was made by counsel, consent, cooperation, and teamwork, prompted by the individual's personal relationship between the king (as feudal lord) and his tenants. During the turn of the twelfth and thirteenth centuries, the seeds for future constitutional development and standing of the individual in society were nurtured.

During this time, early Christian and Greek thought was rediscovered and fertilized and doctrinal background for such developments became a Medieval adjustment of the Platonic system. Major works of Aristotle which had become inaccessible during the twelfth century became accessible again during the thirteenth century, influencing a more vigorous intellectual life. A gradual expansion of people's intellectual horizons awakened a great desire for knowledge, universities began to spring up, a period of artistry began, and there was a remarkable revival of this-worldly interests.

The central problem of the thirteenth century philosopher was to find a place for these "this-worldly" ends as reflected in the science, arts, manners and customs, and political institutions. Plato's personification of the Philosopher King signified that the individual had receded. The Platonic system, through its absorption into Christianity became the backcloth of Medieval political and social organization. This laid the foundation for Thomas Aquinas's further adjustments of Aristotelian concepts within the Christian framework. The philosophical synthesis that finally emerged was the crowning achievement of the Middle Ages.[5]

Thomas Aquinas was born in 1225 A.D. in southern Italy. In 1257 A.D., he obtained the Doctorate of Theology Degree and engaged in lecturing and writing, interrupted by frequent journeys in service of his Dominican Order and the church. He died in 1274 A.D. when not yet fifty years of age, but he stands functionally to the Middle Ages as Plato and Aristotle do to the Classical world. Thomas was more than a theologian and the problems of his time were more than purely theological problems. The supreme good to the early Christian was getting into a right relation with God, but--as society slowly emerged from the darkness of the early Middle Ages and began to rebuild culture and civilization--people inevitably felt renewed interest in this-worldly things. Therefore, the central problem for Thomas Aquinas in the Middle Ages was to reconcile the Christian and Classical views of humanity and the world.

As early as 1210 A.D., fifteen years before Thomas Aquinas's birth, church authorities forbade teaching Aristotle's natural science. Thus, it took considerable courage to maintain, as Thomas Aquinas did, that one-sided Christian insights required supplementation and that people were also natural animals. In this Thomas Aquinas too was a true individualist; it was one thing to recognize that the Classical mind had made significant discoveries that could be noted to supplement the Christian view, but quite another to actually work out the needed synthesis. The difficulty of the task to which Thomas Aquinas set himself should not be underestimated, because the Christians had radically altered the conception of every part of the Classical scheme. For the Christian, people were, in Augustine's words, crooked, sordid, bespotted, ulcerous, helpless and depraved. The synthesis required between two such radically differing views went far beyond any earlier thinker.

Thomas agreed with Aristotle that humans were natural beings with natural ends described by Aristotle, but to Thomas God created a world with many different degrees of truth, goodness and reality. The many different levels of reality, or species of creatures demonstrated the infinite variety of the divine nature. Like photographs taken on a different angle which show an object from different viewpoints, the diversity and multiplicity of the creatures echoed the infinity of the original. Despite divine providence both foreseeing all that would happen and causing it to happen, Thomas maintained that some events were contingent. Free will and freedom from coercion is not to say that will was uncaused. Rather, there was a dual causality according to which human will was attributed to free choice and to God. This contingency, without which human freedom was illusory, necessitated moral responsibility. Good was not simply whether an act fulfilled some desire or provided happiness, but whether it was in accord with the objectively characterized form common to all. Because the individual was in this sense more than Aristotle thought him to be, the supreme good was individual happiness through knowledge of God.

To Thomas Aquinas, the notions of the individual and the Christian corresponded to two different categories of thought. People were a part of nature that demanded attention, which then brought about man's political community. *Fidelis Christianus* corresponded to the supernatural and the citizen to the natural. *Fidelis* had to share attention with the *civis*. The individual became a full participant and a member of the State, or the congregation of all. Accordingly, the gulf in Pauline doctrine between the natural and the Christian was bridged. The natural, washed away by baptism, was reborn and viewed as a constituent member of the State. The core of the new doctrine was that the natural individual emerged independent and autonomous within the framework of the natural order. Government was no longer laid down by law given to a subjected mankind, but instead was the servant and protector of the interests of liberated individuals. He who had been overshadowed by the Christian was now resuscitated and reinstated. The full value and potential of human dignity was well on its way to be recognized.[6]

Renaissance and Reformation--Age of Reason

Beginning in the Renaissance period, defined here as 1400 to early 1600 A.D., beliefs gradually began to change.[7] The hierarchical relationship of the individual to God was eventually replaced by horizontal relationships connecting individuals to their social milieu. The good life changed from a right relationship with God to a working relationship with one's fellow. Medieval political thought, with its emphasis on sin, could not satisfy Renaissance people. Shaped by capitalism, new money, the ideals of Humanism, and the Protestant Reformation, this new person was an individualist that turned attention from godliness and heavenly matters to concerns with the world and its values.

The success of the scientific method and the importance of mathematics grew immensely, measurement and experimentation became the source of all truth, and the world was conceived of as a giant machine. At the same time, Naturalism--as old as Thrasymachus, but buried for centuries beneath the religious orientation of the Middle Ages--arose again during the fifteenth century and became an accepted part of the complex changes called the Renaissance. Defined as the disposition to ignore moral considerations and to concentrate on ascertaining the facts about power and the means of attaining it, Naturalism re-emerged as a legitimate philosophy. In place of old values, power became the focus of attention. At the beginning of this period, Niccolo Machiavelli, the spokesman for realism, introduced reason as the reality in politics.[8] He urged rulers to use force, severity, deceit and immoral acts to achieve national goals. In the latter part of this period, human reason was elevated to the position of highest authority and people's interests shifted from the supernatural to the natural.

Machiavelli was an Italian statesman and student of politics who lived between 1469 and 1527 A.D. Born in Florence as a son of a jurist, he became a leading figure in the Republic of Florence after the Medici family was driven out in 1498 A.D. He served as head of the second Chancery and first secretary of the council of the Republic for fourteen years. The Medici family returned to power and dismissed Machiavelli from his office in 1512 A.D. when King Ferdinand of Spain in Holy League with the Pope took control of French Milan and Florence. Accused of conspiring against the new regime the next year, Machiavelli was at first arrested, tortured, imprisoned, and finally released on order of Pope Leo X. The last fourteen years of his life were spent writing books on history and politics, as well as poems and comedies, becoming a leading literary figure of the Renaissance. Best known for his book *The Prince*, which established him as the father of the modern science of politics--what came to be called *realpolitik*--he set down rules that the prince should follow to keep political power.

In *The Prince*, Machiavelli espoused the idea that a ruler need not trouble over means, but must use any means, no matter how wicked, to strike down his enemies and make his people obey. The book was dedicated to His Magnificence Lorenzo de Medici and was undoubtedly intended to bring to Machiavelli the favorable attention of the Medicean government. Machiavelli's purpose for dedicating *The Prince* to the Medicis did not work and he was never entrusted with public office again. However, largely as a result of his book, his name has come to stand for all that is deep, dark, and treacherous in statesmanship.

For him, there were only two questions: Whatever people aimed at was good and their acts toward attaining their aims were virtue. Machiavelli addressed the leading element of what became a new political ideal in the West, the idea of power politics. The essence of this ideal was his conception of people as stupid, irrational, and incapable of governing themselves intelligently and effectively. He believed people were moved by passion and ambition rather than by reason. They were so selfish and short-sighted that a strong power was required to keep them from destroying themselves. It followed that the only feasible government was a strong monarchy. This is the point of view of the political Naturalists.

Machiavelli's doubts about traditional virtues arose out of his darkly pessimistic view of human nature. In his view, people were so deeply self-interested that they broke the bonds of love whenever it was useful. They could never be expected to keep faith, and only fear of punishment and the consequences of behaving badly controlled conduct. He conceded it would be praiseworthy if indeed princes exhibited the full range of qualities usually held to be good, but the way people lived was so different from how they should live that this was impossible. If a ruler persisted in doing what he ought, his power would be undermined rather than maintained. Therefore, a prince who wished to maintain his position in the world must act immorally when it became necessary.

In Machiavelli's principate, public office seekers did so only for the power, prestige and future profit that it offered. No one in the principality was overly concerned with the common interests, because no sense of commonalty or shared humanity existed. Rather, individual self-interest, a preoccupation with personal rights, and accumulation of wealth drove the entire nation, including the rulers and the ruled. Decisions were not made in the long-term interests of the nation as a whole, but for short-term interests and profit taking. Economic interests were the first and foremost considerations, and every question, public or private, was decided on that basis rather than a shared belief in what was right or good for the whole.

As Naturalism was revived, new political and social ideals--money, power, and the physical expansion of Europe to America and to Asia--created an unstable society in which the energetic and ambitious could rise. Early in this process, the church urged scholarship and contributed to the depth and pervasiveness of the Renaissance spirit by an active patronage. As the movement developed, however, the new ideal gradually replaced the old Christian conception and even the papacy took measures to increase its revenues when traditional sources were no longer sufficient in the changing economic scene.

Early in the fourteenth century, the Popes having become hardly more than an instrument of monarchical policy in France, a source of new revenues was developed in the sale of benefits and offices. As disputes over title to the offices resulted in expensive lawsuits, the

Roman pontiff made a threefold profit; the benefice was awarded, then the annates were collected, and finally court costs were assessed. Thus, the papal court became a useful source of revenue, and the Popes gave it primary jurisdiction over cases formerly heard in Episcopal courts.

Offensive as these practices were, the selling of indulgences came to be the historically crucial abuse. This practice had its roots in the primitive church where a backsliding member repented and either fasted, suffered lashes or made a contribution to charity, whichever the congregation chose. Over centuries, passion became private and determination of the nature of the satisfaction passed from the congregation to the priest who imposed a penance to be worked off as punishment. To avoid difficulties arising from decentralized administration of this penance system, the notion of a treasury of merit was developed. As the moral standards of the papacy declined, the market value of indulgences was not overlooked and the Popes launched into the large-scale business of selling what amounted to an insurance policy against possible inconveniences in the life to come. Payment of a sufficient sum insured the purchaser of safety, regardless of the inner-state of one's soul.

For 1000 years the church had laid down the rules for economic, social and religious life and all were subject to the Roman Pontiff. Around 1396 John Huss gave communion to worshippers, let them drink wine from the chalice, and encouraged them to read the bible themselves. For this challenge to Catholic Church dogma he was summoned by the Pope to explain himself, which he ignored. His next challenge was to oppose the sale of indulgences, for which he was excommunicated by the Pope himself. Later imprisoned for heresy, he was ordered to surrender to authority by recanting his beliefs. Upon his refusal, he was burned at the stake for his dissent against church dogma.

One hundred years later, Martin Luther's beliefs and his dissent ultimately resulted in freedom of choice to the commoner after 1000 years of being told what to do and what to believe by the church. Born in 1483 A.D. as the son of peasants, he attended one of the leading universities of Germany, a center of Humanistic studies. Like Augustine and so many other Christians, Luther was oppressed by a sense of sin and believed that his primary need was to find God. He tried every conceivable manner to achieve union with God and failed, but soon found in Paul a doctrine of salvation by faith alone rather than by the works of penance, alms giving or asceticism. Therefore, salvation was available as a matter of faith by belief in the Lord Jesus and in the mercy of God.

A depressive, Luther entered an Augustinian monastery to please God. While practicing his prayers he came to the vision that salvation was for all who believed. Each person had a direct relationship to God and did not need the church to mediate that relationship. He too became outraged at the Papal indulgences being sold to remove guilt, and he posted ninety-five reasons against the practice. In the mid-1400s Luther used the new printing press to persuade the general public to his teachings against the church. For this he was excommunicated and given sixty days to present himself. Luther answered the call when summoned but refused to retract a thing. For his obstinacy, Charles V condemned him as a heretic, after which he was kidnapped by Frederich the Wise. Alone with his beliefs, he set about translating the bible and published the new testament for the priesthood of the common people.

Luther's doctrine undermined the whole hierarchical system of the church and legitimized a universal priesthood of believers which made sacraments and priests unnecessary to mediate between the worshiper and his God. The authority of the Bible, as interpreted by every individual, substituted for the authority of the church. Once Luther had taken this stand, the church immediately set about trying to destroy him. Though few Princes dared to protect Luther, some did so because they sympathized with his attack on papal abuses. He, nevertheless, had an immense popular following that would have been dangerous to oppose, and they could use the religious revolt to free themselves from ecclesiastical control and extend their own power.

Luther's doctrine of justification by faith accepted Augustine's denial of free will. Literally, Luther believed that an end to be sought by the state was the preservation of peace. To him, people were so sinful and vicious that without a sovereign to keep them in order they would quickly dispatch one and another out of this world. He concluded that people sin if they lie to government, deceive it or are disloyal to what it has ordered and commanded. Moreover, Luther taught that wicked authority was authority still in the sight of God. This political theory was poles apart from the Medieval ideal of the limited monarchy, and it fully underwrote the most extreme claims of the new-type sovereign.

While insisting on the subject's absolute duty of obedience to the prince, Luther tried to extricate the Protestant princes from a corresponding duty to obey their Catholic emperor. In 1525 A.D. peasant revolts threatened his teachings, and he sided with the Princes who slaughtered the new dissenters 120,000 fold. With this decision, Luther became one of the harshest reactionaries of his time. He also found himself in the position of the earliest Christians, having to choose between individual religion and the requirements of institutionalism. Essential for the preservation of the movement, the new church nevertheless created a dilemma, because a church organization required a definite doctrine as a mark of membership. Accordingly, the new theology soon became as inflexible and orthodox as the old, and those who opposed it even by a hair's breath were cast out. Refusing to allow any new thinking, his dogma achieved a new establishment to rival the old, and his reformation caused a counter-revolution leading to the bloody Crusades that ended only when openness, toleration and dissent became values during the Renaissance as protections against orthodoxy's descent into tyranny.

The core of Luther's Protestant insight was in the certainty of every individual conscience, and Protestantism rested on the immediate, felt-data of conscience. This commitment to the primacy of conscience was an expression of one of the basic motifs of the dawning new world--Individualism. The emphasis on the subjective and private, the dictates of the individual conscience, and the politics of subjective feeling, were new dimensions in modern culture. Now economic and social developments fashioned an individual who was intent on this-worldly affairs, and a completely secular universe revealed to this new individual how he could satisfy his new desires. This created the fundamental problem of how to balance the need for order, discipline and obedience against freedom and spontaneity, and how to achieve the controls necessary for economic and political survival without destroying civil liberties. Thus, the great strengths of Protestantism were also its greatest weaknesses, and the questions it failed to answer persistently plague society to this day.

Faith in Science

Development of the scientific method was a part of a widespread movement of thought reflected in the transformation of political and moral ideals in the weakening of the church. At work was a growing passion for exploration and artistry that delighted in the sounds, smells, and sights of nature. One theorist who taught science and artistry was Leonardo da Vinci (1452-1519 A.D.). He demonstrated that there were uniformities in nature that close observation, coupled with experiment would reveal. One hundred years later the same spirit led William Gilbert to improve the compass, determine measures of latitude, and develop other navigational aids. His work helped bring the earth down to scale, showed it as a natural object among others, and demonstrated the pervasiveness and simplicity of natural law.

After Gilbert came Francis Bacon, who acted as a publicist for science as he sought the power and the good things it brings and rejected deductive methods in favor of inductive. Bacon sold the value of science to others on the theme that knowledge is power. Born in 1561 A.D. in the full tide of the Renaissance, he undertook a total reconstruction of the sciences, arts, and all human knowledge. Bacon saw that a purely deductive science was not a natural science and rejected the main tendency of Medieval science to favor the deductive method by starting from propositions of the highest order of generality. He concluded that, though observation was fundamental, it was insufficient. To fulfill this need to guide observation at every step, Bacon developed the inductive method. This method involved experimentation to establish lower orders of generality upon which higher orders were then based. Using Bacon's method, Copernicus developed his heliocentric hypothesis and Kepler his three laws. Not until Galileo, however, were empirical observations organized into a deductive and demonstrative structure. This scientific concept of reality substituted a quantitative mechanistic view of nature for the qualitative and theological look of the Middle Ages.

By the time Galileo died in 1642 A.D., the Western world had changed radically from the Medieval. Faint outlines of modern culture began to appear in the form of territorial states and capitalist type economies. Colonization in America was progressing at a rapid pace and the conception of a single, unified Christendom was shattered. The person fashioned by this culture was an enterprising personality. A loosening of the old social structure was making an individualist, dedicated to the acquisition of wealth and power, alert to the possibilities for self improvement, and determined to compete more or less successfully in a capitalistic economy. The Greek ideal of all-around development of the individual no longer held great appeal as a quantitative and mechanical view of nature was increasingly substituted for the teleological conception from the Middle Ages.

Early modern philosophers that followed the Renaissance sought to solve the problem of mind versus matter with a dualism in which immaterial reality was provided a sphere outside the material reality being rapidly explored by the new science. In this sphere of immaterial reality, they proposed to locate God and the human soul. However, at least one of these early modern philosophers adopted a different course; Hobbes, a Monist, rejected the notion of immaterial reality.

Thomas Hobbes (1588-1679 A.D.), an English philosopher and political theorist, served as secretary to Sir Francis Bacon and tutored the Prince of Wales, later Charles II, in mathematics. He fled to the

European continent during the English Civil War, traveled widely, and met many European philosophers and scientists. Two developments in his time influenced his thought; one was the new system of physics being worked out by Galileo and others; another, was the English Civil War. Hobbes was unsympathetic with Parliament's struggle against the Crown's invasion of ancient rights and the religious sentiments of the Puritans. He believed the freedoms about which they shouted cloaked their own selfish interests. The Parliamentarians, for example, sought a grip on supreme power rather than liberty and justice for the people. To Hobbes, inhumanity made an all-powerful government essential.

His most famous work, *Leviathan*, was published in 1651 A.D. and demonstrated both these early influences on his thought.[9] Hobbes' materialistic and mechanistic philosophy was founded on the emerging laws of physics and motions of heavenly bodies. He believed the whole universe could be analyzed as behavior of material particles moving in accordance with simple mechanical laws, and he applied the same rationale to earthly bodies. Nothing but a body in motion, each individual was no more than a region of the material realm, distinguishable only by the motions occurring there, consisting purely as changes in spatial relations of the parts of human bodies. These changes were completely determined by prior events, by changes in the region we call ourselves, or by other changes in contiguous regions. Activities within the mind, such as thinking, perceiving, imagining, and remembering, were all simply motions in the body.

Hobbes also attempted to place moral and political philosophy on a scientific basis, and he based his philosophy on a fear of anarchy. In *Leviathan*, he denied the social being of humanity and described the state of nature as anarchy, which he said every person sought to escape. Man, driven by competition, defiance, and glory, was unfit to live in communities, and was moved chiefly by selfish considerations, desire for power, and fear of others. Hobbes believed in the general inclination of individuals to pursue power ceaselessly until death. He believed that people lived communally for survival, even though they were wholly unfit to do so, only to avoid the destructive consequences of their own greed. The question became how to control these unruly mobs and, for those like Hobbes who rejected the authority of the church, final authority was found in the secular arm--a strong sovereign.

The mechanistic analogy employed by Hobbes had no room for values, which he saw as purely subjective. Since values could not be interpreted in materialistic terms, they were relegated to the status of mere appearances. As such, they existed only in individual experience, and there was no public realm for them; no place for value in Hobbes' world of fact. Hobbes' views are important because they disclose what a philosophic synthesis must avoid. If Medieval philosophy is placed at one extreme where the scientific view of reality was ignored and concentration was given to the valuational view, then Hobbesian philosophy is at the other extreme where the valuational point of view was ignored in favor of the scientific. Hobbes' successor philosophers asked how--in the physical world of matter in motion where selfish interests, personal rights, and economic decision-making dominate--can one find a place for human spontaneity, significance of human life, and validity of thought.

Rene Descartes (1596-1650 A.D.) was a contemporary of Thomas Hobbes, but held to none of the Hobbesian principles of self-interest. Instead, Descartes underwent a mystical experience from which he believed he discovered a new scientific method for achieving absolute certainty. This was a universal and infallible method of reasoning that he worked out over a period of years and that became a set of twenty-one rules for directing the human mind toward a solution to all human problems. Like Hobbes, Descartes fell in love with mathematical certainty but where mathematics had been a manipulation of signs for Hobbes, for Descartes mathematical reasoning was the basis for a great metaphysical structure upon which a system of values and a god could be erected. Descartes believed in an objective, rational order to the world that the mind infallibly discerned in clear and distinct intuitions, and in native power to know a reality that is fundamentally rational. By making reason adequate and equal for all, Descartes laid an intellectual foundation for democratic social and political institutions. His theories and understandings of the human nature permitted education to raise all to the level of enlightened and responsible citizen. Thus, for him mathematical knowledge was an absolute that provided insight into an objective and rational real.

Attempting to find a *via media* that would accept the new physics without ending in a completely secular, amoral, and Hobbesian view of the universe, Descartes developed a compromise. This *Cartesian Compromise* was exceedingly simple: Descartes argued that mind and body were separate--mind was concerned with spiritual truths, while body was governed by the laws of physics. Inevitably, objects of sense perception were less than real, if mind and matter were completely distinct substances, but sense perception could be explained by proposing their interaction. If mind and body are completely different kinds of things, and if the truths about each follow from the distinct nature of each, it is impossible for the science of minds and science of bodies to contradict each other. Theology, therefore, had no reason to interfere with the study of physics, and physicists no reason to claim special competence regarding spiritual truths.

The new scientific method had both an empirical and a mathematical element, but the inferences that philosophers drew about the nature of knowledge were distorted by the exaggerated role of one such element and minimization of the other. Thus, for example, Descartes emphasized the mathematical element, made mathematical certainty his ideal, and formulated his criterion of truth and reality accordingly.[10] John Locke (1632-1704 A.D.) and his followers also relied on sense perception to obtain knowledge about the world, emphasized experimental verification, and exhibited skepticism about the possibility of achieving absolute certainty. Locke, as much a Rationalist as Descartes, made rational thought of the kind he employed as a physician his prototype.

Built into his belief was a familiar Cartesian assumption that the world consisted of two different kinds of things, minds and bodies. Locke called these states of mind ideas and believed they somehow represented the world external to bodies. Contrary to the complexity of Cartesian dilemmas, Locke aimed at a common sense philosophy preferring the concrete and practical, and starting with reason. Locke assumed that truth was experience, and the mind was a surface on which experience writes. This theory was called *historical plain method*, according to which one's mind begins as an empty surface, a *tabula rasa*, and all its ideas come from experience. Only this experience confirms or disconfirms beliefs, and the mind knows nothing but its own states.

The ethical theory that Locke developed in connection with these understandings, held that good was not the knowledge of God that St. Thomas and other Medieval philosophers had surmised, but pleasure. For Locke, the ethical problem was simply one of ascertaining which act, of all those in any given situation, was productive of the greatest positive good. Of those various acts, the one that maximized pleasure was the greatest good. However, the world of fact with which *historical plain method* was designed to deal, contained no universal or necessary connections. Locke often seemed to suggest that doing one's duty was a good in itself, but insofar as pleasure was the sole good, the motive for obeying moral law was not a sense of duty, but self-interest. Because obedience had no intrinsic worth, the motive was simply a calculation of personal advantage.

Nevertheless, Locke took a more flattering view of humanity than Hobbes, crediting him with a social nature and a high capacity for enlightenment. Locke's political theory rested on an assumption that natural law guaranteed everyone certain inalienable rights and imposed certain duties. Man's chief duty was to avoid interfering with other men's rights, defined as life, health, liberty, and possession. The shortest way to state Locke's position is that people, a collection of autonomous and independent individuals, were and remained sovereign. However, people were not sovereign in the Hobbesian sense, because Locke believed political power was limited by the laws of nature. Accordingly, one could not be compelled to join a community and could be compelled after joining only because one consented to accept the decisions of the majority upon joining the community. Under such circumstances, force against recalcitrant minorities was morally justified, providing no fundamental rights were violated. Locke was thus one of the first political thinkers to emphasize the importance of consent of the governed; a concept later used by Jefferson to undermine loyalty in the colonies to the King of England.

Locke's insistence on fundamental rights reflected the growing sense of individuality that became one of the marks of the new age. Another mark of Locke's new age thinking was the right to property, which he believed arose as an extension of bodily labor. He also gave an analogous account of the origins of money. Ironically, though Locke believed one could collect too much property, he believed that because money does not spoil it is not immoral to accumulate more than they can use. Accordingly, Locke advocated economic inequality through a political theory based upon equality. For Locke the function of a state was to implement and secure for the people those rights they ought to have; that is, life, liberty, and property. The spirit of the Declaration of Independence, the Constitution, and the Bill of Rights were thoroughly Lockean: Indeed, the American ideal today is still the Lockean state. His emphasis on maximization of pleasure, rights, experience, and laissez-faire all contributed to the growth of Individualism.

David Hume (1711-1776 A.D.) reformulated Locke's theory into the *empirical criterion of meaning*, an account of reality in which knowledge came from experience rather than rationality, and empirical data and perception formed the basis for reality. Hume saw no reason in the nature of things why any event should be followed by any other event. For example, there is no more reason why the sun should rise tomorrow than there is any reason why writing the word "necessary" should cause cars to backfire. Therefore, it followed that the pretensions of natural sciences to demonstrable reality were false. If Hume was correct in his thesis, the sciences would be limited to historical statements, that is they could report only past observations. The net result of Hume's analysis was that all knowledge of objects was merely knowledge of spatio-temporal relations among simple ideas or impressions. This kind of knowledge Hume called knowledge of matters of fact. Concepts like reality, mind, and substance, Hume dismissed on grounds that they are unobservable. This philosophical position is known as empiricism. Nevertheless, Hume agreed with the Rationalists that there are absolutely certain, demonstrable truths. The view that morality can be grounded in reason is still widely held, but is one against which Hume rebelled. He argued against Egoism on three grounds: First, he believed that it contradicted facts about conduct, by not taking into account such dispositions as benevolence, generosity, love, friendship, compassion and gratitude. Second, to hold that real motivation is always self-interest commits to a very complicated psychological theory that always rationally calculates self-interest in all situations. Third, self-love could not be the only good, for its satisfaction depends wholly on the satisfaction of various particular desires. In other words, self-love is an abstraction invented by an overly rationalistic psychology. Therefore, the ultimate basis of moral judgment could not be reason, but must be some sense of feeling. Moral judgments were not independent of subjective feelings, not in the sense that an agreement about moral appraisals was impossible, but in the sense that they could not be demonstrated by a process of deductive reasoning like that employed in mathematics. Disagreements over moral appraisals could nevertheless be overcome, because people living in a social world found it advantageous for them to agree on common, or standard evaluations. Hume's atomistic views of experience further encouraged growth of individualism by appealing to experience, perception and subjectivism, rather than to reason and unitary identity.

Hume's attack on Rationalism aroused Kant. At that point, philosophy could choose to conclude that something was wrong with the premises from which it had started and begin to work out a rational philosophy on a different basis, which is what Kant chose to do. He was followed in this project by philosophers as unlike as Hegel and Whitehead, who continued Kant's effort to rehabilitate Rationalism. Another choice for philosophy was abandonment of the quest for certainty, acceptance of provisional solutions as long as they work, and readiness to discard them when changing conditions make them no longer appropriate, which has been the solution favored by Pragmatists and radical Empiricists. The theory that knowledge occurs as a result of human interaction with the environment did not appear until much later.

CHAPTER FOUR

The Individual of Modernity

In a word, the seventeenth and eighteenth centuries were optimistic, so it is not surprising that this Age of Reason came to be called the Enlightenment. Europe emerged from a long period of superstition and bigotry and the new science revealed the universe as a fundamentally simple mechanism. In this orderly universe, behavior could be predicted and controlled in the interests of improving material and social well-being. Unlimited progress seemed possible, and philosophy followed the character of the age.

Descartes aimed at putting the new physics on a firm philosophical foundation by providing a field in which physical inquiry could be carried on undisturbed by theology. He believed that he had accomplished this by dividing reality into the distinct substances of matter and mind. However, the Rationalists carried Descartes' rationalistic bias to its logical conclusion, aiming at certainty. Starting with mathematics--the ideal of all knowledge--they wrote off perception as mere confused thinking. Locke and his followers pursued an opposite course, ending up with an equally frustrating conclusion which was concerned less with certainty than with the actual world of experience. Unfortunately, the assumption that people are aware only of their own mental states leads nowhere, because one does not know an external world, only ideas. Meanwhile, the working scientists, unperturbed by philosophical doubts about the nature of their work, continued making advance after advance that seemed to confirm the

Hobbesian vision of the world as thoroughly mechanistic. As a result, Hobbes' challenges to the traditional religious view of the cosmos were more formidable than ever.

The Philosophes, with nothing but contempt for Christianity, could be regarded either as a body with formal philosophical beliefs or an institution wielding political power. These philosophers rejected the concept of divine intervention in the world and developed common views of order to deal with the closed, completely regular system represented by the universe of the new science. For example, Montesquieu believed that laws determined human conduct, that these laws could be discovered by essentially empirical methods, and that they could be utilized to resolve social conflicts making life better in every respect. Given adequate education, humanity would be able to solve all the problems that arose in the course of life. Because they were, by and large, capable of running their own affairs, laws could be kept to a minimum, laissez-faire political and economic systems could survive, and moral theories based on self-respect, decency and the human dignity were logical outcomes. These enlightened thinkers believed reason could fashion a social order that would reflect the rationality of the cosmos.

Collapse of Confidence

The optimism did not last as industrialism resulted from application of science and technology. A process that was expected to result in unlimited improvement, actually led to urban slums where many workers were far worse off than unenlightened peasants of feudal times. The French Revolution, which rode high on issues regarding the "rights of man" and heralded a new Age of Reason and democratic freedom, collapsed into a reign of terror. Far from rational creatures controlling their destinies, humanity seemed driven by hate and fear, moved less by enlightened self-interest than irrational and destructive aggressions. The individual who emerged in the nineteenth century was very different from the one that appeared during the Renaissance and dominated Europe for two centuries. While the latter had been self-confident and self-assured, capable of mastering the environment, the new image for the nineteenth century was uneasy, anxious, alienated and introspective. Increasingly unsure, this person doubted the validity of values, and showed lack of self-knowledge and an inability to communicate in a meaningful way with others.

This was Dostoevsky's *Underground Man*; masochistic, living by his feelings, profoundly pessimistic, passionately fond of destruction and chaos, endlessly introspective, and afraid or even unable to divulge himself. A major change that led to this shift was Hume's *discovery* that there was no necessary connection among matters of fact, which drove a wedge between reason and nature. These views were far more revolutionary than he realized and, among his contemporaries, Kant-- deeply committed to the Enlightenment ideal--was almost alone in recognizing the destructive force of Hume's attack on reason. Realizing that some compromise was necessary to answer Hume, Kant's resulting philosophy constituted one of the fundamental turning points in the history of Western thought.

Immanuel Kant (1724-1804 A.D.) was born to Pietist parents, members of the Protestant left who believed that true religion was a matter of inner-life that emphasized simplicity and obedience to moral law. Kant's principle work, *Critique of Pure Reason*, sought to remedy a bad situation into which he believed eighteenth century philosophy had fallen. It was obvious to Kant that the Cartesian compromise had failed; the only question was where it had gone wrong. Accordingly, Kant began a more rigorous and sophisticated analysis of the scientific method, by emphasizing the striking contrast between natural science before and after Galileo. He accepted the empiricists' premise that all knowledge begins with sense data--our experiences with the world-- except for an *a priori* knowledge necessary for any thought to take place at all. According to his hypothesis, knowledge is a cooperative affair in which both mind and object make a contribution, and mind contributes the relations while objects contribute the *relata*. To Kant, this consideration completely altered the conventional notion of the mind's relation to objects. It meant that the mind was not passive, but active and that Locke's metaphor of the blank tablet was profoundly mischievous.

Kant solved the problem of pure reason that he saw in prior philosophy with the hypothesis that the mind sorted experience into standard patterns. Although all knowledge begins with experience as Locke and other Empiricists had insisted, it did not necessarily follow that it all arises out of experience. Indeed, all knowledge, not just scientific knowledge, contains elements that are drawn from experience, but supplied by the mind itself. To Kant, self and objects were neither distinct nor mutually independent, but ordered elements in experience; elements in the *spatio-temporal manifold*. Kant drew a distinction between what is within and what is outside the spatio-temporal manifold. In his view, one cannot know the moral self, because knowledge is limited to what is within this manifold. Values are not in Kant's spatio-temporal manifold, but are a separate part of experience with faith, belief or other practical sources of knowledge. Thus, Kant actually proposed to replace the Cartesian dualism of substances with a dualism of kinds of experience, where there existed things called knowledge, values, and faith.

Kant's moral theory was based on primacy of right, rather than on a concept of good or happiness, in which duty was a central theme. He developed three formulations of duty: (1) the categorical imperative (an act by application of a rule), (2) treatment of persons as ends, never as means only, and (3) acting with an autonomy of will that recognizes shared humanity. From this perspective, a moral act is one that is taken from principle; a regular, explicitly formulated, and carefully thought out rule to be obeyed whenever the situation is seen as an instance of the rule. The capacity of the human mind to form categorical imperatives, such as telling the truth, keeping promises and repaying debts, was of immense practical importance to mankind. It instilled in one a sense of duty to perform actions by reviving a maxim. Kant also described another imperative duty to treat humanity as having intrinsic value just because one is human. Whereas Locke for the most part emphasized the rights of individuals, Kant emphasized their duties. These duties could be thought of as deriving their obligatory character from one primary obligation; the duty to treat people as ends in themselves. Kant's third account of duty was autonomous will, which made autonomy the basis of the dignity for every human and every rational creature. It required one to act in accordance with the principle that the laws to which one was subject were those of one's giving, even though they were at the same time universal. Autonomy was respect for personality which in turn held respect for ourselves; not, of course, for private selves but for the humanity we share with others.

By rigorously limiting knowledge to the spatio-temporal manifold, Kant made room for an appreciation of individuals as moral beings with rights and obligations to others. Freedom was thus entirely in accord with the general solution to the problem of pure reason. Freedom too fell within the province of what Kant called faith, which was not an ungrounded belief in something that contradicts science, but a sensitivity to and appreciation of values. Put differently, freedom conformed to Kant's central theme that knowledge of objects and appreciation of values, including the value of being a person, are simply modes of experience too different from one another to ever conflict. Kant's fundamental thesis was that these were two kinds of reality and hence different criteria of meaning and truth. Values could not be assessed by the criteria proper to facts unless values disappear. This analysis of a spatio-temporally organized manifold paved the way for rehabilitation of the valuational point of view that had been lost in Hume's philosophy.

Accordingly, nineteenth century philosophy came to be seen as a series of attempts to deal with problems created by a collapse of the enlightened world view during the Age of Reason. The new complex of attitudes could be brought under the rubric of Romanticism and could be viewed as an action against the mood of the Enlightenment, in particular, against its conception of knowledge. One of the first writers to support Romanticism was the French philosopher Jean-Jacques Rousseau (1712-1778 A.D.) whose career ultimately had a great impact on education, literature, and political philosophy.[1] Suffering through most of life with emotional distress, inferiority, and guilt, he came to be called a perfect example of an outsider in society, but he nevertheless became the most important writer during the Age of Reason. Growing more vain, inconsiderate, and suspicious, he became an opponent of society in the 1750's and quarreled bitterly with former friends in a group of philosophers called the Philosophes. In 1762, the French government condemned his work and he fled to Switzerland to escape persecution. The next year he accepted refuge in England from the Scottish philosopher David Hume. The year after, he quarreled with Hume and returned to France where he wrote autobiographical works justifying his conduct. His work prized feeling over reason, impulsiveness, and spontaneity over self-discipline, and self-expression over conformity. Some of his ideas greatly influenced the development of the French Revolution.

Rousseau believed that people in a state of nature (isolated, without language, and without motivation or impulse to limit one another) was good, but people were not social beings. As soon as people began to live together in society, they became corrupt and evil from society's tendency to nurture aggression and egotism. He believed society should be reorganized into completely controlled communities, where training, guidance, propaganda, censorship, elimination of privacy, and suppression of special interest groups were used to control ideas. Individual ambition alienates people from the state and places them in competition as in the state of war. The enlightened ruler, therefore, uses education to make possible a *contrat social*, or society by consent, and brings to bear science, will, and action.

Rousseau was primarily concerned with the union of wills to form a collectivity or sovereign, without standardizing or diminishing the uniqueness of each, in which the wills are no longer alone but become parts of a whole. Because property is easy to use and hard to defend, Rousseau saw it as directly tied to preservation of life, and motivates most citizens to give law an emotional hold over their actions, it is the most sacred of all rights of citizenship and in some respects more important than liberty itself. Nevertheless, property, possessions, pleasure, and power were not to be guaranteed by society above the subsistence level. Liberty in the form of association to defend and protect the whole, while recognizing the precise relation of each individual to the congregation, was guaranteed. Freedom of the self-- separation from other selves or usurpation by them and isolation as in the state of nature--is guaranteed. Each citizen was viewed as a free-wheeling individual who helped shape the whole through uniqueness, but did not allow the whole to reduce one to conformity.

Though a diversity of views burgeoned among the Romantics, there was considerable unanimity. The Romantics focused on an attack against reason, which had imposed artificial provisions destroying the natural living whole of reality. All were impressed by the largeness of the universe and an immensity to reality that baffled the methods of science, against which the human enterprise seem petty and trivial. Romantics rejected the Enlightenment view of humans as unique from the rest of nature because humans alone possessed reason. Downgrading reason, Romantics thought of people as dependent on it for bodily sustenance and for high thoughts and aspirations. They also rejected the Enlightenment view of a universe of separate entities, and viewed the universe as one continuous living and dynamic being. This Romantic idea of reality was too complex to be exhaustibly explained by the neat conceptual schemes of eighteenth-century Rationalism.

One of the most complex philosophies of this period is that of G. W. F. Hegel. Before discussing Hegel, however, it must be noted that there is no agreement regarding the nature of those views. It does seem fair to say that he carried the Kantian analysis of mind and matter even further, taking a developmental view of the mind changing, evolving, extending and unfolding itself. Like Kant, Hegel believed self and object were not distinct and unchanging entities, but were structures that arise within experience. There can be no object without self and no self without object. However, while Kant's conception of mind was largely static, Hegel's was developmental; mind was not a disinterested judge contemplating a realm of already existent objects, but an inner force creating and shaping the outer, observable forms. For Hegel, the ultimate truth was consciousness, and the notions of an independent and unchanging self disappeared. The mind was not independent because it could never get away from its own content.

Hegel believed that traditional Rationalism, or *Raisonment*, as he termed it, consisted in classifying everything willy-nilly into one or another of science's pigeonholes. *Raisonment* ignored the nuances that make each thing an individual.

Hegel's social philosophy of right was concerned throughout with human freedom, where the substantive aim of the world was to be achieved. In its first stage, freedom was concerned with the concept of personality, the level at which all problems appeared merely as problems of maintaining certain abstract rights. At this level, individuals were complete and autonomous: They continuously developed and were replaced by higher forms of themselves, but all had certain abstract rights. The next level was morality, in distinction from the lower level of abstract right. Here, in a synthesis of morality and right which Hegel called the ethical life, the notion of right is negated by the notion of good, and individuals enter into a compact with others for the benefits to be gained and also for the good of society.

Hegel believed an individual finds good in the larger whole of which one feels a part, beginning with the family, then the civil society, and above that the State. Hegel believed that organizations developed an externality of will, in which individuals find their good in the larger whole of which they feel a part that was absorbed into the supreme type of social order which he called the State. For Hegel, the State was the true individual; it was not a collection of independent individuals; its members were related to it as an organ of an organism; citizens lost their independence in the unity of the state; the absorption of the citizen was complete and nothing survived that was good for the individual in isolation.

Hegel's revision of Kant's doctrine was important because it shifted from an essentially static view of the universe to one as evolving through time. Also, Kant had valued not what people actually achieved, but the motive from which they acted; the purity of their will. But those philosophers who came after Kant were much more practically oriented. They recognized that Europe faced major economic and social problems as a result of the failure of institutional structures to adjust to immense changes occurring in values, expectations, and ways of living.

When Hegel died in late August of 1831 A.D., agitation over the Reform Bill before the British Parliament was at its height. In 1840, the work day still averaged twelve to thirteen hours and occasional holidays had to be made up. Children entered factories when they were nine years old and were expected to perform the hardest labor. Nearly as many children were employed as adults in mines; 167,000 compared with 191,000. Pay was pathetically low and owners reduced their labor costs further by arbitrary fines for breakage and bad work. People were shocked by such conditions, the laboring class itself began to agitate for reform, and passage of the Reform Bill in 1832 was a great victory for the middle and lower classes. In continental Europe, repression instead of Parliamentary compromise was the order of the day, and dissent had no outlet, eventually welling up into outbreaks of open violence in 1848.

Out of reform-minded thinking emerged the Utilitarian philosophers, whose interests lay primarily in social theory and basic first principles which they believed could be proved by empirical means. In Utilitarian philosophy, the end aim of a legislator should be the happiness of the people and general utility should be the guiding principle. John Stuart Mill's essay *On Liberty* is a typical application of the greatest happiness principle. Instead of arguing, as eighteenth-century Rationalists had, that liberty is a self-evident right, he tried to show the greatest good for the greatest number was promoted by a Utilitarian calculation of the consequences of outcomes. "Individuality is the same thing with development, and it is only the cultivation of individuality which produces, or can produce, well-developed human beings" (Jones 1970, 168). Accordingly, Mill showed antipathy toward the Hegelian ideal of transcending finite individuality in that larger self, the State. Mill's argument exhorted every individual to fashion one's own destiny unrestrained by public opinion.

Comte, who could be considered the founder of Positivism, applied empiricism and pragmatism more systematically than his predecessors, the Philosophes. Comte believed that emotion dominated most people, and only a few were capable of setting down and using scientific methods to ascertain answers to problems. The entire difficulty, in Comte's view, was to enable administrators to put scientific knowledge to work in improving the conditions of society. Hence, Comte was the administrator par-excellence. Although the social world looked immensely complex to the layman, to the administrator it fell into a relatively simple pattern. Comte thus followed the Platonic tradition both in the sense that there was a definite set of answers, and that he believed only relatively few people were capable of discerning and acting on them. However, Comte went further, applying the empirical methods of the natural sciences to the study of humans. He advocated a highly organized and tightly controlled society of the kind economic planning has made familiar today.

Similarly, Marx's reality was Kant's spatio-temporal manifold; that is, there was no transcendent realm beyond the world to be encountered in experience. In these respects, Marx belonged, like the Positivists, to the empirical and scientific tradition that combined belief in the inevitability of progress with a belief that human nature and the physical universe conformed to simple laws discoverable by science. But for Marx, as well as Hegel, alienation was a central concept. The Enlightenment philosophers did not experience alienation as a problem, because their world was basically congenial. In contrast, the nineteenth century saw alienation as an inevitable part of the human condition. It arose from the sense that the individual, alone in an indifferent or hostile universe, was estranged from nature, others, and even from one's self.

The nineteenth century was full of tension and change with upheaval so great that even today we struggle to adjust. The Industrial Revolution produced distress, poverty, disease, and alienation as features of the human condition. Nineteenth-century philosophical thinking abandoned Enlightenment truths and inalienable rights in favor of the scientific method. For many years this ethos dominated Europe and America but a counter-movement, hardly noticed at first, emerged to make the self a decider and chooser.

With the advent of world war, and the callous injustice done to blacks in America, the dominant philosophy of reasonableness and progress began to appear naive. In the early twentieth century, the individual again began to feel estrangement from the natural world and philosophers began to regard Augustine as an unusually honest and perceptive psychologist. The new counter-movement represented by Soren Kirkegaard and Friedrich Neitzsche condemned the culture that produced such alienation and estrangement. They thought that becoming a complete self was more important than improving one's relation with one's environment. This focus on subjectivity of self was a part of mainstream Western thought since Descartes. But now Existentialism would focus attention on the Enlightenment's failure to bring anything of value to the individual.

Kirkegaard's philosophy was an intensely personal one that grew directly out of his deeply felt life experiences, and this Existentialism dominated his philosophy. He believed things existed to be encountered and mastered. He asked the question, "What am I to do?," rather than "What am I to know?" He equated existence with an agony of being in a predicament and thought that people were faced with either-or choices, that the individual was finite, God was infinite; people were sinful, God was merciful. It was essential for each person to recognize these relations, act on them, and give oneself utterly and completely to God. Kirkegaard's philosophy embraced radical subjectivity in which no rational, scientific or economic procedure could heal the self: nothing could be proved: only a leap of faith could accomplish that: God was this faith.

Neitzsche, whose life spanned almost exactly the second half of the nineteenth century, was born when Hegel had been dead only thirteen years. At that time, Mill was thirty-eight years old and Kirkegaard was thirty-one. During his life, the optimism of the Enlightenment was ending and the democratization, industrialization and urbanization of Europe were having unpredicted consequences resulting in commercialization, vulgarization, and impersonalization of life. He believed even more than did Hegel that thinking and perception were acts of interpretation in which desires, memories, and passions effect the object perceived or thought about, reflecting a focus on the individual's needs and problems.

Neitzsche saw the vast majority of people as weak, merciless, greedy and murderous. He held nothing but contempt for Kirkegaard's leap of faith, advanced the hypothesis that God was dead, and found fulfillment precisely in the hardness and courage with which he faced up to the terrible truths he had discovered. To him, religion and transcendent ethics were instruments preserving the unfit and subordinating the strong to accept small virtues of small people. He called this a slave morality and saw it as one way the weak waged battle against anxiety. He believed only a few perceptive individuals--the Overmen--recognized this, exploited it, mastered themselves, suspended the ethical, and exerted their will, power, hardness, courage, and creativity.

Both Neitzsche and Kirkegaard reflected attention to the individual person and individual needs and problems, as the name of their philosophy (Existentialism) suggests. This point of view is passionate, not neutral, practical not speculative, and subjective not objective. It thoroughly rejected the Enlightenment belief in self-respect and high regard for human nature.

William James (1842-1910 A.D.) lived about the same time as Neitzsche, but his philosophy retained some earlier optimism from science. He believed philosophy should inform people about the world and help them make a successful adjustment, which depended less on holding beliefs that were true than on holding beliefs that suited individual temperament. For the entire history of philosophy from Descartes to James, there had been in effect a series of efforts to overcome Cartesianism. Starting with James's doctrine of pure experience, one could solve the mind-body problem through consciousness, because dualism seemed plausible or inevitable only if minds are conscious and bodies are not. James held that in pure experience no distinctions exist between mind and matter:

> My thesis is that if we start with the supposition that there is only one primal stuff or material in the world, a stuff of which everything is composed, and if we call that stuff 'pure experience,' then knowing can easily be explained as a particular sort of relation toward one and another to which portions of pure experience may enter. The relation itself is part of pure experience. (Jones 1970, 4:304-305)

James was one of the first philosophers to adopt what subsequently came to be called the phenomenological approach; that is, an approach that seeks to start from, and confine itself to, a description of experience as it comes.

James's vision was one of an open universe, growing, incomplete, and unpredictable in its outcome. To live in such a universe people needed flexibility, resourcefulness, a sense of humor, and readiness to gamble on their convictions and to live with insecurity while enjoying it. These are qualities James prized, but in his pluralistic universe individuality was prized above all other values. James anticipated some of the major themes of twentieth century philosophy with his Existentialist emphasis on the centrality of choice and phenomenological emphasis on pure experience. Pure experience saw no moral absolutes, justified belief in whatever works, gave value to whatever can and whatever suits. In doing so, it boosted individuality and made reality highly subjective.

One of James's contemporaries was Charles Sanders Pierce (1839-1914 A.D.). He too rejected idealism and positivism and was empirically oriented. Pierce propounded: (a) Tychism, which takes the universe as an evolutionary development according to habits which the selves develop; (b) Synechism, which he said sees mental life as a continuum rather than encapsulated events; and (c) Community, which teaches that interests do not stop at our own fate, but must embrace unlimited devotion to collective rather than individual pleasure. Pierce became a formidable critic of individualism.

Quest for Objectivity

While nineteenth-century philosophy moved largely within the Kantian paradigm, the twentieth century can be viewed as a series of attempts to break out of the Kantian framework. Kant proposed that minds and objects were mutually involved, and truth appeared in agreement of objects with minds. To put it differently, knowledge of nature was possible, but only because the mind did not merely react or respond to a completely independent external world, but constructed the form--the structure, not the details--of the world of its experience. This hypothesis promoted mankind into a place of prominence as the constructor of experience. For Kant, the mind was no longer a Cartesian substance contemplating other Cartesian substances from outside and at a distance. Now the objective world became a construct, a product of the synthesizing activity of mind working on and organizing the senses. The immediate response to Kantianism that emerged strongly in the beginning of this century was to re-establish an objective reality and escape the relativism of Hegel and Neitzsche that seemed to follow Kantianism. This pursuit of objectivity took three main paths: (1) a revival of Realism, (2) a revolution in logic, and (3) a phenomenological method.

Though differing markedly among themselves, Henri Bergson, John Dewey, and Alfred North Whitehead are three thinkers that may be grouped together under a philosophy of process. Bergson and Whitehead represented the metaphysical trend that survived Kant's criticism and dominated much of nineteenth-century thought. Dewey represented the empirical, anti-metaphysical trend that became an increasingly powerful influence on Western thought. Bergson's metaphysics was Romantic in its emphasis on dynamism and continuity, its denial of reason as a means to know the inner-nature of reality, and its assertion that reality can nonetheless be known--in intuition. Whitehead reaffirmed the capacity of reason to know reality, and he sought to establish a new categorical scheme of metaphysically valid concepts. Dewey was skeptical of both the possibility and the desirability of building philosophical systems, and he represented the great drive for social reform that had developed in the late Nineteenth Century. All three of these philosophers were reformers who believed in the possibility of progress, which they thought could be promoted by intelligent action on the part of individuals.

Kirkegaard and Neitzsche had been deeply suspicious of the Enlightenment's idea of progress. Bergson, still committed to progress, though not to the Enlightenment's belief in reason, believed that mankind might be on the verge of making a new creative advance. For centuries men and women had made a cult of comfort and luxury, but he believed that they were approaching a new period of Asceticism and Mysticism. Bergson believed in a superior kind of knowledge called intuition by which people have direct and immediate access to the nature of reality. Taking self as the starting point, he viewed self as an active, not a static encapsulated substance. The self was revealed in intuition as a continuous, unfolding new experience that would incorporate the past while moving steadily into the future. He believed that reason and intelligence cause individuals to think of themselves as distinct from the community of which they are really an organ, which disrupts morality and order and must be counteracted by other forces.

Dewey's theory was a version of ideas loosely identified as pragmatic. It is sometimes said that Pragmatism is a typical expression of the American ethos. William James popularized Pragmatism by trying to show that the conclusions of science are not as authoritative as they may seem. Instead, he espoused the principle that truth existed if a particular activity works. Dewey's Pragmatism was called *Instrumentalism*.[2] It reflected his view that the mind is directive and active rather than merely an observer or recorder of information. In this respect, he shared Kant's and Hegel's belief that experience is a product in which mind plays a decisive role. However, Dewey emphasized a world to be lived in and acted upon. He saw human beings not as passive spectators of a neutral world, but as organisms plunged into an environment that infiltrates their very nature. For him, no final adequate descriptions (or laws) could be found, only more and more adequate instrumentalities for dealing with change and growth. Yet, Dewey embraced freedom of intelligence, or mind, but rejected freedom of action:

> Unless freedom of individual action has intelligence and informed conviction back of it, its manifestation is almost sure to result in confusion and disorder. The democratic idea of freedom is not the right of each individual to do as he pleases, even if it be qualified by adding 'provided he does not interfere with the same freedom on the part of others. . . .' The basic freedom is that of freedom of mind and of whatever degree of freedom of action and experience is necessary to produce freedom of intelligence. (Jones 1970, 5:83)

Dewey saw values as simply the practical, social, and human problem of intelligent choice, as facts to be discovered in nature just as any other fact. Dewey placed significant faith in the advocacy of bold intelligence and believed that problems created by technology could be solved by technology. The acceptability of his account depended to a large extent upon people being content to live relativistic and uncertain lives.

Dewey said individualism was born in a revolt against established systems of government, deeply tinged by fear of government, and activated by desire to reduce it to a minimum and limit the evil it could do. Since established political forms were at the time tied up with institutions, especially ecclesiastical, recourse was by appeal to inalienable sacred authority resident in the protesting individuals. Examples of this are the efforts of John Locke to limit the powers of government by calling forth prior non-political rights inherent in the individual. Its classic expression is found in the writings of the French Revolution which at one stroke did away with all forms of association, leaving the bare individual face to face with the State.

For Dewey, life was impoverished not by predominance of society in general over individuality, but by domination of one form of association over other actual and possible forms. To learn to be human is to develop, through give-and-take communication, an effective sense of being and an individually distinctive member of a community who appreciates its beliefs, desire, and methods, and contributes to its conversion of powers into human resources and values. Dewey put philosophy to the service of society. He sought public ends, not private, and believed truth was what worked for the group, not the individual. Morality was social, not individual and was observed by cooperative action. He became the guide, the mentor, the conscience of the American people.

Whitehead's basic orientation was quite different from that of Dewey's. Whereas Dewey thought of his task primarily in terms of solving a variety of immediate, concrete problems, Whitehead thought about a long range and systematic interpretation of experience. If Dewey is seen as representing the empirical spirit of the modern mind, Whitehead represented the Rationalist tradition. He reaffirmed objectivity and conceived of philosophy as simply a search for a pattern in the universe. Though he was convinced that one could never formulate it completely or finally, there was a pattern. Since humans are finite beings, he believed that complete grasp of this pattern is totally denied us. In the final analysis, belief in an order of nature is an act of faith; not Kirkegaard's leap of faith, but a faith in the continuity of things, in an objective truth, in a cosmological principle.

Whitehead advocated a philosophy of organism, that sought to reunite Descartes' separation of mind and matter and restore the reputation of the latter. An organism was defined as a "unit of emergent value, a real fusion of the character of eternal objects, emerging for its own sake" (Jones 1970, 5:83). Thus, all things are interfused. He also founded the so-called process school of theology which rejects creation out of nothing in favor of a universe with no beginning. Instead of creation *ex nihilo*, God's creative activity is manifested in the ongoing process and creative advance in nature's activity. The main advantage of this philosophy was a place for value in a world of fact.

A feature of twentieth century philosophy was a re-emergence of an analytical tradition in philosophy that can be traced as far back into the past as Hobbes. Characteristic of this analytical tradition is a commitment to Atomicity; the belief that the universe consists of a very large number of independent and encapsulated entities. Common to all of the philosophers of this tradition is the conviction that these entities of which the universe is composed are only externally related; in Hume's language, loose and separate. One of the leaders in the revival of the analytical tradition was G. E. Moore (1873-1958 A.D.). Division of complex entities into simple ones and inspection of these simple items were two steps in his method. Moore's universe consisted of a vast number of simple items upon which analysis, if carried far enough, would always terminate. Analysis, then, was the process of isolating for inspection one or more of the separate entities which collectively made up the universe. Unlike philosophers who started from the assumption that reality is a complex unity, Moore believed that understanding of any item comes from inspecting that item in isolation from every other item. He is generally regarded as one of most influential philosophers in the first half of this century and his view carried forward, through Bertrand Russell, to the Positivists.

Moore and Russell, almost exact contemporaries at Cambridge, were friends as well. Both held the universe to be a collection of wholly independent, discreet entities and believed analysis to be the method by which humans could come to know the nature of these entities. Thus, they were both reductionists. Nevertheless, because they differed so much temperamentally they developed very different philosophical positions. Driving Russell was an interest in mathematics and pursuit of certainty, an interest as powerful as that which had animated Descartes.

For Dewey the important element of the scientific method had been its experimentalism and its tentativeness. In contrast, Russell believed that science yielded the truth about things. Therefore, there was nothing to be said about ethics, because all knowledge is limited to science and science had nothing to say about values. In his view, values constituted only individual desires which differed from culture to culture. Despite these views, Russell was deeply interested in metaphysics, which distinguished him from the Logical Positivists.

In the early 1920s, a group of Viennese intellectuals consisting of mathematicians, physicists, sociologists, and economists met weekly and called themselves the Vienna Circle. After acquiring popularity elsewhere in Europe and the United States, they began to call their movement variously Logical Empiricism, Scientific Empiricism, and Logical Positivism. Positivism was one of the last survivors of eighteenth and nineteenth-century culture and was passionately anti-metaphysical. This movement insisted that knowledge is limited to experience, reliable information about the world can only be obtained through use of the scientific method, and everything transcendental, other worldly or supra-natural should be eliminated from philosophical consideration. They wanted to use philosophy to destroy philosophy, except for that part that could be called the logic of the sciences. To them, all problems were technological, not intrinsically human, and could be solved by the application of rational intelligence and scientific methodology.

Generalizing from the principle that only the sciences can properly be called knowledge, the Positivists formulated a criterion of meaning that came to be called the *verifiability principle*. This principle stated that propositions for which no means of verification existed were literally meaningless. In this, the Positivists possessed an instrument that totally destroyed metaphysics. Since according to the verifiability principle all meaningful assertions must be capable of verification by empirical observation, ethical assertions must be either empirically verifiable or nonsense. According to the principle itself, all meaningful assertions were either tautological or empirical. This meant that the principle itself had to be an empirical hypothesis to escape circularity. Because the Positivists could not easily attempt to verify the verifiability principle, they lost their nucleus. But their Emotivist theory of ethics--that ethical expressions assert nothing but feelings--was Positivism's greatest weakness and later led to it being transformed beyond recognition.

Call of Being--Phenomenology

Along side analysis grew another set of basic assumptions called the Phenomenological Tradition. Philosophers of the Phenomenological Tradition inhabited a totally different world in which it seemed possible to agree with Kant that human experience was limited to phenomena, while at the same time denying that the objects thus experienced were constructs. In contrast to the encapsulated simple items of the analytical tradition, Phenomenological philosophers were impressed by the interconnectedness of things. For them, experience was a river, not a collection of loose and separate sense data. The Phenomenologists were unwilling to write off the experiential world, the life-world as they called it. They rejected the bifurcation of nature to which physics had committed modern culture, and they shared the sense expressed by Romantic poets that all things are interfused together, the sense of the presence in everything of everything else.

One of these Phenomenologists, Edmund Husserl (1859-1938 A.D.), believed that the natural sciences seem to exclude subjective, or spiritual, aspects of humanity.[3] This point of view has come to be the model by which all true science is judged. Only sciences of fact are viewed as true sciences, and a science of fact treats the world in the same manner as the natural scientist. This paradigm is easily adopted in human sciences, because human science is always entangled with nature. But the domination of the natural scientific paradigm distorts the human sciences by supporting a naturalistic attitude that conceives of nature not as a real world of everyday life, but as a collection of ideal structures arrived at through elaborate procedures of idealization, abstraction, and formalization. Thus, the objective reality of the natural sciences is itself a theoretical construct, which means there are not two realities of nature and spirit, objective and subjective. Rather, there is one world viewed from two different attitudes. In Husserl's philosophical view, there should be a clear priority of spirit, because natural sciences conceal their very origin in human subjectivity.

Husserl thought of people as chiefly observers, or spectators of reality. Other Phenomenologists saw the individual as a doer, not merely a knower, but they perceived the individual as an alien, cast into an indifferent universe and forced, willy-nilly, to act and to chose. The Phenomenological movement thus underwent a dual development. One of those directions was taken by Martin Heidegger (1889-1976 A.D.), who believed that Phenomenology was the science of Being, rather than the science of beings that Husserl had made it. In contrast to Husserl's view of the individual as a knower, Heidegger saw people as concerned creatures; concerned above all for their fate in an alien world. Humans stood in concerned relation to the object of their knowledge. Thus, in Heidegger's view, Phenomenology became the science of human existence.

Heidegger employed the analytical term *dasein*; human being or mode of being human. For Heidegger, to be an authentic person was to have a world; to be in the mode of *dasein* was to have a nature that endures through time; to possess the ability of being something different at some future time, of choosing, of facing possibilities. Humans are being-in-the-world by showing concern, living ahead and facing a future of alternatives and possibilities, seeking to understand,

and finding a world of things (ready-to-hand) as potentialities for human use in various ways. *Dasein* does not passively react to its world, but does something to, with, or about that world.

Heidegger totally rejected all theories of the spectator type that assume knowledge as a matter of beholding from the outside. *Dasein's* mode of being-in-the-world was toward the world and being-toward-the-world was essentially to be concerned. Ultimately, then, all meaning was for all--not for you or me personally--but for *dasein*, for human beings. This was a unitary theory which emphasized the whole and, where analytical philosophers put their emphasis on the articulated parts, Heidegger emphasized the structured whole and believed an understanding of the whole made the parts understandable. Heidegger also believed in a human predicament called facticity, thrownness, and fallenness (inauthenticity); to live authentically is to avoid seeing others as a competitive they and to live in the *dasein* by perceiving others as having being like your own. Authenticity is understanding one's own mortality and of one's freedom to live up to one's innermost potentialities. It is an ability to live genuinely in the mode of being-with-others and to perceive men and women as others having being, instead of allowing one's experience of others to collapse into an anonymous they. Inauthenticity is that mode of being in which people are lost in and dominated by the world; the condition in which people believe they understand everything, but in which they really understand nothing, because of superficial and external understandings. It is the scientific attitude, being busy, preoccupied and manipulative.

The scientific attitude that Heidegger deplored is called *technik* and makes a fundamental distinction between calculative thought and contemplative thought.[4] The former was connected to a type of thinking motivated by measurement and search for results. Its most powerful expression is the aim of modern science at manipulation and control. A calculating person is one who seeks to gain advantage, to get ahead, to plan for the future, to quantify, to take stock, and to keep everything in order. This thinking betrays a fundamental need of certainty and security that wants to know exactly where things are and precisely what they are doing. Contemplative thinking seeks neither measure nor control, but questions the meaning of things and encompasses the essential task of philosophy, the thinking of Being. *Technik* embodies a logic of domination which underlies technical, calculative thought, and a tendency always to think only in terms of role or function.

Heidegger repudiated the development of another branch of Phenomenology represented by Jean-Paul Sartre. Despite a common

Phenomenological orientation and a shared conviction in the human state of alienation, Heidegger and Sartre had very different motives and experiences. Phenomenology appealed to Sartre because it revealed harsh Existential truths that every individual needed to face and overcome to become an authentic individual, reconciled to living with uncertainty.

In order to become an authentic individual Sartre believed one had to face real moral decisions, see through the social self, and surmount the moral crisis that this revelation entails. When this was done one would not find an authentic self or an immortal soul or transcendental ego, but simply consciousness. To be authentic one had to experience doubt and suffer anguish in an attempt to discover one's self and what one ought to do. Authenticity was not a category of being, but a category of acting, or becoming. Since the authentic self was not a category of being, the only self that *is* was the reconstituted social self. A person is an authentic self in choices made through initiative without adopting other's standards or following other's advice.

One is only insofar as one acts and action is not simply behaving or having things happen, but involves being an authentic social self. Sartre held that the project one chooses determines the actual world one lives in. Since one's choice of project was absolutely spontaneous, one was wholly responsible for and could not pass this responsibility on to others or be excused by blaming the time, place, or circumstance. This was freedom, there was no way to escape, and one could not evade responsibility by refusing to choose. In this view, there was one kind of life that was categorically wrong, the life that tries to escape responsibility by retreating into and never emerging from the social self. Sartre argued that to escape responsibility was to involve oneself in a logical contradiction of choosing not to choose.

Albert Camus was a contemporary of Sartre's born in Mondavi, Algeria in 1913[5], but his philosophy was less intensely Existential than Sartre's. When he died in 1960, Camus had achieved fame as a writer and public figure. He grew up among simple people, many of whom were illiterate. He witnessed their enduring dignity through hardship, hunger, and physical suffering and retained a strong sense of empathy for those whose lives were consumed by unrelenting labor and whose aspirations were rarely fulfilled. His father died during the battle of Marne in World War I. Though his family and friends knew poverty, they lived in a beautiful and sunny environment in Algiers, close to the sea. Their poverty did not necessarily imply misery and desperation. Though he witnessed the brutal evil of which human beings are capable, he found hope that came from the hills over-looking Algiers where the blue sky merged with the blue of the ocean.

Camus brought a perspective on things which dwarfed human drama by an unseeing, unhearing, and uncaring planetary and cosmic process. Awe and love for the myriad beauties and graces of nature permeate his view of natural human context. He saw no conflict between this view and the obstacles that suffering and death imposed. When nature inflicts hardship Camus resists it and tries to alleviate its destructiveness, but he passionately rejoices in and embraces nature's beauty, healing, and liberating dimensions.

Camus was critical of Christianity, blaming belief in an all-powerful God for Totalitarianism, and pleading for a return to pre-Christian, Classical Greek idea of measure, or limits to human action grounded in a common human nature. He saw the twin Christian affirmations of an omnipotent God who wills the torture and death of Jesus, as encouraging resignation to injustice and the sanctification of suffering. In contrast, he called for revolt against injustice and suffering and taught people to look at human life and their natural surroundings to find sacredness. He thus replaced a Christian God with nature, universal guilt with specific responsibility, Christ with all victims of oppression, neighbor-love with limits and moderation, salvation with amelioration, and the Kingdom of God with the Kingdom of the human heart. God's church was the human community whose reality is not Christ but the solidarity of persons in their common life and suffering.

Camus agreed with Socrates that evil is the result of ignorance, or lack of knowledge, rather than corrupt inclinations or malevolence. Similarly, he affirmed the intrinsic value of individual life in its full humanness and the dignity and integrity of personhood. He espoused a philosophy of limits founded on the value of individual human life, fully human values, and the finiteness and fallibility of our knowledge. A philosophy of limits, he wrote, is a philosophy "of calculated ignorance and risk. He who does not know everything cannot kill everything."[6]

Conclusion of Part One

The individual from early Western philosophy is characterized primarily by religiosity. Though this characteristic alternately expanded and waned, it seemed to peak with Hesiod, Homer, and again with Augustine, later with St. Thomas, and still later with Luther and Calvin. During these periods of influence, the individual was submerged or made secondary as obedience of God's commands or the Church's edicts ascended to dominate reality. In the interim periods, individualistic tendencies emerged and re-emerged with increased popularity of science and/or restored faith in rationality. While an individual's religious character predominated and dampened one's individualism in the seventeen centuries between 750 B.C. to 1600 A.D., it should not be concluded that individualism did not exist. Individualistic attitudes and characteristics emerged and can be identified that indelibly influenced the Western concept of human nature that later coalesced in the 400-year period, 1600-2000 A.D.

The individual in early Western philosophy began a transformation from first religious superstition and mythology, to transcendent ordered change and world process, to practical reason, rational understanding, and secular politics. From the worship of all powerful Gods and burgeoning economic dominion over others, evolved an individual primarily motivated by self-interest, who saw war as a means of advancing privileged status. Hesiod, Socrates, Plato, Aristotle, and the Roman Stoics all fought against this excessively individualistic point of view, stressing in opposition the notion that individuals were part of a greater good in the associations with and interrelationships among one another. The true individual embodied an essential human nature, in which resided the moral integrity to choose and social responsibility to place inner-discipline, self-restraint, and unity ahead of personal gain, oppression of the weak, or accumulation of power. However, their points of view did not prevail in Greece or Rome as evidenced in Athenian society's condemnation of Socrates to death by drinking poison Hemlock and in Western society's own demise as the wreck of fallen Rome. During this time, precious little individualism in the true sense was practiced. Socrates lived and taught an authentic individualism that challenged the prevailing view. He pitted strength of character and fulfillment of humanity's essential nature against accumulation of power and he lost out to tyranny of the majority in an ultimate test of strength for individual human will. For a short time, the radical individualism of Thrasymachus prevailed and success was defined as social, political, and economic status, but this humanly constricting view soon led to social malaise and loss of energy culminating in a tired and discouraged society seeking peace of mind and relief from the human predicament, rather than passionate anticipation of and preparation for the future. When Alexander the Great swept down from Macedonia, divisiveness, arrogance, and opportunism--the shadow side of radical individualism--left Western society unprepared to meet the challenge. The penalty for embracing radical individualism and rejecting essential human kindness, compassion, and caring was 800 years of social, artistic, and cultural degeneration. Not until the writings and teachings of Socrates, Plato and Aristotle were rediscovered did Western culture begin to recover.

By the mid-1600s an individualist emerged that was no longer dependent body and soul on institutionalized religion and uninterested in all-around development of mind through contemplative collection of knowledge. Accumulation of wealth and acquisition of power replaced concerted development of character, integrity and compassion. A competitive, calculative, naturalistic attitude dominated thinking, supported and nurtured by the success and popularity of the scientific method. Failure of institutional structures to adjust to social changes led to revolution, revolt, rebellion, and war. The individual that survived was pessimistic in an unconcerned and uncertain cosmos. Not surprisingly, therefore, individual concerns intensified as attention was directed to problems of consciousness, experience, freedom, autonomy, happiness, and rights. The warrior archetype dredged up by Machiavelli was carried on by Christian soldiers of the Reformation and was transformed into the modern fighting man through the imagery of Dostoevsky's destructive, masochistic underground man and Neitzsche's hard, powerful, and courageous Overman.

The most striking aspect of modern Western philosophy of the last 600 years is that the individual came fully to the fore, dominating philosophy throughout the period. From Machiavelli's power politics based on self-interest of the ruler to Hobbes' anarchist; from Locke's pleasure principle to Rousseau's *contrat social*; and from Hegel's interest in human freedom to the Existentialists' preoccupation with individual existence, concerns of the individual have occupied center stage in modern philosophy since Renaissance times. The Socratic individualism against conformity has enjoyed precious little popularity in practice, while economic man prospers in seeming perpetuity. The unavoidable consequence of this narrow, singular reality is that humans are left isolated, unconnected, fragmented, and unfulfilled in their own particularity. With some exceptions during this period, only the

Phenomenologists have departed significantly from this predominant view of the individual's unassailable primacy in the world and the universe.

The Age of Reason's misplaced faith in the scientific world of fact soon led to a Collapse of Confidence in the nineteenth century. The industrialization arising out of science and technology produced slums, poverty, and abuse instead of unlimited improvement. With the advent of World War came the Existentialist frustration with an absurd world in which God was dead and the preoccupation with the individual continued. During the twentieth century, philosophy attempts to escape Kantian subjectivity and return to an objective reality. Some philosophers offer a lifeworld in which self is not a static encapsulated substance separated from all other encapsulated substances, but a continuous, unfolding, evolving, developmental organism interconnected with others. In this world view, individual particularity is recognized as having corrosive effects upon self as well as the social fabric. As a result, it advocates a more responsible individualism in which collective concerns are accorded increased priority, and the unrelenting pursuit of utilitarian pleasure is replaced by the personal satisfaction that comes from raising moral choice above efficiency and economy.

PART TWO

A Model of the Individual in the United States

Synopsis

European values were from a society of rich and poor, controlled by priests, governors, and male heads of family which sought to beat down stubbornness or stoutness of mind. The Puritan First Comers emphasized faith, works, duty, property, self-interest, and doctrine, and taught a passion for righteousness and for getting at the root of everything. Because the early Puritan colonies were primarily trading posts, they developed a distinctly mercantile perspective in which economic feasibility and reality controlled the decision-making process. This view hardened class lines and the distinctions between rich and poor, and made possible pecuniary profit and sale of slaves or other indentured servants. As a result, this nation was not born free but born servant and master, slave and free, tenant and landlord, poor and rich.

Private property as a primary force developing the growth of the country cannot be underestimated. Colonial governments acquired property from Native Americans and offered it at bargain prices to settlers, so little national separatist feeling arose in the colonies prior to 1775 as colonists wanted to preserve the expansive freedoms they had already acquired. The Constitution itself was a conservative document designed to preserve, secure, maintain, develop and correct those freedoms already enjoyed only by some and those things political and religious that already existed. It and the Bill of Rights put property in the place of happiness, accepted the Hobbesian war of one against all, adopted Hamilton's mercantile image of life, and saw humans as Machiavellian and Hobbesian creatures of rapacious self-interest.

Little surprise toleration declined as the power of the "common man" arose to the fore during Jacksonian Democracy. Old Hickory, rough hewn out of live oak, reinforced the rugged individualist image of frontier life. Westward movement, building, creating, inventing, urbanization and new methods of transportation hastened industrialization and spurred the corporate form. Dollar worship and materialism became the most significant American values. Despite these manifestations of greed and self-interest, there existed also a belief in the divinity of human nature that appeared in some as intense individualism. This was one of America's busy ages, in which everyone had some semblance of work, but it was marked by fear of expressing unpopular views, less independence and more bending to majority rule.

For millions of farm hands, clerks, teachers, mechanics, flatboatmen and rail-splitters, Abraham Lincoln represented the traditional ideal of the Protestant Ethic: hard work, frugality, temperance, and a touch of ability applied long and hard. In his time, an inability to rise on the economic scale was individual failure, an outward sign of an inward lack of grace--idleness, indulgence, waste, or incapacity. This conception of the competitive world was intensely and even inhumanely individualistic.

A rags-to-riches mythology in America matured between Appomatox and 1900, an era of public scandals, corporate profiteering, unequaled economic growth, and financial ruin--the age of Robber Barons and Rebels, cynicism and Spoilsmen. Economic analysis of problems--begun on Plymouth Plantation--came of age and began to dominate public and private decision-making. With a taproot in the Protestant Reformation, the doctrine of industrious life pervaded society and a conviction developed that everyone had a right to come into their own.

Manifest Destiny, born from a philosophy of survivalism and Christian righteousness, provided the rationale for profound cruelty. The year of the massacre at Wounded Knee, 1890, was officially declared by the Bureau of the Census as the close of the internal frontier. The nation had changed character; it was on the threshold of a new age in which the Captains of Industry would lead the people to unparalleled wealth and modernity, but it all collapsed in the fecund 1890s. The coarse, materialistic civilization that emerged from the Civil War produced a practical breed of political reformers. Determined to restore the American spirit he called the fighting edge, Teddy Roosevelt advocated the heroic, soldierly virtues of the hunter, cowboy, frontiersman, and naval hero. The reformers he represented tried to remedy by more individualism the evils that were the inevitable result of already existing individualism.

The Progressive Era ended with the outbreak of WW I and the Roaring Twenties emerged as a time of prosperity and fun only at the top. On the surface there had been over thirty years of prosperity, and it was the dawn of a Golden Age. Hoover declared a final triumph over poverty and wrote a book expounding his philosophy of untempered individualism. Yet wild financial speculation was prevalent in the financial markets, the conditions for American workers were grim, and the economy was fundamentally unsound. The Jazz Age was merely a diversion from the serious social and economic problems, and preoccupation with personalities served as a convenient source for collective self-denial about true conditions.

The Great Depression resulted in grinding poverty for millions and began an inexorable march toward further reforms. Hoover restrained the government by his laissez-faire philosophy that nature would cure all, and his survival-of-the-fittest Secretary of the Treasury Andrew Mellon wanted it to go right to the bottom. He believed people would work harder and live moral lives, values would be adjusted, and enterprising people would pick up the wrecks of less competent.

Helpless, humiliated and deceived by these politicians, the country voted for welfare and security of simple folk--the transfer of wealth from rich to poor by action of government. There was never a stronger mandate in American history for repudiation of laissez-faire and the individualism of business and finance. Freedom of action justified in the simple life of the last century could no longer be tolerated. The age of the New Deal dealt a death blow to American individualism as it had been practiced up to that time.

Soon, growing Soviet strength and the Korean War fueled national paranoia about communists. McCarthyism whipped it to a feverish pitch and other abridgments of individual liberties soon became common place. A conspiracy theory that creeping Communism would smother the American Way of Life haunted a generation of Americans. Ultimately, this fear led to the Cold War and forty years of influence for the military-industrial complex. Post-war economic prosperity pushed these fears to the back of the collective unconscious, America was able to get about the business of business, and a fat consumer market was born.

The nifty fifties, a rock and roll age, tough and sexy, bloomed to shunt aside the fear and danger in Khrushchev's promise to bury the West. While images of mushroom clouds dominated their unconscious and plans for fall-out shelters and civil defense sought room in their consciousness, the American people went on a decade long spending binge to divert their attention. Appearances, style, conformity and popularity became passions as the population became more alike in housing, dress, habits, possessions, problems, and number of children. In spite of widening prosperity, old inequalities of wealth remained and rising intolerance experienced a revival. Consensus existed in the U.S. that America was the greatest country on earth, superior to all contemporary, and even to most past, civilizations. Criticism of the effects of capitalism, the government, or the American Way of Life made the speaker suspect and was to be avoided.

Chief Justice Earl Warren resigned in 1969, ending an era of the court that brought individual civil rights to the forefront of every American's consciousness. From its desegregation decisions to the school prayer, criminal rights, abortion and one-man-one-vote decisions, the court aroused fervent passions and boosted individualism again, this time by making everyone aware of their personal rights. The Sixties involved civil rights and political activism, but there was also a general upheaval against the artificial, oppressive ways of living from the Fifties that touched every aspect of life: marriage, sex, child birth, dress, music, art, sports, language, religion, literature, death and schools. Individualism, suppressed for a decade or more, reasserted itself in the Sixties and early Seventies.

When John Kennedy took office in 1964 there was a short-lived feeling of vigor, public interest and renewed optimism, but Kennedy's assassination contributed to moral questioning and loss of faith. When the assassination of M. L. King was followed closely by the assassination of R. F. Kennedy, the country began coming apart. The Watergate scandal continued a decline in politics from which the nation has yet to recover. In its place was substituted a high-tech, consumer-oriented mass society that wanted more money for less work, more government benefits with less government and taxes, and greater individual freedom without responsibility.

Attention to self pushed out attention to others as the narcissist personality seemed to spring from the American public. Living for yourself and the moment, not for your predecessors or for the future, became the prevailing passion in government, society and business. As success came to require more attention to youth, glamour and novelty than it did to conscientious and competent handling of job assignments, creation of self became the highest form of creativity.

In the 1980s, this self-indulgence of the Seventies was carried a step further, as self-interest was put into action. The values of public purpose, insofar as they were reflected in the traditional institutions receded, and the values of private interest moved forward. Americans wanted their share of the pie and devoted themselves to attaining it. A crisis in ethics began in the decade: from recruiting college athletes to trading stocks and bonds, from Watergate to Soonergate, from the TV evangelist to the sports training room, from Savings and Loan boardrooms to the halls of Congress, and from police chief to mayor, America underwent a national crisis in ethics, but America was not paying attention. It was a decade of excess that ended with society in paralysis, unable to address the important issues of the day. Widespread problems existed in ethics, global warming, environmental contamination, disposal of toxic and nuclear wastes, drug abuse, ineffective education and the widening gap between rich and poor. Instead of aiming at solutions, the public practiced self-deception.

This madness continued in the Nineties as the newest crime fads became drive-by shootings, car-jackings, and dropping heavy objects from highway overpasses onto cars passing below. The ill effects of a growing ethic of purely personal rights and concerns became even more apparent. Truth became as disposable as a candy wrapper, and the lie became expected in the automobile showroom, in sports, in advertising, in politics and in the courts. By 1990, public officials were no longer leaders, but were expected to be CEOs of a corporate body and rational technicists, slashing budgets and personnel, as voters refused to pay even the cost of services then in place. In 1992, two out of three Americans believed the nation was in decline--economic, moral and spiritual. The Nineties also saw atomization of entire societies as personal rights and parochial interests defined action rather than tolerance and common humanity.

CHAPTER FIVE

Rugged Individualism of the Revolutionary U.S.

While Renaissance Europe was dominated by the religion of Popes, the government of Kings and the frenzy of money, another culture evolved rapidly along different lines. Native Americans were known for their hospitality, humanity, belief in sharing, and unfamiliarity with the concept of private property. Columbus wrote in his log that the Arawaks of the Bahama Islands ran to greet him and brought food, water, and gifts as he and his men came ashore. He wrote that the Indians willingly traded everything they owned and were quite submissive, and yet Columbus's first thought upon encountering this group of simple people was to enslave them. He noted in his log that they could be subjugated entirely and made to do whatever he wanted with as little as fifty men.[1] He concluded that they would make very good servants: "They are fit to be ordered about and made to work, to sew and do aught else that may be needed" (Cohen 1992, 104). These Arawaks were much like the North American Indians, whose culture taught solidarity with the group, equality in status, sharing of possessions, individual autonomy, and refusal to submit to overbearing authority. When Columbus and his successors arrived on the North American continent, they did not enter an empty wilderness, but a world that was as densely populated in some places as Europe itself and that held a complex culture embracing human relations more egalitarian than in Europe.

About a thousand years before Christ, while construction of extraordinary structures was occurring in Egypt and Mesopotamia, the Zuni and Hopi Indians of New Mexico built comparable structures in villages consisting of large terraced buildings. Before European explorers arrived, these people used irrigation canals and dams, and produced ceramics, weaved baskets, and made cloth out of cotton. By the time of Christ and Julius Caesar, a culture of so-called mound builders developed in the Ohio River Valley whose fortifications exceeded three and half miles long and enclosed one hundred acres. These Indians planned and executed a complex trading system extending from the Great Lakes to the Far West and the Gulf of Mexico. As the mound builder culture declined about 500 A.D., another arose to the west in the Mississippi valley. These Indians built huge earthen mounds as burial and ceremonial places near a vast metropolis that may have housed thirty thousand people. One hundred feet high, these mounds were constructed on a rectangular base larger than that of the Great Pyramid of Egypt. Also, from the Adirondacks to the Great Lakes in Pennsylvania lived the league of Iroquois, which included many tribes and thousands of people bound together by a common language. They owned land in common and worked in common, hunting together and dividing the catch among members of the village. Houses were common property shared by several families, and the concept of private ownership of land and homes was foreign to them. A French Jesuit priest who encountered them in the 1650s wrote, "Their kindness, humanity and courtesy not only makes them liberal with what they have, but causes them to possess hardly anything except in common" (Zinn 1980, 20).

Colonial Heritage

The Pilgrims arriving in New England were not coming to vacant land, but to territory inhabited by many tribes of Indians. Those Indians had cleared and tilled innumerable stretches of open fields and made the land easier to hunt game. The Pilgrims at Plymouth were assisted by those Indians who had survived smallpox caught from European fishermen. These Indians taught the new settlers how to plant corn, helped feed the colonists, and taught them to adapt old customs to a new environment. There were only two Indian attacks on the Virginia colonists in the first thirty-five years of their presence here. Clearly, the land was not desolate wilderness occupied by wild men. It had been made productive of food and shelter by the Indians already in residence there. Yet their failure to divide it up into private plots for individual, as opposed to community, use became an excuse for purloining the land.

John Winthrop, the Governor of the Massachusetts Bay Colony, created an excuse to take Indian land by declaring the area legally a vacuum. Proclaiming the Indians had not subdued the land, he concluded they only had a natural right to it, which had no legal standing, rather than a civil right. Moreover, the Puritans appealed to the Bible, Psalms 2:8: "Ask of me, and I shall give thee, the heathen for thine inheritance, and the uttermost parts of the earth for thy possession." They also justified their use of force in taking the land by citing Romans 13:2: "Whosoever therefore resisteth the power, resisteth the ordinance of God: and they that resist shall receive to themselves damnation" (Zinn 1980, 14). The desire for and acquisition of land soon became a consuming and motivating force as the colonies expanded and the nation's boundaries were pushed inexorably westward.

Alexis de Tocqueville, traveling America from England for nineteen months in 1831-32, studied the democratic experience here and made it a point to observe social phenomena in this country. Of the treatment afforded the Indians he said:

> The Spaniards were unable to exterminate the Indian race by those unparalleled atrocities which brand them with indelible shame . . . but the Americans of the United States have accomplished this twofold purpose with singular felicity, tranquilly, legally, philanthropically, without shedding blood and without violating a single great principle of morality in the eyes of the world. (Bradley 1945, 355)

Tocqueville noted that great tribes of the east--the Narrgansetts, the Mohicans, the Pequots no longer existed. The Lenapes, who received William Penn one hundred fifty years before had disappeared. Tocqueville himself met with the last of the Iroquois, who were begging alms. He found that a traveler "must penetrate more than a hundred leagues into the interior of the continent to find an Indian" (Ibid., 336). Observing their destruction Tocqueville said, "the manner in which the latter change takes place is not difficult to describe" (Ibid., 337).

The insidiousness of this extermination of a culture is most apparent in the example of Goyahkla (Geronimo), the "Apache renegade" who refused to succumb until 1886 while his band of sixteen warriors, twelve women and six children were being pursued by five thousand U.S. troops. He was not a chief but a medicine man: Nevertheless, he was the last great leader to stand against the tide of Manifest Destiny. Even he was lied to by General Nelson Miles who told him he would be reunited with his family within five days, his sins would be forgiven, and his people would be settled on a reservation if only he would give up and surrender. Few of them ever saw their homeland again and Geronimo would spend his remaining years signing autographs and performing The Last Buffalo Hunt in expositions where prominent Apaches were exhibited like trophies. Finally, after coming to bitterly regret having surrendered to Miles, Geronimo fell from his horse on a winter night in 1909, lay in a ditch till morning, and at age 85 succumbed to pneumonia four days later.[2]

In contrast to Indian shared concerns, European values were molded in a separatist society of rich and poor, controlled by priests, governors, and male heads of family who sought to beat down stubbornness, or stoutness of mind. Still, the Indians were more rugged than any of the Europeans who later came to be called individualists, able to find bounty, survive, and prosper in a land cruel to Europeans. The earliest Virginian and Puritan Old Comers faced insufferable hunger and hardship and were desperate for labor enough to grow food to stay alive. The winter of 1609-1610 was the starving time when, crazed for want of food, these Puritans roamed the woods for nuts and berries, dug graves to eat corpses, and died in batches until five hundred Colonists were reduced to sixty. During that winter, many of the people lived in cave-like holes dug in the ground and were

> driven thru insufferable hunger to eat those things which nature most abhorred, the flesh and excrements of man as well as of our own nation as of Indian, digged by some out of his grave after he had lain buried three days and wholly devoured him; others, envying the better state of body of any whom hunger has not yet so much wasted as their own, lay wait and threatened to kill and eat them; one among them slew his wife as she slept in his bosom, cut her in pieces, salted her and fed upon her until he had clean devoured all parts saving her head. (Zinn 1980, 24)

Even later immigrants did not have to await their arrival to the mainland of America before experiencing such extraordinary degradation. A musician traveling from Germany to America around 1750 wrote of his voyage:

During the journey the ship is full of pitiful signs of distress--smells, fumes, whores, vomits, various kinds of seasickness, fever, dysentery, headaches, heat, constipation, boils, scurvy, cancer, mouth-rot, and similar afflictions, all of them caused by the age and the high salted state of the food, especially of the meat, as well as by the very bad and filthy water. . . . Add to all that shortage of food, hunger, thirst, frost, heat, dampness, fear, misery, vexation, and lamentation as well as other troubles. . . . On board our ship on a day in which we had a great storm, a woman about to give birth and unable to deliver under the circumstances was pushed through one of the portholes into the sea. (Ibid., 43)

These hardships and sufferings, the European values of settlers, and a Western history of slavery dating to ancient Greece made possible pecuniary profit by shipping and selling slaves and other indentured servants, hardening class lines and sharpening the distinctions between rich and poor. As a result, the country was not born free but born servant and master, slave and free, tenant and landlord, poor and rich.

Puritan Ethic

The story of Plymouth Colony started when King Henry VIII made his break from the Pope. Within a century, religious reformers questioned their religion and pronounced new dogmas in both England and on the continent. When King James I succeeded Elizabeth in 1602-1603, England was religiously divided between Catholics, Anglicans, and a great variety of Protestants. Among them were the Puritans, who constituted a movement within the Church of England but were not a distinct sect or denomination, and the Separatists who had modified Puritan thinking until they wanted to be completely separate from the official church. The Puritans had been persecuted in England and hoped King James, who was a Calvinist, would lead them into the City of God, a church/state. When this did not happen, the Puritans looked toward the New World as their New Canaan. Puritanism thus found itself in the position of defying authority. Nevertheless, those Puritans who migrated to the Massachusetts Bay Colony in 1630 rejected the principle of separation altogether, despite the Separatist origins of the congregational polity they defended.

The Colony of New Plymouth was established by approximately one hundred Separatists from Holland who had fled England for religious freedom. Holland had allowed considerable freedom for religious dissent, but had become economically depressive and morally degenerate. The Separatists, later called Pilgrims, were a splinter group of the Puritans and they established Plymouth Plantation, the second nucleus (after Jamestown, Virginia) of the English-American empire. The Separatists were accompanied across the ocean in that 1620 voyage by Strangers not of their faith, but with whom they were required to travel to obtain support for their venture from businessmen called Adventurers, who ventured capital into the New World settlement in the hope of great profits. These Adventurers, some of whom were undoubtedly Separatists themselves or at least of Puritan persuasion, were hard-nosed entrepreneurs who had obtained a patent to colonize the northern part of the Virginia territory.

The Mayflower left the coast of England destined for the northern Virginia territory at a point roughly where Manhattan is today, but it sailed further north, outside the Virginia limits. Since the landing had not occurred as planned in the Virginia territory, some of the group asserted that they had the right to live as they wished and take orders from no one. Because of this first appearance of faction, it was thought good to combine into one body and submit to such government and governors as common consent could agree and choose. Accordingly, all free adult males present signed the Mayflower Compact, which stated essentially that the individual would be subject to majority rule.

According to their agreement with the Adventurers, settlers were to live a socialistic life, sharing everything in common for seven years, when the profits of the company were to be totaled and divided according to the number of outstanding shares. However, before seven years elapsed many were complaining that the industrious were supporting the lazy. At that point, it was decided to give every man, woman, and child the use of one acre of land to be cultivated as they wished for their own crops. They would all still cultivate the remainder as common lands for the company. This was known as the division of land and it began a custom in the colonies, the impact of which cannot be underestimated on the development of the United States. Soon, eight of Plymouth's leaders purchased the shares of the Adventurers and gave new land grants for private use to most of the settlers then residing in Plymouth.

By 1627, the concept for colonizing Plymouth Colony had changed considerably. The settlement had no royal charter to support it and only a patent for residing in the Virginia territory, but Plymouth nevertheless remained outside the jurisdiction of Virginia and assumed self-government. The colonists had agreed in the Mayflower Compact to form a democracy that would not be practiced in their homeland for several centuries. The large non-Separatist population of Plymouth

Colony prevented implementation of a church-state as was subsequently established in adjoining Massachusetts Bay Colony. Consequently, Plymouth obtained a reputation for having less rigid and more moderate government. Moreover, for those who measured progress in terms of large-scale industrial and commercial expansion, settlement on the shallow shores of Plymouth Harbor prevented the Colony from ever achieving the size, prominence, wealth, or importance of Massachusetts Bay Colony or New York. Ultimately, Plymouth Colony was transferred into the Massachusetts Bay Colony, largely as a result of Plymouth's failure to obtain a royal charter and England's displeasure at the way Plymouth persecuted the Quakers.

Plymouth Colony was a poor colony and everyday life was geared to hard economic reality. The first question was always: Who will bear the charge? Economic feasibility also spilled over into the requirements of justice since communities living just above the subsistence level did not have surplus wealth to invest in penitentiaries for long term prison sentences. Economic harshness permitted some families to rationalize putting-out one or more children for servitude under a contract, or covenant, that was to be strictly observed by both parties. Yet, the community could not stand by and see an individual or family without food, shelter, or clothing, and if no one else paid the costs, the community would. Thus, these Puritans intended to establish a community rather than a mere colony, where they could put their ideals into practice. Yet even then, this community had an economic harshness about it, quite unlike the indigent civilization that preceded the Puritans in the New World.

Puritanism was a religious movement dedicated to living a New Testament life while making a living. It taught a passion for righteousness, for getting at the root of everything, and for restoring the church of the early Christians. Puritans claimed descent from Sts. Paul and Augustine, and the main body of their doctrine was medieval Christianity. Puritanism was a reformation not a revolution, a traditional doctrine rather than an innovating doctrine. Later, Calvinism was more revolutionary; Calvinists were the shock-troops of Protestantism, according to Perry (1944). The task of Calvin and his followers was to define Protestantism, whose individualism and sectarianism tended to anarchy. Calvinism was characterized by doctrinal rigidity, the strictest rectitude and rigorous ethics that fixed moral responsibility directly on the individual. It was a hard doctrine that did violence to human nature by confronting people with salvation or damnation. This choice was filled with utmost anxiety for the fate of one's soul was at the mercy of forces over which the individual had no control.

Puritanism emphasized faith, works, duty, and doctrine. Puritans desired to approach God directly without any intermediary, and to glorify God and do God's will as the first concern for receiving future happiness. New England was God's Christian experiment, but the Puritans rejected ritual and ancient pageantry found in Catholic worship. Combined with their religious belief was a pragmatic way of doing and thinking that has had profound effects on the character and mind of U.S. citizens; the birth of what was later commonly called the Protestant Ethic. Puritans placed no stigma on manual labor, so yeoman and workman, blacksmiths, wheelwrights, carpenters, joiners, cordwainers, tanners, ironworkers, spinners, and weavers were the backbone of the community. Puritan doctrine taught each person to think of themselves as a significant, but sinful unit to whom God had given a particular place and duty, a calling. Though Puritanism was a religious movement, the early colonies were primarily trading posts, so they developed a distinctly mercantile perspective in which economic feasibility and reality controlled the decision-making process.

Nevertheless, Puritanism's stress on faith and works proved an excellent implement for subduing the environment and land in New England. "Never waste precious time" became a basic American tenant, and "An hour's idleness is as bad as an hour's drunkenness" became a maxim that kept people busy when the climate did not (Morison 1965, 73). Lacour-Gayet (1969) and Russell (Feinberg and Kasrils 1984) believe Puritanism was responsible for America's economic prosperity. By teaching people the iron will to forego present pleasure for future reward, habits of discipline and saving produced the capital needed for individualism. The necessity and duty of work, the rejection of pleasure, and the refusal to compromise pursuit of eternal life all worked to the benefit of the economic order.

Despite the other-worldly outlook and rigorous ethics, Puritanism also justified human attainment of wealth and earthly happiness. The energy with which one pursued the calling was evidence of godliness and was rewarded in this world and the hereafter. Combined with democracy, which affirmed the coincidence of individual and universal happiness, Puritanism provided legitimation for worldly success. In both beliefs the moral unit was the responsible individual, deserving of reward or punishment. The concrete human individual is the soul of Puritan individualism.

Both Puritanism and democracy also gave their blessing to laissez-faire. It was seen as a doctrine of painless piety by which the individual could seek private gain and serve the will of God and the good of mankind. Puritan individualism's assimilation into the texture of America was possible only because of its affinity with laissez-faire capitalism.[3] The characteristics of Puritan individualism are described by Perry (1944):

> The code of worldly prudence was in harmony with the puritan's self-reliant individualism. It was an application to livelihood and business of the puritan emphasis upon the integrity of the human soul and of its characteristic prerogatives. It was the economic form of the puritan's idea of retributive justice, with its emphasis upon dessert and individual responsibility. And it expressed the puritan's temper of personal independence. For though he was willing to admit his dependence on God, he looked to this as a means of emancipation from dependence on men and on nature. Salvation was the only gratuity that he was willing to accept. Wealth which he earned for himself was both a manifestation and a condition of self-reliance. It was a product of his own will and at the same time an instrument of freedom. (Ibid., 301)

According to Perry, Puritanism may properly be reproached because it confirmed the narrowness and hardness of secular life. It encouraged people to be forever striving, moving, and making, but has not taught graciousness or tenderness. An emphasis on instrumental goods of livelihood and wealth neglected beauty, contemplation, and social intercourse. Despite its rigid ethics, Puritanism represented economic life as retributive and disciplinarian rather than as cooperation through science to provide equitable satisfaction of human needs. The history of Puritanism exhibits as its deepest motives the interplay between two universal goods in conflict; social solidarity and individualism.

Puritanism was the sharp edged instrument which hewed liberty, democracy, and a certain brand of humanitarianism out of the American wilderness. Inherited from religious predecessors, it is the driving force behind the sense of moral responsibility expected from public officials in the United States today.

> Puritanism springs from the very core of the personal conscience--the sense of duty, the sense of responsibility, the sense of guilt, and the repentant longing for forgiveness. No [Western] man, if he grows to maturity, escapes these experiences. Every man, sooner or later, feels himself rightly exiled from paradise and looks for a return. (Ibid., 627)

As an unseen guide in the unconscious, the Puritan "comes aboard, like a good pilot; and while we trim our sails, he takes the wheel and lays our course for a fresh voyage" (Ibid., 268).

Declaration of Independence and Bill of Rights

Through belief in the Holy Trinity and the Bible as divine word, Puritanism sought to sweep away Renaissance practices. But its acceptance of the notion of universal priesthood and individual self-worth, its ethic of having and doing, its economic perspective, and its advancement of private property all helped to pave the way in the New World for rising individualism and capitalism from Renaissance Europe. Once the raging fires of Puritanism were banked in New England, people began to fall away from this antique faith. By the 1720s, Puritanism was losing hold of the colonies as a moral force; however, an emphasis on works, property, and self-interest continued to grow. Though people still attended church "meetings" and kept the Sabbath holy, others became what was vaguely called Arminian, believing that good works and a free Catholic spirit were sufficient for salvation. To combat this soft attitude, a revival of Orthodox Calvinism known as the Great Awakening began in 1734 among New England Congregationalists and Middle Colony and Southern Presbyterians. As the people of the Old West were falling away from traditional churches, the Awakening swept up lost souls, offering everyone a new sense of significance, and expanding with the frontier a strong Christian tradition. Calvinist theology had made God everything and humans nothing, giving people value only through toil, work, and suffering. The Awakening indirectly contributed to the American Revolution by helping develop a new independent American.

Accordingly, many Colonists felt inferior to the average Englishman and sought social status to prove their worth. Ownership of land gave that status, so the growing interest in private property was the primary force developing the growth of the country. Anyone who underestimates the importance of land as an enticement fails to comprehend the value system of the seventeenth-century Englishman. Colonial governments acquired property from the Indians and offered it at bargain prices to settlers who spilled from Pennsylvania down the Shenandoah into the "Old West" of Virginia and the Carolinas.

Crossing the Atlantic could seldom have been a pleasure before the clipper-ship era, but it was never tougher than in the eighteenth century. Bad drinking water, putrid salt meat, excessive heat, crowding, lice, rough seas, sickness, foul air, dysentery, scurvy, typhus, canker, and mouth-rot, all acted to discourage new settlers. Nevertheless, free land enticed tens and hundreds of thousands. Whether 50 acres free in North Carolina, 640 acres for three shillings in Virginia, or 100 acres for 5-15 pounds in Pennsylvania, the migration of immigrants seeking private property propelled the boundaries of the country southward and westward for approximately 150 years.

The vital stake in all the wars and diplomatic maneuverings after 1700 was the American West. The question was whether England, France, Spain, or, as no one could then foresee, an American Republic would rule the West. When George Washington and 150 men from the Virginia militia confronted the Canadian French at Great Meadows in Western Pennsylvania in 1754, shots in that western wilderness sparked a series of world-shaking events (the French and Indian, or Seven Years, War) that reached their culmination nearly thirty years later with the American Revolution. In 1783, Major General George Washington resigned his commission as commander in chief of the United States Army after winning independence for a republic not even dreamed of in 1753.

Nevertheless, little national Separatist feeling existed in the colonies prior to 1775, because colonists wanted to preserve the expansive freedoms they had already acquired. The situation between England and the colonies had its points of friction, but was far from explosive, as British subjects in America were then the freest people in the world. Colonial assemblies had acquired far more autonomy than, for example, Ireland then enjoyed. Indeed, many interventions of the English government and colonial administration had been to protect minority groups against majorities, or small colonies against big ones; for instance, the Quakers and the Anglicans against the dominant Puritans.

Every path of conciliation with England was kept open as Daniel Boone and other long hunters pushed the boundaries of exploration westward through Kentucky. Refusal of the King to grant these new lands to those with land warrants was bitterly resented. In the meantime, Boston bristled with Redcoats brought to help enforce British power over colonial governments, but loyalty to the King was still strong and America as a whole did not want independence. Thus, irrepressible conflict did not ignite spontaneously, and efforts at final reconciliation were made repeatedly. These continued right up until George III proclaimed a general rebellion existed in August of 1775, and commerce was cut by Parliament that December. Belief that the American Revolution was spontaneous among a united people is a myth spun by Thomas Jefferson in the Declaration of Independence.

Discussion of independence was brought about by Thomas Paine's pamphlet *Common Sense.* Espousing principles of American liberty, Paine argued that the King had forfeited his right to loyalty and obedience by failing to honor the compact between him and the people to protect their rights. Drawing on John Locke's *Second Treatise*, Thomas Jefferson later removed honor to the King as a barrier to revolution by basing the Declaration of Independence on this compact theory of inalienable rights whose violation by the Prince dissolves the compact and permits subjects to throw off their allegiance. Jefferson modified Locke's theory that individuals entered political society to protect property, substituting the Greek pursuit of happiness as an example of inalienable rights along with life and liberty. This concession to the well-being of the whole did not survive constitution making.

Though beginning with the word *we*, the constitution put property in the place of happiness. It was essentially a conservative document designed to preserve, secure, maintain, develop, and correct those freedoms already enjoyed by some and those things political and religious that already existed. In a blow to the concept of unity of the whole, the mixed constitution was designed to recognize self-interest and to encourage faction. The theory for this was that the minority would not likely have a common interest separate from the whole or the majority.

Our constitution-makers accepted the Hobbesian war of one against all, Hamilton's Puritanistic mercantile image of life, and a view of humans as a Machiavellian and Hobbesian creatures of rapacious self-interest, but wanted them free to practice Jeffersonian individualism. To assure ratification and further elucidate individual liberties that some believed were already embodied in the Constitution, the Bill of Rights was later adopted. These amendments also nourished self-interest and faction, but sought control over it by fragmenting power and emphasizing individual rights.

At the time, colonial America was a middle-class society governed by its upper classes. Those upper classes bound the loyalty of the middle class during the 1760s and 1770s with the language of liberty and equality which united just enough to fight a revolution against England without ending either slavery or inequality. Thus, the American Revolution was not fought to obtain freedom, but to preserve the liberties that colonial Americans already had. Independence was not a conscious, secretly nurtured goal, but a reluctant last resort to preserve life, liberty and the pursuit of happiness as some Americans had already come to know it.

The American constitution-makers were enlightened people who knew their rights and the limits of power. Unlike any other people before them, they aimed to think before they acted. "Never was there a People whom it more immediately concerned to search into the Nature and Extent of their Rights and Privileges than it does the People of America at this day" (Wood 1969, 5). These Americans sought a comprehensive knowledge of history and all of the various governments of ancient and modern states. This resulted in an outpouring of political writings--pamphlets, letters, articles, sermons Mingled with their historical citations were writings of Enlightenment philosophers and common-law writings of English jurists. Their blend of history, rationalism, and scripture was a synthesis for arriving at precepts about human and social behavior. The records of all peoples in all situations were sources, including those of Aristotle, Plato, Livy, Cicero, Sidney, Harrington, and Locke.

Nevertheless, the colonists were selective by focusing on those writings which expressed an opposition view of English politics. The expressions which they found most attractive and most relevant to their situation and needs were those with the least respectability and force in England. The theory of government that they espoused had a compelling simplicity; politics was nothing more than a battle between the rulers and the interests of the people. Whatever was good for the people was bad for the governors, and vice versa. However, the politics of the Founders were not necessarily the politics of the Constitution makers.

The ideal of politics since Aristotle had been, of course, to avoid either the degeneration into tyranny on the one hand or anarchy on the other. Many concluded that the greatest danger to Republicanism was not magistral tyranny or aristocratic dominance, but "faction, dissension, and consequent subjection of the minority to the caprice and arbitrary decisions of the majority, who instead of consulting the interest of the whole community collectively, attend sometimes to partial and local advantages" (Ibid., 502). "To secure the public good and private rights against the danger of such a faction, and at the same time to preserve the spirit and form of popular government," said Madison, was the "great desideratum of Republican wisdom" (Ibid., 502). Consequently, the American constitution-makers attempted to bring federal authority all the way down to the individual as distinguished from the corporate or collective capacity. It was their intent to extend the authority of the union to the person of the citizen. They believed a government of the union must be able to address itself immediately to the hopes and fears of individuals and must provide a national legislation over individuals. In the end, the Constitution did not attempt to coerce sovereign bodies, or states, in their political capacity, but the convention opted for a Constitution in which Congress would exercise its legislative authority directly over individuals rather than over states. In that way the laws of Congress were thought to be binding on individuals rather than the state and singled out the individual for legal coercion.[4]

Wild, Wild West

Washington's and Jefferson's Republican principles of toleration declined as the power of the "common man" rose to the fore during the period of Jacksonian Democracy. In 1788, Benjamin Franklin remarked that Americans were prone to pay too much regard to their rights and too little to their duties as citizens. He noted that they had amply demonstrated their proficiency in overthrowing governments, but now something very different was required of them; the capacity of submitting to restraints upon their freedom and of yielding obedience to laws of their own making. It was soon found that Americans were not very proficient at accepting limits in a nation of boundless resources. Rejecting the precepts of Republicanism, Andrew Jackson's slogan was: Let the people rule. His administration is credited by many with bringing democracy--long opposed by Madison and the Federalists--to America. No champion of the poor or the "common man", Jackson was loved by the general populace anyway. The "Gineral" proved immensely popular because he encouraged active participation in politics by the common people. Against the ossified Jeffersonian Republicans, he championed the cause of ordinary folk.

Born in a log cabin, Jackson became one of the founders of the Democratic party in 1832. A simple way of thinking--everything black or white--and the habit of command became key notes of Jackson's policies. Old hickory, rough hewn out of live oak, accustomed to being obeyed, with a sense of honor, and a gallant attitude, appealed to the populace and reinforced the rugged individualist image of frontier life. Jackson brought the Spoils System practiced in many states to the federal government. The consequence was more power to party organizations, dilution of politics with the incompetent and corrupt, and catering to mediocrity.

Another consequence of Jacksonian pandering to popular sentiment was the policy of driving the Eastern Indians west of the Mississippi. As a soldier, Jackson had fought the Indians, and he resented the fact that the Indians in the east owned much of the best farmland. By the end of his administration, almost all Indians in the East were moved west of the Mississippi, including the Creek, Cherokee, Choctaw, and Chickasaw. Thousands of Native Americans, cheated out of their land, died during the forced migration along the Trail of Tears. Jackson himself made his money by selling land to new settlers; buying it for as little as ten cents an acre and selling it for as much as three dollars and acre.

Jackson's hair-trigger temper involved him in many duels, and this no doubt contributed to fear of disagreeing with him. The period was marked by fear of expressing unpopular views, less independence and more bending to majority rule. Catering to prejudices of the middle class and the poor whites, a tide of ill-educated, provincial politicians perpetuated slavery and prevented emancipation. Moreover, the westward movement recovered momentum and the fun of building, creating, and inventing dominated consciousness. Urbanization and new methods of transportation hastened industrialization and spurred the corporate form. Because democracy wanted results and stressed useful knowledge, an anti-intellectual spirit developed. This led to glorification of buckskin-clad, bearded, lean fur trappers, traders and trail guides of the Great Plains and Rocky Mountain (Mountainy Men), and the proud, upstanding, independent mountain hunters and fishermen of the Ozarks and Appalachians. These lone operators were admired and revered for their aura of the self-made man. This brand of American reigned throughout the Jacksonian democratic period from 1828 to the Civil War.

During that whole time, American policy toward the natives of North America continued the old world process of one highly developed civilization, race or people pushing out a weaker one that would not be absorbed. In the United States, as elsewhere in the nineteenth century, conquest and expansion became an absorbing pastime, as America became intoxicated by the map. Oregon fever in 1842, the California Gold Rush in 1849, and the Pike's Peak Gold Rush in 1859 began a westward rush of long-whips and Conestoga wagons that did not end until after the Oklahoma Territory was settled. Far from dispensing the blessings of liberty and egalitarianism, the Jacksonian era is more accurately described as an age of inequality, class consciousness, and dominion by the propertied. It was a time of pragmatism and opportunism, when the old politics of ideology by a benevolent aristocracy gave way to the new politics of ambition, demagoguery, expediency, simplistic speech making, and indirection on issues.

This period also saw the intensification of industrial development. One of America's busy ages, everyone had some semblance of work before he had learned to employ leisure. Labor fared poorly, working people during the era lived lives of unparalleled precariousness, and conditions of the laboring poor ranged from dismal to abysmal. Dollar worship and materialism became the most significant American values. The preacher Theodore Parker told his congregation: "Money in this day is the strongest power of the nation" (Zinn 1980, 216). These manifestations of greed and self-interest, appeared in some as intense individualism.

The Jacksonian American character did much to influence the American mind or intellect. That character has been described as

coarseness and strength combined with acuteness and inquisitiveness; that practical, inventive turn of mind, quick to find expedience; that masterful grasp of material things, lacking in the artistic but powerful to affect great ends, that restless, nervous energy; that dominant individualism, working for good and for evil, and withal that buoyancy and exuberance which comes with freedom. (Pessen 1978, 6)

Jackson himself certainly seemed to equate true manhood with violence and a refusal to accept criticism. His contempt for authority and law that characterized his youthful and early adult life in Tennessee is clearly discernible in his later acts:

The arrogance, the disingenuousness, the cruel disregard for the rights of Indians, the highhandedness, the egotism bordering on egomania, the intolerance, the joy in hating, the emotionalism, the pettiness, the vindictiveness, that marked his career before 1828 continued to manifest themselves afterwards. (Ibid., 322)

Jackson's character seemed to parallel the character of the nation at the time.

That character has been described by a number of foreign visitors who do not present a very attractive picture. These visitors described the Jacksonian era American as rude, curious, humorless, and of a dull character. Americans were said to take themselves too seriously and show excessive gravity, making a toil of pleasure. These visitors were not sure whether Calvinism or other factors were to blame for these unattractive traits. Some believed that the cruelty displayed so often by so many Americans was shocking. Violence was a much observed trait and these visitors were amazed that respectable men would throw themselves savagely on someone else who had inadvertently provoked them. Less frightening but no more attractive was American selfishness, about which it was stated that no one was more dedicated to the gratification of his own physical wants than the American. Other characteristics observed by visitors to the United States were lack of self-confidence, self praise, insatiable hunger for flattery, and vanity. Inveterate complainers, Americans were intensely practical, utilitarian, and shrewd. They were concerned with immediate outcomings and success rather than long-range consequences or ethics, more capable of mechanical invention than of theoretical scientific innovations, and clever but not profound.

In the period of changing ethical standards during the 1830s, a thief often passed for an honest person. Americans were also described as anti-intellectual and other-directed with a vengeance. There was no doubt that in small things and large Americans guided their behavior by the anticipated reactions of their neighbors. Social corrosion rather than inner conviction accounted for much and inordinate deference to majority opinion resulted in sterile intellectual conformity. Lack of moral independence, worship of opinion, and fear of singularity were frequent criticisms of the American character. American hypocrisy toward blacks and Native Americans was severely censored as were their own claims that they were a very moral people. The transcendent American value according to most contemporaries was materialism, love of money and a tendency to judge things according to a monetary standard. Many Americans indeed practiced dollar worship described as vulgar materialism, which was accompanied by opportunism and expediency. Moreover, Americans were often criticized as having no respect for tradition, adopting whatever proved to be advantageous, and showing disrespect for the law.[5]

The portrait of the Jacksonian painted by contemporary observers of the time was of a good natured but essentially shallow person

> clever but not profound, self-important but uncertain, fond of deluding himself, living almost fanatically for the flesh (although not knowing too well how), straining every fibre to accumulate the things he covets and amoral about the methods to be used, a hypocrite who strains at gnats and swallows camels, an energetic and efficient fellow albeit a small one, who takes comfort in--as well as his standards of behavior from--numbers. (Pessen 1978, 29)

Aggressively egalitarian in their public relations with one another, early Americans were quite the contrary in their personal relations in private life. Proud and boastful, they took no criticism from foreigners. A tradition of lawlessness went back to colonial times, and became a permanent feature of American life, kept alive and nourished by the frontier. Risk takers in the all-absorbing pursuit of wealth, Go Ahead was the password of American railroads despite rickety roadbeds and innumerable accidents.[6]

In America, people spoke dollars and price more than anywhere else. Public works like bridges, and so forth, were always discussed in dollar terms rather than construction or engineering terms. The American soul was shaped by loneliness, yet strict economic calculation was a concrete reality.[7] Tocqueville (Bradley 1945) said he knew of no country where the love of money had taken a stronger hold on the affections of all people. Conveniences of life were uppermost in every mind. Tocqueville saw America as the most serious nation on earth. Serious and almost sad, even in their pleasures, the source of American disquietude and restlessness in the midst of abundance seemed to be their taste for physical gratifications.

Religious Reform

Arising after the War of 1812, Antebellum reform peaked in the 1830s and 1840s and declined in the 1850s generating what would be the most fervent and diverse outburst of reform energy in its history. The origin of this reform effort lay in the failure of politicians to lead the transformation of the United States in a virtuous fashion. Politicians disgusted reformers by catering to the electorate's lowest common denominator. No promise was too extreme, no spectacle too extravagant, if it resulted in votes. Consequently, Evangelical Protestantism provided most of the ideological and organizational foundation for Antebellum Reform. The second Great Awakening raised expectations that the Kingdom of God on earth was imminent, and similar notions led to religious fervor after 1800.

These social conditions and American characteristics exhibited during the Jacksonian era presented fertile ground for a new Evangelism (a second Great Awakening) based on the salvation of all and the individual exercising free choice to achieve it. Calvinism's innate sinfulness and condemnation to hell could be avoided by a simple, mortal act of will. Revivalism was pragmatic, materialistic, and anti-intellectual, but it took religion out of the hands of clergy, stressed the significance of the individual, and brought religion to the people in a language they understood. In the face of American irreverence, the secularism of a materialistic people, and selfish individualism, the reformers actively tried to improve the social, economic, and political arrangements during the 1830-1870 period.

Encouraged by religious revivalism, confidence in human progress and human will, and the notion that individual efforts mattered, Antebellum reformers first sought total societal change beginning with individuals. Lowering their goals later in the period from attacking sin to seeking civil service laws, honest elections and free trade, reformers tried to harness individualism in the name of responsibility to mankind. However, such goals were only achieved by their later counterparts, the Progressives of the 1900-1916 period and the New Dealers of the 1930s, who believed that solutions to the evils of modern life had more to do with industries and cities than with the sinful hearts of individuals.

A belief emerged that the United States was chosen by God to fulfill a great mission and the idea of a national destiny was accepted and used by reformers. While Calvin had maintained that human beings were innately sinful, nineteenth-century preachers made the claim that human effort could bring about a thousand years of peace, prosperity, harmony, and Christian morality. In doing so, they were abandoning a line of theology stretching from Calvin through early American Congregationalism and Presbyterianism. These beliefs were important for reform because they taught individuals that things were wrong with their situation, and yet gave them confidence that they could make it better and could accomplish almost anything if they really wanted to.

Civil War

Separatist notions that kept the Colonies from uniting against the King, briefly overcome by the Declaration of Independence and the Constitution, flared up again in 1861 with the Civil War. Abraham Lincoln's paramount objective was to save the Union, not to save or destroy slavery. He was first and foremost a politician, creating his own humble image and his ambition was the little engine that knew no rest. The presidency quieted his ambition, shook his image of politics as an exhilarating game, and chastened his exercise of power. This personal transformation allowed him to mold common sentiment to that of his own vision for the United States. The goal was to bring back the South with slavery intact. Only when emancipation became a military necessity did Lincoln relent to radical pressures to free the slaves, and he did so only in those States loyal to the United States. Nearly 540,000 people lost their lives in the pursuit of or fighting against his vision for the nation. As a result, he is a Christ-like legend in political mythology; a great man who shouldered the torment and moral burden for sinful people, suffered for them, redeemed them with hallowed Christian virtues, and was destroyed at the peak of his success.

There was no appetite in the North for a war to eliminate slavery, but fierce agreement boiled with the desirability of maintaining the Union. By manipulating a Confederate attack on Fort Sumpter, Lincoln was able to unify Northern sentiment for a defensive war to save the Union, sacred principles of popular rule, and opportunity for common people. For millions of farm hands, clerks, teachers, mechanics, flat boatman, and rail splitters, Lincoln represented the traditional ideal of the Protestant Ethic; hard work, frugality, temperance, and a touch of ability applied long and hard. In his time, an inability to rise on the economic scale was individual failure--an outward sign of an inward lack of grace--idleness, indulgence, waste, or incapacity. This conception of the competitive world was intensely and even inhumanely individualistic. Moreover, the demands of Christian virtues and the success myth of the Protestant Ethic were incompatible; the ambition necessary for success melded with the Christian sin of pride and clashed with Christian disdain for material worship. In this way, individualism as it had evolved by Lincoln's time was heavily conflict laden and easily a cause of dual-edged guilt for both economic success or lack thereof. The vital test of democracy for Lincoln and his contemporaries was in fact an economic test.

Nevertheless, as the Civil War years approached, slavery could not be ignored. Though Lincoln was a follower and not a leader of public opinion on this issue, he took the slavery question out of the realm of moral and legal dispute and, dramatized it in terms of free labor's self-interest, and accorded it a universal appeal. The slavery issue became politically permanent in the mid-1840s and when anti-slavery forces gained control of the political branches of government in 1860, they aspired to more than abolition of slavery. Many of those associated with the anti-slavery movement decided that the time had come to restore morality throughout government. In that sense, the Civil War became a marker as a moral watershed. Nevertheless, Lincoln moved towards emancipation only after all his other policies had failed. Even then the Emancipation Proclamation of January 1, 1863 contained no indictment of slavery, but simply based emancipation on military necessity.

During the same time frame, the United States was undergoing great changes in other respects as well. By 1860 there were thirty-three States, including two, California and Oregon, on the Pacific Coast, while there had been only eighteen States in 1815, with none farther West than Louisiana. In 1815 the United States had totaled around 1.7 million acres, but by 1860 it had reached its present continental limits and had added about 1.2 million square miles. Similarly, in 1814 there were 8,400,000 Americans, yet on the eve of the Civil War there were 31,443,321. All of these changes led to a fracture in American unity that could not be repaired without a war to preserve the Union, or a permanent division of it and the prospect of an interminable series of internecine wars. Long and bloody as it was, the Civil War probably prevented more wars and the fracturing of the United States into several confederacies. Even as the war raged, the Western expansion continued.

In the mid-1800s, an estimated 300,000 went West in search of free land, escape from crowded cities, religious freedom, gold, or adventure. Along the 2,000 mile Oregon Trail so many trekked across the continent to establish homes in the far Northwest that gouges carved by sliding wagons are clearly visible in the crest of hills and those same wagons carved five-foot-deep grooves in the sandstone, while footpaths from all those who walked beside the wagons can still be seen. The weather on the plains was a brutal 115 degrees in the summer and minus 40 in the winter, and the soil was so hard that wooden plows skittered over it like skates over ice. Yet still they came. After the invention of the metal plow, sod busters moved in and swiftly transformed the Midwest into the bread basket for the nation. As a result, Congress enacted three landmark laws in 1862 to open up the West: the Homestead Act which offered any American citizen or any alien intending to become a citizen 160 acres of western land absolutely free; the Morrill, or Land-Grant Act, providing for the establishment of public colleges and universities throughout the country; and the Pacific Railroad Act which made grants and loans to aid construction of the first transcontinental railroad.

In 1873, Winchester Repeating Arms Company unveiled a .44 caliber repeater rifle that became known as "the gun that won the West." Three years later, the Battle of Little Big Horn occurred ending with the slaughter by the Sioux and Cheyenne of the 7th U.S. Cavalry under Lieutenant Colonel George Custer. Then, fourteen years later about 300 Sioux were massacred by the Army in the Battle of Wounded Knee, the last major Indian resistance to White expansion in the West. This brought to an end the carnage begun in 1830 by passage of the Indian Removal Act which allowed President Andrew Jackson to move the eastern tribes westward. At that time, Jackson replied to critics of this policy by saying, "[Once we] open the eyes of those children of the forest to their true condition, [they will realize] the policy of the general government toward the Red Man is not only liberal, but generous."[8] Ralph Waldo Emerson thought otherwise when he wrote, "the name of this nation will stink to the world."[9]

CHAPTER SIX

Rational Individualism After Romanticism and Reform

The late 1800s was also an era of public scandals, corporate profiteering, unequaled economic growth, and financial ruin--the age of Robber Barons and rebels, cynicism, and Spoilsmen. Corruption in and out of government was commonplace, and everyone tried to make a fast buck. The Daddy Warbucks rags-to-riches mythology in America matured between Appomatox and 1890. The notion grew that being poor was a sign of personal failure and being rich was a sign of superiority. Thinking in economic terms and solution of problems by economic analysis--begun on Plymouth Plantation and nurtured during Lincoln's time--came of age and began to dominate public and private decision-making.

Innovations in transportation, manufacturing, and farming swept the country. The greatest march of economic growth and transformation in human history capitalized on a country rich with minerals and a huge supply of human beings bent to unhealthful, back-breaking and dangerous work. As a consequence, people learned obedience to authority and work became the core of the moral life. The Puritan Work Ethic, equating work and Godly virtue, combined with feverish development and ruthless competition to perform a transvaluation of life. Early artisan shops, farms, and counting houses gave way to mills, factories, sweat shops, machinery, and subdivided labor. Mass wage earners gave the moral primacy of work a place of unequaled commitment.

This era produced an ethos reverberating with the word duty and spread an infectious model of active conscientious doing. With a taproot in the Protestant Reformation, the doctrine of industrious life pervaded society and politics. It was nurtured by universalizing the obligation of work and methodizing the time of workers. A passionate conviction developed that everyone had a right to come into their own, and the industrialists stood squarely on the myth opportunity for the common people. Survival of the fittest was applied in philosophy and industry, public opinion idealized unscrupulous attainment of wealth, and "it's just business" became a term used to describe unsavory activity justified by the exigencies of economic expansion.

Industrialism--The Gilded Age

Observers from other countries have noted American fascination with business.[1] The idealization of businessmen--like its opposite the unconcern for the intellectual--has been blamed for America's inability to create a group of people who make public service a lifetime concern. Commenting that the U.S. rarely develops such dedicated public servants in positions of administrative power, one foreign observer states:

> It is undeniable that the archetype of North America, the model or hero to be imitated, is not the scholar or even the intelligent man, but the successful businessman . . . who succeeds, through his tenacity and cleverness, in amassing a fabulous fortune.   . . . Moreover, all education that the child receives, from his parents or in the school, is conducive to building the model. The youth spends his vacation not in rest or in intellectual self-improvement, but in earning money, selling magazines, or washing dishes and glasses in soda fountain. (Joseph 1959, 295-296)

Bertrand Russell, described by the newspaper press of his time as "one of the world's most extravagant individualists," deplored the American ethic that "what we do is get on in our business, and get a fortune which we can leave our descendants" (Feinberg and Kasrils 1973, 1:98-99). In preparation for one of his New York lectures in 1929, he said:

America has more respect for businessmen than it has for learned men. The economic opportunities in America are so tremendous that the businessman is bound to have far more prestige than the learned man. When the time comes in American that money-making will be more difficult and earnings will be less, then I think we will see that the people will turn to education. (Ibid., 111)

This business worship occurs despite the fact that working people of the railroads, mines, textile mills, steel mills, and auto plants faced the clubs of policemen, the machine guns of soldiers, and the contempt of strike breakers to get an eight-hour day and a living wage.

But Americans are known for their double standards,[2] in business ethics and whole areas of life that lack moral responsibility, or purpose.[3] Bertrand Russell's (Feinberg and Kasrils 1973, 1984) visits to America found, in a land where human rights were idealized, gross inequalities in wealth and power, interference with academic freedom and civil liberties, racism and persecution of minorities. Anthropologist Margaret Mead described another disquieting American view:

The traditional picture is perfectly clear. The self made man, while he is rising from newsboy to multimillionaire by his own efforts, is drivingly ambitious, loyal mainly to his own interests, and ready to ride roughshod over his employees and his rivals. (Mead 1967, 288)

Sharp business practices were admired by the mid-Nineteenth Century American as well. It was *slick* to outdo another. The Midwest expression for having been cheated was *yankeed*.[4] Mead believes that such disparity between American expressed ideals and American behavior breeds cynicism, self-indulgence, distrust, apathy, fear, and corruption. Russell agrees that Americans are unable to face reality except in a mood of cynicism. He blames a far too strict set of ideal rules for virtuous politics that can be met by no one and, therefore, permit no politician to be virtuous. Clearly, the standards of behavior for politicians and businessmen are contradictory and contribute to cynical attitudes.

Mead also believes such cynicism "could well form the basis of an American fascism, a fascism bowing down before any character strong enough and amoral enough to get away with it, to get his" (Mead 1965, 203). Others too have recognized this tendency in Americans who are "eager to put their trust in one, two, or three Great Men who would lead them to salvation and relieve them of the anxiety of the unknown" (Joseph 1959, 78). This is conformity in its most pernicious form, born not of meekness, passive acceptance of dogma, or strong centralized government, but of industrious, competitive striving for superiority and victory over others. Conformism is said by outside observers to lie at the core of American life.[5] Every traveler to America in one study was struck by the uniformity of ideas.[6]

Tocqueville saw American conformity as little independence of mind and inadequate securities against tyranny of the majority.[7] He also saw it in separation among people:

> Despotism, which by its nature is suspicious, sees the separation among men the surest guarantee of its continuance, and it usually makes every effort to keep them separate. No vice of the human heart is so susceptible to it as selfishness: a despot [Machiavelli's prince] . . . stigmatizes as turbulent and unruly spirits those who would combine their exertions to promote the prosperity of the community; and, perverting the natural meaning of words, he applauds as good citizens those who have no sympathy for any but themselves. (Bradley 1945, 2:102)

Zinn (1990) recognized American conformity in the 1960s Milgram experiment in which two-thirds of the volunteers gave what they thought were electrical shocks to human subjects, even when the latter feigned agonizing pain. Experimenter Milgram said the fundamental lesson of his study was that ordinary people simply doing their jobs can become agents in a terrible destructive process. Both Henry Commager (1950) and Bertrand Russell (Feinberg and Kasrils 1983) observed that twentieth century America was remarkable for the decline of significance of the individual. Russell saw a submission to leaders, loss of individual responsibility, and the habit of individual thought, hysterical fanaticism, and a condition of servility, indifference, persecution of people of independent mind, and tyranny of the herd. It was not new, having its roots in Puritan colonies, but Russell thought it the worst feature of America.

Commager (1950) described the nineteenth-century American as impatient, accustomed to prosperity, resentful of anything that interfered with it, and outraged at any prolonged lapse of it. Whatever promised to increase wealth was good, which brought tolerance of speculation, exploitation of natural resources, and the worst manifestations of industrialism. This gave a quantitative cast to American thinking on everything. A person's worth was material worth, solution to problems were therefore always quantitative, and everything yielded to the sovereignty of numbers. Accordingly, no philosophy that got much beyond common sense was ever of any interest, except practical instrumentalism.[8] Tocqueville (Bradley 1945) attributed this boundless passion for wealth to an inexhaustible supply of natural riches and resources. Commager (1950) agreed that America rarely had need to build for the future because it was easier to skim the cream off the soil, forests, mines, or business investments, abandon them and go on to something new. Boundless free will, optimism, infinite possibilities, and confidence in the ability of the next generation to look after itself came from inexhaustible resources, a spacious universe governed by immutable laws, and a benevolent God. Similarly, writing in 1949 Bertrand Russell (Feinberg and Kasrils 1973, 1984) also attributed the American preoccupation with utility and material outlook to a large country, not yet over-populated, with immense resources and greater wealth than any country in Europe or Asia.

Energy and order, freedom and regimentation, individualism and conformity warred with one and other. While the American joiner arose from growing uniformity, a mission-like desire for distinction and a sense of self perpetuated the howling wilderness image of the frontier. As a part of the vision that a moral life was hard work and hard-bitten determination, the most picturesque phase of the Wild West was glorified, led by cattle droving cowboys. Just when the demands of industrialization drained America's soul, the spare frame, pithy speech, bow-legged stride, and six-shooter of the authentic American cowboy captured the popular imagination. This taste for the great open spaces and the free hardy life, with horse and rifle accounts for the popularity of Teddy Roosevelt and his Rough Riders of 1898. Unfortunately, it is also largely responsible for the feeling that the only good Indian is a dead Indian and for wiping out the Indian villages of the Great Plains. Manifest Destiny, born from a philosophy of survivalism, provided the rationale for profound cruelty. In fact, the year of the massacre at Wounded Knee, 1890, was officially declared by the Bureau of the Census as the close of the internal frontier.

By the 1890s America had changed character: It was on the threshold of a new age in which the Captains of Industry would lead the people to unparalleled wealth and modernity. However, it all collapsed in the fecund 1890s. The year 1893 saw the biggest economic crisis in the country's history. After decades of wild industrial growth and uncontrolled speculation, 642 banks failed and 16,000 businesses closed. Caverns of discontent opened, politics lost equilibrium, and the people groped for a remedy. The popular esteem for wealth that sanctioned and blessed industry also rewarded cunning and hardness of heart. Industrialization heaped desperation and despair on the working class, casting seed for the rise of organized labor.

Marxism, Socialism, and Reform

Anger from the realities of ordinary life emerged as the twentieth century opened. Elihu Root in his presidential address before the New York State Bar Association in 1912 described the difficulty being faced at that time:

> In place of the old individual independence of life in which every intelligent and healthy citizen was competent to take care of himself and his family, we have come to a high degree of interdependence in which the greater part of our people have to rely for all the necessities of life upon systematized cooperation of a vast number of other men working through complicated industrial and commercial machinery. Instead of the completeness of individual effort working out its own results in obtaining food and clothing and shelter, we have specialization and division of labor which leaves each individual unable to apply his industry and intelligence except in cooperation with a great number of others whose activity conjoined to his is necessary to produce any useful result. (Morison 1965, 811)

Based on Frederick W. Taylor's scientific management, division of labor theories and time motion studies, industry tried to control every minute of the worker's energy and time. This system, which treated workers like standard parts, was well fitted for the emerging auto industry, but it further eroded individuality, humanity, and conditions of the work place.

Perry (1944) has noted that after the middle nineteenth century growth of the cult of materialism and positivism, America grew queasy as the flavor of life became unsavory. It was the apotheosis of the Captains of Industry, symbols of the self-made individual, the march of technological progress, and the social benefits of competitive ambition. However, their sordid motives, unscrupulous behavior, exploitation of labor and unholy alliance with political bosses belied their professed public service and painted them as monsters rather than demigods. As a consequence, Socialism prospered, Socialist candidates began to succeed in local elections, and fear of spreading Socialism increased the pace of progressive reform to head it off.

Disillusionment from failed promises of the industrialists led to a succession of leaders that came to be called Progressives. They realized that interdependence had replaced the independent life of early America, requiring government action to curb the arrogance of organized wealth and poverty amid plenty. During the administrations of Theodore Roosevelt, Taft, and Wilson, legislation passed state and federal levels to regulate railroads, pipelines, banks, monopolies, hours and wages, meat packing, and to provide for income taxes, worker's compensation, and safety inspections of factories. The Progressives replaced the laissez-faire creed of the lawyers, bankers, and industrialists with government action. As a result of abuses by the Robber Barons and Spoilsmen, the people were in an angry mood, permitting American revivalism of the Great Awakening to sweep away much of the cynicism and apathy that had characterized politics for the previous thirty years. The coarse, materialistic civilization that emerged after the Civil War produced a practical breed of political reformers with steady nerves, strong ambitions, tenacity, and flexible scruples. Many of these Progressives were college graduates who believed in the perfectibility of humans, and an open, non-deterministic society capable of changing for the better.

Foremost among them was Theodore Roosevelt. Roosevelt believed, for example, in the Hamiltonian notion of making the federal government truly national through a broad interpretation of the general welfare clause of the Constitution. Determined to restore the American spirit he called the fighting edge, Roosevelt fought the fat materialism of the wealthy and the lurking menace of the masses by advocating the heroic, soldierly virtues of the hunter, cowboy, frontiersman, and naval hero. He displayed a passion for sudden violence and a trigger-like willingness to use troops for putting down strikes. With no passionate interest in the humane goals of reform, he saw himself as an arbiter between rich and poor and custodian of the stern virtues necessary for the United States to play its destined role of mastery in the world theater. Create, act, take a place, be somebody, was his advice. He believed only a warped, perverse, and silly morality condemned conquest of the American West. Thus, Roosevelt and the reformers he represented tried to bolster individualism; to remedy by more individualism the evils that were the inevitable result of already existing individualism. Achievements of two generations of boundlessly individualistic and ambitious entrepreneurs eclipsed the old, individualistic workshop economy and replaced it with a new, faceless world of system, large scale enterprise, and intricate bureaucracies.

World War I, Communism, and the Age of Heroes

The Progressive Era ended with the outbreak of World War I. When that war ended in 1918, fifty thousand soldiers had died, and bitterness spread through the country. The first efforts at organizing labor were downed by force, and the Socialist party was falling apart from the impact of the drive for national unity during the war. With the Socialists weakened, a Communist party was organized, and trade unionism began to develop in earnest. On the surface, there had been over thirty years of prosperity between 1897 and 1929, which had seen a marked increase in American wages and standard of living. It was the dawn of a golden age. In 1928, Herbert Hoover declared a final triumph over poverty and wrote a book expounding his philosophy of untempered individualism. In it he declared equality part of the claptrap of the French Revolution. But the Roaring Twenties was a time of prosperity and fun only at the top. Wild financial speculation was prevalent in the financial markets, but the conditions for American workers were grim, and the economy was fundamentally unsound. The Jazz Age was merely a diversion from the serious social and economic problems just below the surface. Hero worship and preoccupation with personalities served as a convenient source for collective self-denial about true conditions.

Rural America was moved to the city and the invention of the internal combustion engine was a material key to a Great Change as horsey America was becoming motor-conscious. In 1900, automobiling was one of those things, like playing golf and smoking cigarettes, which politicians did not dare to be seen doing. Woodrow Wilson believed that there was nothing more a picture of the arrogance of wealth, or anything likely to spread socialistic feelings in the country more than the snobbery of motoring. Nevertheless, Henry Ford's assembly-line of mass production made the Model T, called the Tin Lizzy or flivver, affordable to farmers and skilled workers like. It was not long before the Ad-Men made motoring a respectable pastime. Before the auto revolution was over, the automobile would give each individual the freedom of movement never before experienced, permitting the worker to live miles from his job.

Depression, World War II, and The Ad-Men

At times nothing is more misleading than personal experience, as when it embraces only success. Herbert Hoover was a bright and energetic businessman and believer in the unregulated profit system. For thirty-two years covering Hoover's entire maturity, from the end of the 1893 Depression to the crash of 1929, this system suffered no major set-backs. Since his childhood, Hoover had seen a marked rise in American wages and standards of living and to him the system plainly worked, and it worked well. In his book, *American Individualism*, he admitted that untempered individualism would produce many injustices, but asserted that individualism in the United States had been tempered by equality of opportunity:

> Our individualism differs from all others because it embraces these great ideals: that while we build our society upon the attainment of the individual, we shall safeguard to every individual an equality of opportunity to take that position in the community to which his intelligence, character, ability, and ambition entitle him; that we keep the social solution free from frozen strata of classes; that we shall stimulate effort to each individual to achievement; that through an enlarging sense of responsibility and understanding we shall assist him to his attainment; while he in turn must stand up to the emery wheel of competition. (Morison 1965, 812)

To Hoover, human progress was the result of opportunity for the individual to use his personal skills as best he could. The most an individual could expect from the government was liberty, justice, intellectual wealth or common equality of opportunity, and stimulation. Opportunity, individualism, laissez-faire, and personal success were all in the dominant American tradition of the time. In the language of Jefferson, Jackson, and Lincoln such ideals were fresh and invigorating, but in the language of Herbert Hoover they became stale and oppressive.

During the crisis of the 30s, Hoover's essential beliefs became outlandish and unintelligible almost overnight. He was the last Presidential spokesman for the hallowed doctrines of laissez-faire, until revived by Ronald Reagan in 1980. When the stock market crashed, most of the nation's wealth was concentrated in the hands of only a small percent of the people, and large depressed segments of society-- farmers, textile workers, and coal miners--lacked sufficient income to meet much more than their minimal needs. Corporate profits were up, production was up, and income was up, prompting President Coolidge to declare in 1925 that the business of America is business. The full flush of fiscal euphoria brought swollen profits and abundant credit to bear in wild get-rich-quick speculation, but when it came down, it came down fast.

The stock market crash of 1929 marked the beginning of the Great Depression, ended the self-deception of the Twenties, resulted in grinding poverty for millions, and began a march toward further reforms. For six months, no one even admitted the existence of a Depression, while Hoover's laissez-faire philosophy that nature would cure all restrained government action. His survival-of-the-fittest Secretary of the Treasury, Andrew Mellon, wanted it to go right to the bottom: "People will work harder, live a moral life. Values will be adjusted, and enterprising people will pick up the wrecks of the less competent people" (Hofstadter 1973, 387). Business and government leaders repeatedly stated that the worst had passed, but the worst did not pass until mid-1932 when stocks hit rock bottom.

Indeed, a readjustment of values did occur. Sociologist John Dewey considered the condition of the American public as early as 1927, when he said the public seemed to be lost and bewildered. Disillusioned by the Robber Barons and Spoilsmen, the public created a crisis in American individualism. There was never a stronger mandate in American history for a new program, or a clearer repudiation of laissez-faire and the individualism of business and finance. Feeling helpless, humiliated, and deceived by the Capitalists, the country voted for welfare and security of simple folk--the transfer of wealth from rich to poor by action of government. Fearing the American system needed desperate measures to be saved, they were ready to take a chance on the New Deal.

Almost everyone of wealth, with resources to weather the Depression, wanted the downward spiral to hit rock bottom, smash the labor unions, and re-establish the free labor market of the previous century. However, what they got was quite different from what they wanted, as the age of the New Deal dealt a severe blow to American individualism. Freedom of action justified in the simple life of the last century seemed no longer tolerable. The Welfare State was born in the United States and it probably saved the capitalist system. The thesis that government is ultimately responsible for the welfare, employment, and security of the populace became generally accepted. The State became a medium for humanistic self-expression and the New Deal demonstrated that there was no inherent conflict between authority and freedom. Expansion of governmental functions shored up and buttressed a capitalist system tottering on the brink. Rather than weaken or destroy it, the New Deal saved American capitalism by ridding it of its worst abuses and compelling an accommodation of the larger public interest. Though big business and finance lost status while labor and the ordinary citizen gained power, the New Deal still left so much to private enterprise that the entire economy was strengthened.

The period just prior to the stock market crash was also the Golden Dawn of total advertising. A torrential output of consumer goods began, including such new products as radios, electric refrigerators, faster cars, shinier bathroom fixtures, and plusher caskets. The soft sell that had dominated advertising began to harden as competition increased pace with the volume and variety of manufactured goods. A great post-war boom ushered in the age of advertising and by 1925, magazines and newspapers owed a large part of their total income to ad revenue. The ads of the Twenties shared several traits with the decade itself, such as brashness and lack of scruples, as many ads pushed quasi-factual and pseudo-scientific claims. But the decade's dominate and identifying trend in advertising was the use of psychology by appealing to secret emotions that motivated people to buy. Rather than facts, advertisers planted in the readers' minds a connection between products and pleasant feelings of freedom, excitement, and romantic adventure. Psychological insights were applied with increasing effectiveness as the decade wore on, and advertising and mass production became twin cylinders keeping the motor of modern business running smoothly.

Consumerism, Conformity, and McCarthyism

As conditions in the nation improved, advertising still encouraged continued consumption by holding out the promise of leisure for all. After 1935, Keynesian economics and the Roosevelt administration made serious efforts at improving mass purchasing power. Some believed that the glorified producer--economic man--had thwarted the promise of Capitalism and what the nation needed was to treat the worker as consumer. These market oriented critics argued that the Declaration of Independence recognized the primacy of consumption in the right to life, liberty, and the pursuit of happiness. Likewise, Adam Smith took the position that consumption was the sole end and purpose of all production. Abundance would assure a decent level of consumption for everyone and permit devotion of one's energies to non-economic interests in life. As a result of these pressures, government and business policy began to focus upon the expansion of private choice and the acquisitive impulse, which survived the Thirties and Forties, and blossomed again in the Fifties.

Jean-Jacques Rousseau proposed two responses to modernization: One rested on an ideal of individual autonomy, the other on the collective city-state. Both constituted a critique of modernity that stressed its corroding effects on the authentic self, civic participation, and community. Key themes in the debate were authority, true individuality, authenticity, and the need for institutions to address the imbalances of modernity. Rousseau laid out a dream of secular happiness that has haunted the West since.[9]

Emersonian individualism daringly proclaimed that only the individual was natural, while society was artificial and corrupt. John Dewey wanted to reverse this value. He hoped that the United States could find room for an ideal of individual autonomy, or true individuality, in a vision of community, cooperation, and independence. A rebel against the solitary excesses of nineteenth-century individualism, Dewey searched for the great community which would restore the lost individual. He undertook an Emersonian effort to fuse the contraries of the one and the many--to consolidate material abundance, rationality, science--and develop new possibilities for cooperation, communal and participatory modes of learning, and civic action in impersonal cities.

At about the same time the Progressives and David Riesman added their voices to the ongoing dialogue. The nub of the debate between the Progressives and Riesman was the nature of true individuality in the modern world. The Progressives set into motion a series of shifts in American social character that Riesman called other direction. Their search for community to replace the obsolete, but powerfully entrenched individualism was a significant reversal of American intellectual life. In the name of autonomy, Riesman rebelled against the Progressive social thought.

At the height of his Progressive phase, Dewey was a booster of progress and other Progressive ideals. Though he was committed to an ideal of fulfilled individuality, his Progressive insistence on the group character of all life celebrated group life in ways that showed the Progressive blind spot toward conformity. He found inner directed morality lacerating and believed its ideal of conscience responsible for loneliness, alienation, and inner desolation; opposed the morality of self-scrutiny, rigid character, obsession with motives and inner purity; attempted to replace the dark isolation of private, individualistic conceptions of morality with sunlit, public standards; and replaced

Emersonian inner torment with social, communal, and objective standards. In place of rhetoric and guilt, he wanted action ethics that focused on visible consequences. This instrumentalism shared the Progressive confidence in the application of industry and science to all of life, and expressed the Progressive ideal of efficiency. He explored the possibility that science and technology would create new shifts in society and values away from economic individualism. He argued that the scientific outlook by itself was inadequate. In this he joined Emerson, Thoreau, and Whitman to denounce economic individualism as a threat to the human soul. Competitive individualism eclipsed true individuality under the force of oppressive inequality.[10]

Riesman thought Dewey a magnificent example of the kind of autonomy possible in the age of inner-direction. These inner-directed people were of unbending principle equipped with an inner gyroscope. Work, success, independence, manliness, character and internalized guilt equipped them to master a continent. The other-directed in contrast represented a world of other people, rather than a material environment, as the chief arena in which to strive. Instead of a gyroscope, these people employed an infinitely sensitive radar screen. Relentless concern over the judgment of the group was their mechanism for enforcing right behavior. This conformity most concerned Riesman, who believed Tocqueville was right that the American disease was conformity. His cure was a subdued, chastened ideal of autonomous individuality. Yet the true nature of individuality eluded a definitive answer in Dewey's age of the lost individual and Riesman's era of the lonely crowd.[11]

No personality expressed the American popular temper during this age better than Franklin D. Roosevelt. Roosevelt was warm, personal, concrete, and impulsive, and his capacity for change, flexibility, experimentation, and growth was enormous, whereas Hoover had been remote and abstract. When FDR came to power, the people wanted experiment, activity, trial, and error, because stagnation had gone dangerously far. Roosevelt accurately read the mood of the country when he said, "The country needs and, unless I mistake its temper, the country wants bold, persistent experimentation. It is common sense to take a method and try it. If it fails, admit it frankly and try another. But above all, try something" (Gans et al. 1979, 6). Only a leader with an experimental temperament made the New Deal possible.

When he took office, the economic machinery of the nation had collapsed and its politics was disintegrating. Therefore, during the emergency, Roosevelt effectively had dictatorial powers. People who had something to lose were fearful and sought any way out that would still leave them in possession. In 1945, FDR told Congress that power must be linked with responsibility and could defend itself only within the framework of the general good. The New Deal provided a heart-warming relief of distress and imprinted its values so deeply that Republicans were compelled to endorse it in their election platforms. After moving into the oval office, Roosevelt is said to have sat alone for a few moments and then shouted for his aides. One of his first acts was calling a special session of Congress which strengthened the financial system by passing his emergency banking bill unchanged in just thirty-eight minutes after convening. Deposits exceeded withdrawals when the banks opened four days later and the immediate panic was over. Sensing opportunity, FDR kept lawmakers in session for the next one hundred days and used a firmer rein on an uneasy nation than it had felt since the days of FDR's cousin, Teddy Roosevelt. In the process, he permanently altered the conduct of American life. When Congress adjourned approximately one hundred days later, fifty new laws assured government action and fifteen major messages streamed from the White House to Capitol Hill. These acts sought to employ the jobless, to develop the backward Tennessee Valley, to support crop prices, to repeal Prohibition, to stop home foreclosures, to insure bank deposits, and to stabilize the economy. In response, Alf Landon reportedly said that the iron hand of a dictator is preferred to a paralytic stroke.

The country was on a permanent war economy during the next thirty years, but it had big pockets of poverty. Though there were enough people at work, making enough money, to keep things quiet, the distribution of wealth was still unequal and had not changed much from 1944 to 1961. During that time, the lowest fifth of the families received five percent of all the income while the highest fifth received forty-five percent. In 1953, 1.6 percent of the adult population owned more than eighty percent of the corporate stock, and nearly ninety percent of the corporate bonds, and about two hundred giant corporations dominated the business scene.[12] Nevertheless, corporations and industrial might gained respect, Capitalism remained intact, and hysteria about Communism built a climate of fear.

The left, influential in the hard times of the Thirties, declined as World War II weakened labor militancies and patriotism pushed for unity of all against enemies overseas. Growing Soviet strength and the Korean War fueled a national paranoia about Communists, whipped to a feverish pitch by McCarthyism. Loyalty oaths, fear of speaking out, and other abridgments of individual liberties soon became common place in a contagion of fear. McCarthy called the terms of Truman and FDR twenty years of treason during which he said they conspired to deliver America to the Reds. As utterly preposterous a theory as this was, the country was almost torn apart. Efforts to root out subversives from government, colleges, and businesses ruined the careers and reputations of thousands. McCarthy was one of the most colossal liars in history and perpetuated a conspiracy theory that haunted a generation of Americans with the thought that creeping Communism would smother the American Way of Life. Ultimately, this fear led to the Cold War and forty years of influence for the military-industrial complex.

By the mid-Thirties, American workers were headed toward a deadly showdown with management. When a Senate committee wanted to know in 1928 why a coal company kept machine guns in its coal pits, Chairman of the Board Richard B. Mellon replied you could not run the mines without them. In 1935, hired guns still loomed over the toughest company towns, where a word about the union could get a person beaten up or killed. In those harsh times, losing one's job as opposed to losing one's life, was about the mildest punishment given a union organizer. Businesses routinely hired strike breakers both to fill the jobs of strikers and to wield machine guns, night sticks, and tear gas. These tactics permeated industrial management, including Ford Motor Company and General Motors, who used policeman to beat picketers with clubs and spray them with buckshot and tear gas. After John L. Lewis told Michigan Governor Frank Murphy that the latter should listen to the spirit of his grandfather rather than employ the National Guard to evict the strikers, Murphy--whose grandfather had been hanged in the Irish Rebellion--tore up his order to activate the Guard. After forty-four days of losing profits at a rate of a million dollars a day, General Motors finally agreed to bargain with the United Automobile Workers in the seventeen plants that had been struck. In four months time, the UAW had won its drive for acceptance and organized the majority of General Motors workers.

Never in American history was an event more anticipated yet more of a surprise than the attack on Pearl Harbor. When it happened, it seared the American consciousness and propelled the United States into a war that it had been desperately trying to avoid. No sooner had Americans managed to accept the shocking reality of Pearl Harbor than they faced another grim circumstance that never before experienced; that is, continuing disasters on the battlefield. In Guam, Kuwait, Hong Kong, Borneo, Singapore, and the Philippines, America and its allies endured a series of defeats. The allies were not able to start onto the offensive until late 1942, and when the flow of the war did shift, American marines and GIs leapfrogged from one obscure Pacific outcropping to another: Guadalcanal, Tarawa, Eniwetok, Saipan, Eulithi, Hiroshima, and Okinawa. America conducted war on land, sea, and air while production of armaments and equipment proceeded apace back at home.

Nevertheless, not all wartime sacrifice was received popularly. Even though Americans did not have to suffer the excruciating effects of war on their homeland, their individualistic nature chafed at WPB Directive No. 1, which instituted rationing in January 1942. It came as quite a shock to Americans and almost everything they enjoyed was affected-- meat, coffee, butter, cheese, sugar, and gasoline. In accordance with by now well-known characteristics of American pragmatism, it was not long before gas chiseling and ration stamp fraud became a national scandal. While the war raged, Joe Louis became a boxing great, bobby soxers attained high fashion, the football hero was cheered and fussed over, the fraternity initiate went his perilous rounds, and most high school and college kids indulged in time-killing that was inelegantly but accurately known as messing around. Pep rallies, smooching, making-time, roller skating, hanging around, listening to records, and striving to become or pursue the big-man-on-campus occupied American teenagers.

Writing in 1943, Margaret Mead described the American character as follows:

> We have a certain kind of character, the American character, which has developed in the New World and taken in a shape all its own; a character that is geared to success and to movement, invigorated by obstacles and difficulties, but plunged into guilt and despair by catastrophic failure or a wholesale alteration in the upward and onward pace; a character in which aggressiveness is uncertain and undefined, to which readiness to fight anyone who starts a fight and unreadiness to engage in violence have both been held up as virtues; a character which measures its successes and failures only against near contemporaries and engages in various quantitative devices for reducing every contemporary to its own stature; a character which sees success as the reward of virtue and failure as the stigma for not being good enough; a character which is uninterested in the past, except when ancestry can be used to make points against other people in the success game; a character oriented towards an unknown future, ambivalent towards other cultures, which are regarded with a sense of inferiority. (Mead 1967, 193)

At war's end there was considerable readjusting to be done, which did not proceed at all well. A large portion of the public in 1950-52 saw nothing but failure--the Soviet prominence, loss of the Korean War, and conflict with China. Malaise, suspicion, and frustration were heightened by the charges and innuendoes of the House Committee on Un-American Activities and the demagoguery of Senator Joseph McCarthy. In 1953, "Ike" the World War II hero, became President and rather than becoming a dynamic initiator of policies, he smoothed over difficulties and mediated conflicts. While he presided, international upheaval changed the old world order. At a terrible price of forty million killed worldwide by the war, the United States and the USSR, second rate powers in 1939, emerged as the world's economic and military superpowers.

The war had accelerated revolutionary developments in atomic weapons, jet airplanes, rockets, computers, and other technologies, which contributed to a vast social, economic, and technological revolution that transformed the face of the nation. After a brief recession in 1957, post-war economic prosperity pushed the decade's earlier listlessness to the back of the collective unconscious. As a result, America was able to get on with its business of business and mammoth organizations with international operations ceased being merely corporations and became institutions. Without a guiding principle, but with terrific power, they affected people's lives enormously. In 1910, major industries had not wanted college graduates, but now young organization men sought jobs in big firms, hoping to become an executive. By 1956, one hundred thirty-five corporate giants owned forty-five percent of all industrial assets and business's star was on the rise again as people bought executive rugs and rented executive apartments.

The Cold War, Civil Rights, and Vietnam

The Fifties, like the Twenties, salved a national hangover from the war years. First, the atomic bomb, then the H-bomb, the Cold War, Russian ascendancy, and Khrushchev's promise to bury the West replaced permanent peace and led to puzzlement with world events. Yet the Fabulous Fifties, the Nifty Fiftys--the Rock-and-Roll Age, tough and sexy--bloomed to shunt aside the fear and danger. The economic boom was about to transform American ideals and a fat consumer market was just being born. While images of mushroom clouds poisoning the atmosphere dominated their unconscious and fall-out shelters and civil defense plans sought room in their consciousness, the American people went on a decade long spending binge to divert their attention. Television was only one of hundreds of appliances for the home that were developed in the late Forties and the Fifties. But it opened a mass market never before available, and the Ad-Men wielded remarkable influence. America preoccupied itself with baseball, Marilyn Monroe, 3-D movies, cramming Volkswagens and telephone booths, the hula hoop, sack dresses, short shorts, crinoline, and pop-it-beads. Appearances and style became more important in politics and out, conformity and popularity became passions, and the population became more alike in housing, dress, habits, possessions, problems, and number of children. As basic civil rights were suspended, as the FBI investigated job applicants for low-level government positions, as McCarthy employed Hitler's big lie technique, and as suspicion and intolerance pervaded life, America bought washers and dryers, toasters, can openers, TVs, freezers, vacuums, incinerators, air-conditioners, and a myriad of other products that they did not need for their health or happiness. Keeping up with the Jones's preoccupied America and materialism, already an obvious American characteristic, reached new proportions.

The automobile's importance to the Fifties cannot be exaggerated. As it became responsible for one-sixth of GNP and provided mobility, status, freedom, and privacy, forty-one thousand miles of roads were built with public funds to accommodate it. Yet in spite of widening prosperity, old inequalities of wealth remained, and the poor could now see through the TV what it was missing. Segregation was outlawed, but there was still only token integration and rising intolerance permitted the KKK to experience a revival in the mid and late Fifties. It was going to take a popular movement to change the effects of hate and fear. Religion boomed in the Fifties, but worshippers wanted comforting and inspiring sermons, not appeals to shun materialism or advance social justice. This lack of concern for larger issues paved the way for social activism in the next decade.

Consensus existed in the United States that America was the greatest country on earth, superior to all contemporary and even to most past civilizations. Criticism of the effects of Capitalism, the government or the American Way of Life made the speaker suspect and was to be avoided. Moreover, the nation was shocked by Sputnik into believing that General Eisenhower had let the United States fall behind the Russians and that America was now losing the world-wide war against Communism. Reinforcing the paranoia generated by McCarthyism, the Korean War, and the Cold War, Sputnik set the stage for acceptance of the domino theory that propelled the United States into Laos, Cambodia, and Vietnam during the Sixties.

In the decade of turmoil and instability that was the 60s, a few things seemed to have dominated over all others: the Kennedys and their deaths, the arms race, the black emergence, the Vietnam War, and the Beetles. When the decade opened, Ike was still in the White House, but the campaign for President between John F. Kennedy and Richard M. Nixon was in full swing. When JFK and Jackie entered the White House in 1961, they exhibited a magical blend of elegance and vibrance which brought a short-lived feeling of vigor, public interest, and renewed optimism. However, before long the feeling grew that events were slipping out of control. On May 5, 1960, relations with the Soviets worsened when Francis Gary Powers was shot down in an American military U-2 flight over that country. Moreover, when J. F. Kennedy took office, people believed relations with Cuba could hardly get worse, an error soon to be corrected. On April 17, 1961, Kennedy launched an invasion of Cuba so poorly planned that Castro needed only four days to destroy it. Also, on August 13, 1961, a wall went up between East and West Berlin and later in October, 1962, the United States, the USSR, and Cuba were involved in the most dangerous moment of the Cold War. Until this Cuban missile crisis was resolved, school children began practicing hiding under their desks again. This crisis, the Bay of Pigs, the Berlin crisis, civil rights violence, Vietnam, and Kennedy's assassination soon led to moral questioning and loss of faith in the establishment.

The 1960s enjoyed the longest period of sustained economic growth in modern history, making years of real progress for ordinary Americans. This success led some to believe that prosperity would be so great that real poverty would be largely abolished in the United States. Everything in the country seemed to be getting better and better, and minorities were generally invisible. Civil rights laws were passed in 1957, 1960, and 1964, but they were enforced poorly or they were ignored. That began to change in 1963, when Martin Luther King's "I Have A Dream" speech thrilled two hundred thousand Black and White Americans. Yet certain sentences critical of the national government and urging militant action intended to produce stronger note of outrage were censored by the march leaders. Nevertheless, in 1965, Congress again reacted to Black revolt and turmoil and world publicity with more civil rights legislation. The plight of Blacks in America was precisely and poignantly expressed in signs carried by picketers in the Memphis sanitation workers strike that read, "I am a man." Then in 1967, the greatest urban riots in United States history came from the Black ghettos in Newark, Selma, Detroit, and Watts.

The mid-Sixties saw young men indicted for refusing to register for the draft. The slogan "Hell No We Won't Go" and "Hey Hey LBJ/How Many Kids Did You Kill Today?" reverberated across the nation. Many registrants burned their draft cards and two even burned themselves. When the bombing of North Vietnam began in 1965, indignation increased and a remarkable change in sentiment took place. It began with teach-ins at the University of Michigan in Ann Arbor, Michigan, but by 1970 hundreds of thousands were appearing for Washington peace rallies, including middle class professionals, and priests and nuns unaccustomed to activism. By 1968, the opposition to the Vietnam War was pressing in from all sides and the campuses were feverish with sit-ins and strikes during the first semester of the 1967-68 academic year when 204 separate demonstrations were conducted. Indeed, 1968 was indelibly a year of strife and loss, with Tet, Mi Lai, and that awful spring when first M. L. King, Jr. and then R.F.K. were killed by assassins. Another kind of riot also occurred at the 1968 Democratic National Convention in Chicago.

In 1965, when the bombing of North Vietnam began, a hundred people gathered on the Boston Common to voice their indignation. By October 15, 1969, the number of people assembled on the Boston Common to protest the war was one hundred thousand. Perhaps two million people across the nation gathered that day in towns and villages that had never seen an anti-war meeting. By 1970, the Washington peace rallies were drawing hundreds of thousands of people and in 1971 twenty thousand came to Washington tying up Washington traffic while expressing their disgust with the killing still going on in Vietnam. The climax of the protests came in 1970 when Nixon ordered the invasion of Cambodia. On May 4, national guardsmen killed four students at Kent State University in Ohio and another was paralyzed for life. Watching Americans in uniform kill American teenagers on television galvanized public opinion against the war, and withdrawal of United States troops begun in 1970 was complete by 1974.

The Sixties did not involve just civil rights or political activism. Despite another decade of economic growth, there was a general rebellion against the artificial oppressive ways of living that had survived the Fifties. There was new suspicion of big business profits as the motive for ruining the environment, and with the loss of faith in big powers--business, government, religion--there arose a stronger belief in self, whether individual or collective. The belief grew that people could figure out for themselves what to eat, how to live their lives, and how to be healthy. Traditional education was also re-examined and the schools that taught values of patriotism and of obedience to authority were challenged, not just on the content of education, but on the style, the formality, the bureaucracy, the insistence on subordination to authority. Never in American history had there been more movement for change concentrated in so short a span of years. It touched every aspect of life: marriage, sex, childbirth, dress, music, art, sports, language, religion, literature, death, and schools. Many Americans were shocked by the new temper, the new behavior. Individualism, suppressed for the decade of the Fifties or more, reasserted itself in the Sixties and early Seventies.

CHAPTER SEVEN

Radical Individualism From Disillusionment and Loss of Faith

Chief Justice Earl Warren resigned in 1969, ending an era of the court that had brought individual civil rights to the forefront of every American's consciousness. By its desegregation, school prayer, criminal rights, abortion, and one-man-one-vote decisions, the court aroused fervent passions and boosted individualism by making everyone aware of their personal rights. When the assassination of Martin Luther King in 1968 was followed closely by the assassination of Robert F. Kennedy only two months later, the country began coming apart, and by the early 70s, the system seemed out of control. With the Watergate scandal, a decline in politics occurred from which the nation has yet to recover.

The Nixon White House was threatened by action of the masses. After the 1968 Chicago convention, at which no one was safe from the police, Nixon took the police state to new heights. His administration sought to quell disturbances, to defeat demonstrations and to dampen rising individualism by resorting to dirty tactics and illegal means. When these tactics were disclosed to the public and the President was implicated, he was forced to resign or be impeached. Faith in government was never lower than in 1974. A mood of pessimism existed in higher circles, which spread through the rest of society as people lost faith in their leaders. The age of abundance seemed to have ended and past lessons seemed irrelevant or dangerous. A flight from politics occurred and the government, the military, the President, the Congress, and business all suffered diminution before the public. William Simon, Secretary of the Treasurer, urged businessmen in 1976 to show the human side of Capitalism. President Carter directed his appeal to those beleaguered by the powerful and the wealthy, but Americans did not want to attend the poor. They were preoccupied with inflation rising faster than wages and unemployment rates at eight percent and higher.

The Beatles came to represent a counter-culture that embraced everything new from clothing to politics. This culture probably sprang from the Beatniks of the Fifties and early Sixties, who practiced free love, took drugs, and repudiated the straight world. The Beatles' music and lifestyles had a great affect on the young. Beatlemania coincided with a more ominous development in the emergence of the counter-culture--the rise of the drug prophet Timothy Leary. The popularity of drug use among the young induced panic in the old. During the Sixties, drug use remained a deviant practice and a source of great tension between the generations.

Self-Actualization in the 70s

The Sixties counter-culture developed a hedonism that may have contributed to the feelings of need for self-actualization in the Seventies. With the Watergate scandal, politics was replaced by a high-tech, consumer-oriented mass society that wanted more money for less work, more government benefits with less government and taxes, and greater individual freedom without responsibility. Attention to self pushed out attention to others and knowledge about one's self and one's place in the world became an important pursuit. The consciousness movement of the Seventies resulted in mass self-examination and therapy established self as the successor to rugged individualism. Economic man gave way to psychological man; haunted by anxiety, out to find a meaning in life, demanding approval and acclaim, requiring immediate gratification, perpetually unsatisfied and restless, craving without limits, and extolling cooperation and teamwork while harboring deep anti-social impulses. Americans retreated to purely personal preoccupations and what mattered was psychic self-improvement. The narcissist personality seemed to spring from the

American public, and a survivalist mentality where the world view centered solely on self was a characteristic of the Seventies.

According to the University of Michigan Survey Research Center, trust in government was low in every section of the population as early as 1970. Of professional people, forty percent had low political trust in government and sixty-six percent of unskilled blue-collar workers had low trust. Those polls were said to show "widespread, basic discontent and political alienation" (Zinn 1980, 530) Even after Nixon resigned in August of 1974 and other actions were taken to purge the rascals and to restore the country's health, America was still suspicious and hostile toward government leaders, the military, and big business. A July, 1975 Lou Harris poll looking at the public's confidence in the government from 1966 to 1975 reported confidence in the military had dropped from sixty-two percent to twenty-nine percent, in business from fifty-five percent to eighteen percent, and in both President and Congress from forty-two percent to thirteen. In 1973, another Harris poll reported the number of Americans feeling alienated and disaffected with the general state of the country climbed from twenty-nine percent in 1966 to over fifty percent. After President Ford succeeded Nixon, the percentage of alienated was fifty-five percent. Even so, that survey showed that the people were troubled most by economic circumstances, specifically inflation. This was confirmed by public opinion analysts testifying before Congress in the Fall of 1975, who reported "that public confidence in the government and in the country's economic future is probably lower than it has ever been since they began to measure such things scientifically" (Ibid., 545).

These surveys demonstrate that the feelings of discontent went beyond Blacks, the poor, and the radicals. It spread among skilled workers, white-collar workers, and professionals. Perhaps for the first time in the nation's history, the lower and middle classes were also disillusioned with the system. This all led to decreasing government legitimacy:

> The essence of the democratic surge of the 1960s was a general challenge to existing systems of authority, public and private. In one form or another, this challenge manifested itself in the family, the university, business, public and private associations, politics, the governmental bureaucracy, and the military services. People no longer felt the same obligation to obey those whom they had previously considered superior to themselves in age, rank, status, expertise, character or talents. (Ibid., 547)

All this produced problems for governance of Democracy in the 1970s.

Living for yourself, not for your predecessors or posterity or even for the future, became the prevailing passion. Older traditions of self-help atrophied, eroding everyday competence, and the individual became more and more reliant upon the State, the corporation, or other bureaucracies. Authority figures in modern society lost credibility and aggressive impulses arose to replace empathy for others. The organization man was cast aside by the bureaucratic gamesman, who avoided intimacy, pitted himself against others, felt little loyalty to the organization, and tried to use it for his own ends. The upwardly mobile shifted their focus from technical mastery to control of players' moves. Ambitious young men now had to compete with their peers for the attention and approval of their superiors, and inner-direction of previous generations was replaced by the other-directed type. As success came to require more attention to youth, glamour, and novelty than it did to conscientious and competent handling of job assignments, creation of self became the highest form of creativity.

This describes a way of competitive life that carries the logic of individualism to the extreme of a war of one against all and pursues happiness to a dead end, narcissistic preoccupation with self. It has been contrasted with the rugged individualist of early America:

> In the nineteenth-century American imagination, the vast continent stretching westward symbolized both the promise and the menace of an escape from the past. The West represented an opportunity to build a new society unencumbered by feudal inhibitions. But it also tempted men to throw off civilization and to revert to savagery. Through compulsive industry and relentless sexual repression, Nineteenth-Century Americans achieved fragile triumph over the id. The violence they turned against the Indians and against nature originated not in unrestrained impulse but in the white Anglo-Saxon's super ego, which feared the wildness of the West because it objectified the wildness within each individual. While celebrating the romance of the frontier in their popular literature and practice, Americans imposed on the wilderness a new order designed to keep impulse in check while giving free rein to acquisitiveness. Capital accumulation in its own right sublimated appetite and subordinated the pursuit of self-interest to the service of future generations. In the heat of the struggle to win the West, the American pioneer gave full vent to his passivity and murderous cruelty, but he always envisioned the result--not without misgivings, expressed in a nostalgic cult of lost innocence--as a peaceful, respectable, churchgoing community safe for his women and children. (Lasch 1978, 10)

Early Americans lived a vigorous, instinctual, self-interested existence, but people nowadays have become so dependent upon the State, the corporation, and other bureaucracies, that they tend to be consumed by rage and inner anger for which the bureaucratic society can devise few legitimate outlets. Defenses against desire cause anger, and that anger gives rise in turn to new defenses against rage itself. The result is a people that are bland, submissive, and sociable on the outside but who seethe within.

Self-Aggrandizement in the 80s

In the 1980s, the self-indulgence of the Seventies was taken a step further, as self-interest was put into action. Anecdotal examples of such self-indulgence throughout society are legion: seemingly random killings on the highways and in the movie theaters from coast-to-coast; children neglected, abused, and murdered by their parents; houses and other buildings burned in our cities for fun on Devil's Night; abortion bombings; ex-President Reagan accepting two million dollars from the Japanese for implementing policies favorable to them while he was President; the HUD/Silent Sam Pierce scandal; defective military equipment provided by dishonest suppliers; investigations of judges at all levels of the court system; destructive parties by college students numbering in the thousands; Material Girl as rock star of the 80s; the drug scourge; college football heroes fighting with police and sponsoring beer parties for the hundreds in attendance; administrators of colleges paralyzed by the civil rights of offending sports players; debate over flag burning while so many important issues go wanting; the ethics package in Congress tied to a thirty percent pay increase; bumper stickers that read "Whoever Dies With The Most Toys Wins"; TV evangelists bilking their flock out of millions of dollars in the name of salvation; the Iran-gate sale of arms to the Ayatollah and, of course, the inability to reduce the deficit, cleanup toxic wastes, or dispose of nuclear wastes because neither special interest nor the citizenry can reach agreement.

Moreover, a 1989 survey of college students at one university shows evidence of alienation and self-indulgence: twenty-eight percent of the students almost never discussed issues of deep personal significance with an adult; fifty-two percent said that they want to learn on their own terms; fifty-five percent reported that they know someone who has values and beliefs that cannot make any sense to them; thirty-two percent stated they know someone who has made or talked about making a suicide attempt; and sixty-five percent report spending equal or more time in the social side of college than in the academic one, while only twelve percent report spending more time on the academic side; fifteen percent reported that members of the minority should adopt the values of the majority; fifty-one percent responded that they do not care about university policies concerning alcohol consumption because they consider that to be a private matter; and seventy-two percent report that the reason for their career choice is that it earns them enough to be reasonably comfortable.[1] A similar survey in 1990 of college freshmen found "making more money" was a "very important factor" (Huer 1990, 16). This attitude toward money was a big jump from twenty years earlier.

This lure of money also invades the schools, traps minority students and others, and robs them of their future. Veronica Vega, age 16, of Robert E. Lee High School in San Antonio has 20-hour days in which she spends 6.5 hours scanning groceries, six hours in school, takes care of her four year old brother, and tries to find time for homework. Finally home by 11 PM, she starts her home work at midnight and by 2 AM she is asleep on her books. The alarm is set for 6 AM, when she will dress her brother, take him to day care, and start all over. By week's end she will spend 35 hours at school, 36 hours at work, and eight hours on homework.[2]

Last year she was getting A's in school and played a clarinet two hours a day. She once dreamed of going to MIT and exploring the heavens for NASA, but she took a $5 an hour job not because she needed to but because she wanted to, her grades have now turned to C's and D's, and she received her first F. "I'm really messing up," she says. "I used to love school. Now I hate it" (Bensimkon 1993, 76). She has started sleeping through classes, she gets sick often (mostly from stress she thinks), she has missed seven days in the last six weeks, and a volatile relationship with her mother is exacerbated by exhaustion. "I started working because I wanted to get out of the house. It's addictive. I can't stop," she says. "I have major bags under my eyes, but I don't want to give up the little luxuries I have" (Ibid., 78). But Veronica is not unusual: 66 percent of U.S. high school students work and it is jeopardizing their futures.[3]

The 1980s saw an administration loosely controlled by an old, forgetful, uninspiring, but extremely popular President who had been elected twice on a platform of trickle down economics that favored private interests over the public interests. In a world where one percent of the nation owned one-third of the wealth, envy and class anger burgeoned in America. Americans wanted their share of the pie and devoted themselves to attaining it. Self-indulgence became the American credo. Economization of the world diminished and denigrated the public sphere. The values of public purpose, insofar as they were reflected in the traditional forms of government, receded as the values of private interests moved forward. Competition, greed, and domination of the individual by rational organizations strangled consideration of the common good.

Life conceived of as a competitive struggle in which joy is getting ahead of one's neighbor has been called the major cause of unhappiness in America. A secondary cause is the necessity for subservience to large organizations. The bureaucratic impersonality of vast collective units submerge the individual by failing to provide for independence of mind.[4] Moreover, the Profit Ethic--economic consideration as the central feature of American culture--became a "subconsciously internalized state of mind" in which politics and everything else was subordinated to economics.[5]

Beginning and ending with individual self-interest, the Profit Ethic is an all encompassing and overwhelming "generalization of life and thought" that has no obligation to be human. This economic ethos has become such an established fact in American life that saying anything uncomplimentary about it is positively un-American and few are conscious of greed as a factor. It cannot conceive of a value in anything unless it is "visible, measurable, and obtainable in specific terms." Therefore, this ethic has no need for spirituality, morality, or humanity. What began as an explanation by Adam Smith of economic exchange in a marketplace is now the driving force behind a society and a cultural obsession. We are "selfish and we are proud of it."[6]

Huer (1991) notes that the Profit Ethic has advanced so far in the United States that capitalism has been replaced by commercialism. As an advanced form of capitalism, commercialism is more psychological and cultural than real. It is a widespread practice and belief that money-making is the single most important purpose of life and self-interest is the God-given nature of mankind. The total resources of government, science, and technology are devoted to the enterprise of making money:

> It is the general cultural adulation of money--an almost theological acceptance of money as the supreme purpose in life. It is in the definition of life for every decent young man and woman in America; it is in the curriculum of schools and colleges . . . it is also in the theoretical and intellectual assumption of human nature that self-interest is a natural part of existence. It is . . . [not] a moral struggle between good and evil . . . [for] the issue has been generalized and

moralized as an ethical system and established as a national commitment. (Huer 1990, 19)

Commercialism is a national creed that rules the soul to such an extent that freedom is perverted into a struggle to dominate, to enlarge oneself over others.[7]

The modern commercial American even distrusts competition out of an unconscious association of it with the urge to destroy:

> Hence he repudiates the competitive ideologies that flourished at an earlier stage of capitalist development. . . . He extols cooperation and teamwork while harboring deeply antisocial impulses. He praises respect for rules and regulations in the secret belief that they do not apply to himself. (Lasch 1979, xvi)

This brand of American has had his own way for so long that he has no heart for the difficulties of attaining happiness. Rather, he wants it bestowed upon him because he thinks it is one of his personal rights.

Finally, the primacy of competition in the global marketplace drove out all concern for the human effects of economic decisions. Responding to criticism for moving production to Mexico to cut costs, one corporate president expressed the business credo for the Nineties: "We live in a global economy. We have to be competitive. We always hate to close a plant, but *we have to do anything to survive* [Emphasis supplied]" (Oniski 1993, 1E). Answering a critic who raised the lack of humanity for Americans in such decisions, the same executive said, "He doesn't understand the global economy at all" (Ibid.). To the lack of humanity in paying Mexican worker's an average of $2.50 per hour, he said their wages were not significantly lower than their U.S. counterparts.

Self-aggrandizement in the Eighties is exemplified by the Leveraged Buy Outs (LBO) of corporate raiders. In such LBOs, top management would borrow heavily to complete deals then to repay the debt they typically sold junk bonds, dismembered the companies, and eliminated jobs to cut costs. In pursuit of huge speculative profits, these new managers added no value to the corporations they dismembered, but often left them saddled with such large amounts of debt that they never recovered. For example, the twenty-five billion dollar leveraged buy out of R.J.R. Nabisco that took place in the last year of Ronald Reagan's presidency has become a symbol of greed in the decade of the Eighties. Reportedly, R.J.R. Nabisco was making a billion dollars a year before the buy-out then it nearly went broke after. The size of the

R.J.R. Nabisco deal stunned even the greedmeisters like R.J.R.'s former president. Nevertheless, other companies, such as Safeway, went through similar deals, then rushed to shrink operations and fired thousands of workers. Other riskier deals were financed with high-interest loans that were nicknamed junk bonds. Michael Milken, the darling of the Wall Street set, defrauded hundreds of millions of dollars from investors seeking profits in the private sector in junk bond deals.

Unabashed greed was a sign of the times in the Eighties and is no better illustrated than by such exploits. On April 10, 1992, Savings and Loan Officer Charles Keatings was given the maximum sentence of ten years for fraudulently selling bonds from his American Continental Corporation which he knew was unstable at the time of the sale. The decade of Oliver North's impudence and unabashed defense of his lying, and of Charles Keatings' and Ivan Boeskcy's valueless rides at the top, featured the longest, uninterrupted period of growth on record, the taming of inflation, modest unemployment, modest interest rates, and entrepreneurial dynamism. However, it was also the decade when fundamental social problems were ignored, the rich grew richer, the poor got poorer, and middle class got squeezed while the deficit multiplied more than it had in all of the previous American history combined.

A crisis in ethics also began in the decade of the Eighties. From recruiting college athletes to trading stocks and bonds, from Watergate to Soonergate, from the TV evangelists to the sports training room, from the Savings and Loans boardroom to the halls of Congress, and from police chief to mayor, America underwent a national crisis in ethics, but America was not paying attention. During the same period, widespread problems existed, such as ethics, global warming, environmental contamination, disposal of toxic and nuclear wastes, drug abuse, ineffective education and the widening gap between rich and poor. Instead of engaging in broad and continued public debate aimed at devising solutions, the public practiced self-deception. Public consciousness was consumed by trivialities as a diversion from the stark reality of daily existence. Examples of trivial issues that received wide spread attention were Aspen, Colorado's ban on wearing of furs, a Constitutional Amendment to ban burning the flag, and whether or not to keep Chief Illini at the University of Illinois.

These diversions seem to act as palliatives which suppress the nagging necessity for having to decide larger issues. Daily reports of drug abuse, child abuse, highway violence, shootings in theaters, Devil's night burnings, abortion bombings, and drugged destruction on college campuses numbed the mind. Twenty years of the affects of untrammeled individualism stupified the general public, leaving them lethargic, apathetic, and completely cynical. The attitude of the Eighties is personified in the nomination of the Material Girl as the rock star of the decade and epitomized by building the 96-acre, 4.6 billion square feet, 350-store Mall of America in Bloomington, Minnesota, which some have called the last gasp of the Eighties excess. With its fourteen cinemas and seven-acre amusement park, it is a fitting example of a decade of excess that ended with society in paralysis, unable to address the important issues of the day.

Malaise in the 90s

The madness of the Eighties continues in the Nineties as drive-by shootings, car jackings, and dropping heavy objects from highway overpasses onto cars passing below are the newest crime fads, and billions of dollars in Home Health Care fraud--by doctors, providers, and patients alike--plagues the latest efforts to reduce Medicare costs. Early in the decade people everywhere were hurting, angry, and frightened with little reason to be hopeful after two years of economic depression in 1992. The government leaders, especially the President, had denied that there was even a recession, and people felt utterly powerless and unable to control or influence decisions. In that same year, two out of three Americans believed the nation was in economic, moral, and spiritual decline. Four in ten said working hard did not guarantee fair treatment. A majority believed that getting a good education did not insure getting a good job. Almost half said they could not count on their views being considered in the political process.[8] Voting rates declined as most Americans obtained their political information from thirty-second sound bites. Lacking information to evaluate political claims, they were more susceptible to manipulation by emotion-laden campaign commercials, manipulative political slogans, and divisive appeals to fear and prejudice and this is exactly what the public received from the candidates. As Clinton and Gore pandered to the middle class, Bush and Quayle centered their efforts on emotional appeals to winning the peace and being an economic super power. The ill effects of a growing ethic of concern with purely personal rights became even more apparent.

By the time the 1990s arrived, public leaders were expected to be more efficient managers rather than bold leaders; they were expected to deal more with the budget's bottom line than with ethical leadership. Risk taking and controversy were to be avoided as were public statements on social issues and a passionate advocacy of principles. Public organizations likewise were thought of merely as corporate entities with the need for efficient delivery systems. Public accountability came to be defined as minimal expectations and narrow efficiency rather than social advancement and human understanding. Public officials were expected to be CEOs of a corporate body, rational technicists, slashing budgets and personnel, as voters refused to pay taxes even to cover the costs of services then in place. Civil Service systems began to adopt private sector Pay for Performance incentive programs, raisnig animosity and pitting worker against worker in competition for scarce public dollars to fund salary increases. This lamentable scenario considers public employees and citizens as consumers and requires public officials to deal more with the bottom line than with compassion for pain and suffering.

This condition is directly proportional to a preoccupation with economic questions that descended over a nation already ruled by economic decision-making. As the process of alienation and withdrawal accelerated, special interests filled the breach, shaping public policy outcomes even more than before. Thus, a vicious circle resulted in greater voter cynicism. On the 200th anniversary of the Bill of Rights, the American Bar Association reported the results of a survey that disclosed Americans do not understand freedom, civil rights, or the Constitution.[9] To Americans, truth became as disposable as a candy wrapper in the Nineties and standards were lowered everywhere. The lie became expected in the automobile showroom, in advertising, in politics, in the courts, and in the doctor's office where HIV patients were defrauded with quackery.

The Nineties also saw intolerance and diminution of community as personal rights or separate interests defined action rather than tolerance and common humanity. Despite the fact that the aspirations of our pluralistic society seem to be intertwined more than ever, divisions between segments of society seem to widen. Hate crimes were on the rise nationally and reached an all-time high in 1992 in Michigan, prompting one commentator of the Michigan scene to observe:

> From ethnic cleansing in Bosnia to starvation in Somalia, the gloomy litanies accumulate, shrouded in the guise of war, hate crimes, intimidation, harassment, and subtle acts of insensitivity. Meanwhile, fear and ignorance, coupled with a fair measure of herd mentality, threatened to derail constructive responses to age-old conflicts. (Jones and Baron 1993, 1)

Some, such as Western Michigan University President Diether H. Haenicke and history professor Donald L. Fixico believe the most useful function of a university is to teach various diverse groups that despite separate and unique concerns, humanity shares common experiences and problems. Yet this is apparently not happening. As noted by Western Michigan University professor of public affairs and administration, Peter Kobrak, "Ninety percent of minority students study in schools that are 90 % racially segregated" (Ibid., 1). Kobrak believes this kind of residential segregation contributes to and helps shape bigotry in America.

While these concerns suggest more social mixing is necessary, the trend seems to be the other way. Western Michigan University professor of history, Lewis H. Carlson--who specializes in the historical significance of racism and diversity--propounds a different point of view:

> Throughout history, America has had a single perspective--that of the white Eurocentric male. We've been conservative, nervous, not accepting of change. The melting pot theory was one of the worst myths ever perpetuated; it denigrated cultural heritage, saying 'put aside what you were and become Americans.' (Jones and Baron 1990, 1)

Yet, the cultural diversity hailed by Carlson and teaching of the virtue of tolerance seems to have the opposite effect. From cafeterias to dorm rooms racial fragmentation is spreading on college campuses. Ethnic pride and identification, not assimilation, is the chosen goal by minorities and many other students are confused and resentful.[10]

Arthur M. Schlesinger, Jr. (1992) expounds on this trend in *The Disuniting of America*, in which he says racial and ethnic conflict will replace ideological conflict as the explosive issue of the times. He opines that the point of America was to forge a new culture, not to preserve old cultures. The curse of racism was the failure of this experiment; this glaring contradiction of racism still cripples America. He sees a cult of ethnicity among non-Anglo whites and among non-white minorities to denounce the melting-pot, to challenge the concept of one people, and to promote, protest and perpetuate separated ethnic and racial communities. He argues this philosophy sees America as a nation of groups rather than of individuals, and he believes that these separatist tendencies can only result in fragmentation, resegregation and tribalization of American life.

This self-segregation and rebellion against racism and the homogeneity of the melting-pot is enforced by its own brand of conformity which creates group animosity against minority students who are not for the cause.[11] The legitimate goal is not group against group, but a salad bowl in which each ingredient is distinct in the mix. Minority students, as all humans, do not want to be recognized as part of an amorphous, identity-less conglomeration, but want respect for their individual and personal talents. Says University of Detroit Mercy's Lyn Lewis, chairman of the sociology department, "One of our roles is to guide. While the students may think one thing, it is incumbent upon us to broaden the students' perspective and let them know the long-range effect of certain behavior."[12] Therefore, the effort must be directed toward developing a social and individual philosophy that encourages interaction and commonalty while preserving individuality; one that recognizes human dignity in a social context.

Conclusion of Part Two

Something has to account for the slavery and conquest that dominated the early period of U.S. history. There must be a cause for the ancestral belief in the right to enslave one population and destroy another. Dogged insistence upon pushing the national boundaries in spite of the war, suffering, and hardship that resulted must have an explanation. In this search for meaning, the most significant observation from early U.S. history is the persistent survival of separatist forces that tend to atomize the polity into helpless, functionless, non-principled, solitary drifters without unitary purpose.

These forces were present at the drafting of the Mayflower Compact, they attended the signing of the Declaration of Independence, they relentlessly drove the national boundaries westward, they fueled the Civil War, and they embraced industrialism and laissez-faire capitalism. Separatist forces line the path between individualism and social solidarity continually agitating for excess of the former over the latter. In the developing U.S. these forces were fear, status, rights, property, wealth, conformity, freedom, religion, destiny, and intolerance. They interacted to create certain consequences first leading to independence from Britain and then propelling the U.S. toward anarchy several more times: the rapid expansion of the western frontier and decimation of the Indian population was a lawless frenzy; the Civil War was an obvious rebellion to perpetuate enslavement; the industrial abuses of the late 1800s, depression in the 1890s, and subsequent labor revolts brought bloodshed and suffering; and the 1920s saw criminals become heroes. America seems to have adopted Calvinism's tendency to anarchy without its sense of individual responsibility. These unstable conditions and the separatist forces giving rise to them evolved from beliefs born in the country's Puritan past, harbored during its industrialization, and brought to full bloom in the modern era.

Puritanism's economic reality, or mercantile outlook, and a philosophy of abundance seem to have combined and strengthened one another resulting in idealization of business, a myopic view of the common good, and a degeneration of politics and government. Puritan communalism was abandoned for incessant personal striving. The individual was awarded priority over the collective, but the purely personal was given priority over a transcendental individual. Individualism came to mean personal particularity rather than singularity of thought. The populace became risk takers in terms of physical safety and economic reward, but not in intellectual terms. There was a failure to nurture the Puritan soul of the concrete individual and its internal realities of prudence, self-consciousness, and memory; and human prerogatives were elevated above the integrity of the human soul. A substitution of status as the justification for wealth replaced Puritanism's godliness, without acceptance of the latter's responsibility, duty, or guilt. America adopted Puritan pragmatism, but not its rigid ethics.

The Early Americans were emancipated from dependence, but self-reliance became a disability as inability to accept others led to loneliness and intolerance. They accepted religion, but lacked spirituality and refused to learn anything from the Native American culture except that which worked for survival. The practice of democratic freedoms flourished without democracy's equality of human interests. Hypocrisy, duality, and duplicity were characteristics when it came to either racial equality or tolerance of the native populations. Faction was practiced as a personal right before the Mayflower Compact, after which conformance to majority rule was made a civil obligation.

That which is worth saving from this period are: the Puritan and Native American value of shared concerns; the Calvinist and Puritan sense of individual responsibility; the Puritan recognition of the integrity and soul of the concrete individual; constitutional protections for minorities and direct connection to the individual citizen; the graciousness, tenderness, beauty, contemplation, social intercourse, and singularity of thought of Jeffersonian Republicans; the altruism of the Antebellum reformers; the realism of the Progressives; plus the prudence of purpose, sober reflection and energy of the good Puritan pilot. These qualities of the early American spirit--unlike the usual reverence paid to self-reliance, industriousness, determination, faith, competition, rugged individualism, hard work, and pragmatism--can form a solid foundation for a fresh determination of the proper balance between social unity and unfettered individual action.

In the modern U.S., similar forces seem to drive us apart. Self-interest that was supposed to play the role of virtue in America, became the dominant view for individual action. Instead of recognizing as the Founders did that self-interest was a real but destructive force in the world that required other real countervailing action, modern Americans abandoned any effort to contain it. Ignorance or misunderstanding of the Founders' negative perception of self-interest led modern Americans to mistake that earlier realistic recognition of it in the role of virtue as positive legitimation for a credo of self-interest in public policy and personal conduct. Accordingly, self-interest climbed from playing the role of virtue to being a virtue in American life, and aspiration to moral excellence was eclipsed by the modern conception of self. While self-interest could assume this mantle without debilitating effects when resources were limitless and confrontation of problems could be avoided or ignored by moving-on, it no longer works that way.

Self-interest as it is practiced in modern America has resulted in certain negative forces associated with modernity. In the United States today, an unholy combination between an economic/technological framework for thought and the bureaucratic social system is preempting human responsibility for ethical social behavior with pure self-interest. Racism in modern America has replaced conquest of the Wild West. Hate has replaced the old intolerance, and greed has replaced wealth and status. In addition, the forces of conformity, alienation, and obsession with personal rights have become powerful rivals for predominance in the American psyche.

This study of individualism in modern America discloses a paradox that must be resolved to stay on the quest for happiness in the future. That paradox is as old as humanity itself; that of striking an appropriate balance between stifling conformity and atomistic individualism. During the years of the developing U.S., the balance favored economic expansion and intensive personal striving for material advance. This may have been an appropriate balance for that period of unlimited resources and geographical expansion, though the legacy of black and native Americans strongly suggests otherwise. When one had despoiled or no longer enjoyed the environment then, one could pack-up and leave it behind in that day and age.

Americans and their leaders must confront the forces of modernity and develop methods for ameliorating them. One step in this extraordinarily difficult task is adoption by every American of a philosophy to govern personal action and public policy that honors human dignity and prizes social responsibility. The following explication of authentic individualism is one such model for individual conduct that attempts to alleviate the destructive excesses of conformity and individualism.

Rather, than viewing conformity and individualism as countervailing forces at opposite ends of the spectrum, authentic individualism conceives them as parallel forces. As with electrons spiraling about electromagnetic field lines, these forces intertwine one another in a helical pattern. The function of citizen and public administrator alike is to steer the straight field lines about which these forces spiral. Authentic individualism attempts to avoid dependence on either and draws only enough source energy from each of these forces to make that course feasible.

PART THREE

Synthesis of Philosophies Toward a
More Socially Responsible
Individualist in the
Third Millennium

Synopsis

Many thoughtful people believe science and technology can greatly change the course of economic and social evolution. But science must be coupled with a world view that recognizes the importance of enhancing human dignity before it can be a powerful force for good. Big Bang cosmology, central to all current theories of matter and energy, sees much the same universe as medieval scholars did--a finite cosmos created *ex nihilo*, from nothing, perfection of which is impossible, and which is degenerating to a final end. St. Augustine included this view in his doctrine of creation *ex nihilo*, a profoundly pessimistic and authoritarian world view denigrating all earthly endeavor and condemning material existence. Before quantum physics and Einstein's Theory of Relativity, Western humanity believed the universe to be composed of solid objects occupying empty space. This Newtonian-Cartesian view of matter as inert substance, formed and shaped by external forces, became deeply ingrained in Western culture and led to a view of humans as no more than a collection of material particles--skin encapsulated objects--with no necessary relation to one another.

Changes in cosmology such as particle physics and thermal dynamics are molding a transformation that sees an infinite universe evolving and changing over infinite time. This toward-the-future outlook can encourage social progress, offer renewed hope, and provide the motivation human beings need to join together in collective efforts rather than to fragment into the anarchy of self-centered groups. An evolving universe which includes humankind is a powerful concept for religion and science, but it requires a primary human component as the guiding inspiration.

These new ways of looking at the universe, the mind, and the body demonstrate that, important though it is, a purely objective, scientific, quantitative, and mechanistic framework of understanding reality is insupportable. A new world view is emerging in which reality is more subjective in the sense that people are inextricably intertwined with nature and one another so that he does not conceptually stand apart from it or others and has no right to dominate over it or them. In this vein, two streams of philosophy--one anti-scientific, the other tending toward scientism--merged in Existential Phenomenology, which views humanity intersubjectively, or being-through-others. This making-one-another-be is the indispensable condition for an authentic, personal existence. In such a framework, rights are not personal possessions to be played like trump cards, but are concepts for the way you treat others derived from human dignity.

It seems that individualism is rapidly leading into anarchy, not because of too much attention to nonconformity, but because of losing moral consensus, a sense of community, willingness to sacrifice for a shared future, and understanding that competition, isolation, and top-gun status do not provide meaning or dignity to human life. Creating unique individuals cuts off from others and makes strangers without community or cosmos. This is a clarion call for a paradigm of cultivation to replace the old, outworn Lockean rights and management oriented management paradigms within which our society has operated for nearly two centuries. After all, as Wallace Sayer (Chandler 1987a) has already noted, business and public administration are alike in all unimportant respects. Likewise, Gary L. Wamsley et al. (Chandler 1987a) observed in the Blacksburg manifesto that public administration is more than generic management; it is administration of public affairs in a political context.

A new concept of reality should be substituted for the old that recognizes limits on autonomy and control. In search of such a philosophy, it is paramount to account for the incontrovertible fact that all life is kin and only about .1 percent difference in the DNA of a human (99.9 percent is held in common) distinguishes one from another. We are all vastly more alike than we are different. The age old philosophical problem is to find a syncretic balance between the individual and the collective, the few and the many, the majority and the faction, the Wild Heart and the conformist. The authentic individualism paradigm developed in this paper is an attempt to find such a syncretic balance in a synthesis of the individual from Western philosophy and United States history.

Authentic individualism rejects the Newtonian-Cartesian mechanistic view of the universe and human existence as self-contained objects occupying empty space. Humans are more than mere parts of a machine, or even of a process; they are the process, the focus and the ends-in-themselves. Authentic individualism sheds the pessimism, finality and futility of conventional cosmology and existentialist philosophy in pursuit of a optimistic look toward-the-future view of humanity. It struggles to escape the restrictive effects of pure reason in scientific and economic approaches to problem-solving and decision-making. Competition and particularity demand change rather than reverence; they are part of the problem, not the solution.

Authentic individualism retains primacy of the individual whom it teaches to become other-interested. Instead of social duties owed to society, obligations of freedom, more like Thomism's natural virtues, are owed one another out of respect for human life and individual worth. Though the single individual is the starting point of all humankind, that single individual is the result of a universal process and shares kinship with everything and everyone. As a result, one owes responsibility to others as to one's self for the common origin and dignity all inherit from nature. Within a framework of limits and moderation, rights are concomitant; that is, they are bestowed on one another by individuals who respect their shared dignity and common origin. An individual's chief duty is not to serve oneself while avoiding interference with the rights of others, but to assure concomitant rights are respected by looking out for the well-being of others. While authentic individualism accepts the developmental nature of ethical conscience, it discards absolute freedom as the expression of human essence. Rather, it adopts human dignity as the moral norm and embraces the notion that law is only the minimal expression of one's obligations to others. Instead of Madisonian self-interest in the role of virtue, the harsh, compassionless profit orientation of the business mind becomes the Other-world of human commonalty and public good.

Some ethical considerations flow from authentic individualism and related philosophies. Our moral sense must compete with other senses, such as self-interest. How the struggle is resolved depends on one's character, circumstances and culture. As a result these moral sentiments are partial and incomplete guides to action. There is no single moral principle or trait on which to found moral philosophy or single good for political philosophy, only several partially consistent ones. Neither happiness nor virtue can be prescribed by rule. The universal strategy of aggression coexists in the unconscious with altruism, heroism, compassion, and self-sacrificing love for the young. The key is to elevate the latter over the former.

Failures in the ability or desire to do so mean humans are not consistently reasoning animals. Rather, he is profoundly affected by laws he can only partially understand. He is not fully conscious of what he is and his freedom is not always open choice in a clear situation. Instead, he obtains increasing knowledge of his own real being only haltingly. It is only the full flowering of attributes for good over our shadow side that distinguishes humans. But nothing is preordained, and the project of each individual is the responsibility to bring this balance to bear in life. The fundamental debate over the relationship of personal rights to social obligations is what moral development is about, and the highest form thereof is to maintain the balance, the tension, between rights and obligations.

People in organizations and leaders of organizations need to change the way they think about their organization and the role organizations play in daily life. Organizations need to become a part of society, to take a greater (not bigger) societal role, to show the same responsibility toward others as an individual, and assume the same obligations. Since organizations are treated by the law as individuals, they must fulfill a more responsible social role, within their organizational boundaries and without. The individual derives meaning from the group and vice versa, and any conception that separates their identities fails to address the mutual process of adjustment and integration necessary for balance in the whole.

Members of today's organizations expect to be a part of decisions and to hold a more empowered job. In contrast to the wide acceptance of conformity and social assimilation of the past, people celebrate their differences today. In place of theory that demeans the individual, organizational leaders need to substitute a framework of human dignity. In the process orientation, goals are subject to continual revision as awareness of new information requires change. Instead of moving along a predetermined path, mindful individuals see new choices and endpoints, and unexpected stumbling blocks become building blocks. A tolerance for uncertainty develops in the mindful manager, who sees problems as part of an ongoing process rather than disastrous deviations from the past. The office becomes a place where questions are encouraged, ideas are exchanged, and an error does not mean getting fired.

True individualism is impossible in organizations that demean the individual by treating humans as property. It, therefore, becomes the responsibility of organizations and managers to respect total personhood. They need not actively further it, but must define themselves and their functions in ways that do not obstruct, but facilitate worker's self-integrations. Management is a sacred trust for the well-being of others placed in one's care.

Developmental psychologists, such as Piaget, Kohlberg and Erikson reject the need, wants and passions approach to analyzing individual behavior. Instead, they describe individuals as passing through multiple, invariant, qualitative stages of moral development in which certain principles guide behavior. Individuals must make moral judgments, but they are not sufficient basis for ethical action. Moral judgments require the reasoned assessment of the consequences of human actions for human beings. Work in the community is part of the larger work of self-actualization, and it becomes the organization of diverse value-identification and different stages of moral development in the community. Thus, work becomes the propelling force of the community toward fuller development economically and spiritually.

CHAPTER EIGHT

Need for a New World View

Millions die of anarchy, malnutrition and disease in Africa and, simultaneous with economic decline, comes environmental degradation in the form of deforestation, ozone depletion, air and water pollution, acid rain, and nuclear waste disposal. Modern capitalist countries have reached the limits of expansion. As Rome needed new slaves and feudal kingdoms needed new land, the expanding United States needed ever greater resources, and the capitalists need new markets. When hope is gone and social bonds disintegrate in an individualistic world, an orgy of greed, selfishness, aimlessness, and despair gains influence. The medicine that once healed now threatens to destroy; like the early Greeks, our strength is now tearing us apart.

The Moral Animal

In his recent book, *The Moral Sense*, James Q. Wilson noted that a person who contemplates the endless litany of tragedy and misery in the world would be pardoned for concluding that humans are at best selfish, aggressive animals whose predatory instincts are only partially and occasionally controlled. That person would agree with Thomas Hobbes' observation that the natural human state is a war of all against all. (Wilson 1993, 1). Yet Wilson adheres to a profoundly hopeful view of human nature as fundamentally decent and good. He warns us against accepting a narrow vision of our humanity and against making a world that fulfills our diminished expectations. Despite the daily evidence of human immorality, Wilson argues that humans have a biologically based moral sense.

Similarly, in the book, *The Moral Animal*, Robert Wright also concluded--through the lens of an evolutionary psychologist--that humans have a technical capacity to be moral. Because we have self-awareness, memory, foresight and judgment, we are to Wright potentially moral animals, but we are not naturally moral. Natural selection biases us toward unconscious, hidden self-interest. Self-interest rules us unless we take morality seriously and build on our foundation of decency. It is this foundation and building process that modern American Individualism fails to consider.

Creating unique individuals cuts off from others and makes strangers without community or cosmos. A need for change in point of view from the perspective of public administration could not be more poignantly demonstrated than in the words of the suicide note found in the briefcase of White House counsel Vincent Foster; "Here ruining people is considered sport."[1] This is a clarion call for a paradigm of cultivation to replace the old Lockean individualism.

Whether you adopt the view that a moral sense is biological, or that only the capacity for morality is biological, that sense or capacity must be fashioned, sensitized and honed. It is developmental and must be pursued not ignored. Without conscious and conscientious attention to it the moral sense will whither from disuse, and self-interest will assume the role of prime virtue. Authentic individualism discussed in this chapter is an attempt to develop a working philosophy with a message for sustaining the republic that does not ignore but nurtures the moral sense.

The Good Society

Bellah et al. (1992) sound a clarion call for a paradigm of cultivation to replace the "old, outworn Lockean individualist one" (Bellah et al. 1992, 270). They see the public morality of John Locke as separated from its Calvinist sense of obligation, and they believe the secular aspects of his teachings received attention outside his overall vision. Today, life, liberty and the pursuit of happiness is exemplified by the solitary individual's appropriation of property, and government is instituted for protection of that property. These atomistic beliefs bloomed untempered by Locke's notion of moral order. This unfettered version of Lockean teachings became support for endless accumulation. As a result, we still have a Lockean political culture, emphasizing individual freedom and affluence, but our economy and government are most un-Lockean. Instead, it is dominated by great corporations acting out of self-interest with an economically oriented government in tow. This world dwarfs the self it was meant to serve, which must now submit to market forces. The Lockean language of individualism is still seductive, even though it no longer describes the institutions that govern the U.S. One can no longer create the good life simply by striving for individual comfort and security. This Lockean notion of self-interest has such a hold on American public life that it blocks efforts toward a sustainable future. Under Lockean culture in America, individuals' perceptions of self-interest are more important than republican tradition, community, and history. The Lockean ideal of the autonomous individual embedded in a complex moral ecology and a vigorous public sphere--neither of which exist now--is an outmoded concept, and America has developed needs in the past two centuries that its Lockean ideology cannot describe. "The nominalism that Locke represents both epistemologically and sociologically" (Ibid., 295) no longer appeals to the best thinkers of the time.

Locke's philosophy resulted in the same view as Descartes' where knowledge reflected brute reality and physical science was the system of mirroring images. His view of the mind as *tabula rasa*, an empty slate for experience alone to write on, distinguished ideas of the mind and qualities of the body. This distinction implied that knowledge is a purely passive mirroring of the world divorced from the subject. Only objective mirrorings could be known, and only quantitative aspects could be mirrored, because the individual subject spoiled all other mirrorings by subjective contributions.

According to Locke, property is an ownership right for the sole benefit of the proprietor, and ownership is defined exclusively as an extension of self, a private domain exclusive of the rest of mankind. This notion that property benefits the exclusive individual "is a deep-seated modern misconception of social and personal life" (Norton 1991, 130). It reflects a modern moral minimalism that ignores any higher stages of moral development.

Consequently, Bellah et al. propound the good society rooted in fundamental social understanding of human beings, rather than absolute rights. In it the common bond of humanity demands that government and other institutions respect and facilitate human dignity. Because we are caught in "an inescapable web of relationship with other human beings," personal freedom can only be attained along with the other virtues of care and responsibility. Institutions fail to use all of our capabilities to attain a sense of enjoyable achievement and of contributing to the welfare of others. A relentless focus on individuals as utility-maximizers blinds us to a need to restructure these institutions. The authentic individualism model in the next chapter is an effort to develop a journeyman philosophy based on the common bond of humanity and human dignity rather than rights.

Shared Humanity

Sagan and Druyan (1992) recently addressed the broad question of who we are in their book *Shadows of Forgotten Ancestors*. They set out to find the roots of our stuckness in modernity, with its violence, injustice, nuclear threat, environmental decay, burgeoning population, national and ethnic divisions, and lack of leadership. Some of the questions they asked were: Who are we? Why are we this way and not some other? Are we capable of fundamental change or are we compelled by our remote past? Can we alter our character? Can we improve our societies? Can we make a better world? Are we wise enough to know how to change? Can we be trusted with the future? Beginning with a sense of dread, they found reason for hope. But they concluded that events of remote ages, long before humans came into being, are critical for an understanding of the trap our species seems to be setting for itself.

What they found in their examination of our past was not a nature red in tooth and claw, but a nature of cooperation and harmony. The sky, the earth and the universe are one; indeed, every atom that is down here was once out there. We inhabit a shallow zone of environmental clemency that compared to the size of the Earth is thinner than a coat of shellac on a schoolroom globe. Yet we are not unique among the creatures of the Earth, we are not central in a world made for us, and our Antecedent was not King of the Universe.

Instead, Sagan and Druyan note all life is kin and only about .1 percent difference in the DNA of a human (99.9 percent is held in common) distinguishes one from another. We are all vastly more alike than we are different. The most important conclusion gleaned from anatomical studies is the interrelatedness of all life on Earth. So, not from uncritical sentimentalism, but out of tough-minded scientific scrutiny come the deepest affinity between ourselves and other forms of life on Earth. There is a biological unity to the planet, where organisms live in intimate mutual contact. Moreover, one promising finding in artificial intelligence is that many small computers working in parallel without much of a central processing unit do very well and sometimes better than the largest and fastest lone computer.

Sagan and Druyan also found change was the general order and impermanence characterized Earth's evolution. Physical reality has permanence, stability and regularity to it, but historical reality is fickle and fluid, and change plays a major role. We are each a tiny being who rides the outermost skin of one of the smaller planets for a few dozen trips around a local star. The longest-lived organisms on the planet endure for a millionth of its age. If the Earth were as old as a person, the typical organism would be born, live and die in a sliver of a second.

All forms of life are dependent on one another, but those at the top of the food chain are clearly the most dependent and the most inefficient. One thing, therefore, is abundantly clear: Humans who are at the apex of the predatory food chain are extremely dependent for life upon plants and animals lower down the chain and are accordingly more vulnerable to change. Therefore, it would make more sense to recognize the part of such life in us and to revere and nurture such life rather than claim dominion over it and uniqueness from it.

Wild Heart

A Wildness metaphor is used by many writers to explain reality in terms of expanded individuality and autonomy, or wildness of spirit. Stivers (Bailey and Mayer 1992) brings this theme into public administration literature in the form of Wild Patience borrowed from feminist poet Adrienne Rich. Stivers urges a multiversalist paradigm in which heart thinking replaces head thinking, trust and cooperation replace competition, feelings replace the hardened heart, and interconnectedness replaces autonomy and the separated self. This authentic self recognizes dependence on others and originates in social interaction, which is of equal importance with autonomy. The dual aims of freedom and reciprocity are sought through developing process skills for interaction, social learning, and collaborative activity.

The Wildness metaphor is also used by Keen (1991) to describe the wild man--given to play, fantasy, sensuality, fun, and games--just under the surface of rational man. Here, a man is most virile for Keen when he insists not upon autonomy of will, but harmony with the will of God. Post-modern man is not a candidate for this heroic position:

The 'new age' man who is self-absorbed in his own feelings and committed to 'personal growth' [is not] a candidate for heroism. It is an illusion to believe that the virility men have lost can be recovered by anything except a new locational passion.

Our loss has been ontological, not psychological. A deficiency in meaning and in being. A refusal to care for what matters, a limpness in the face of the challenge of our history. The challenges seem overwhelming, and we are understandably to retreat into professions and corporations that swallow us, into private pleasures and high consumption. But let's call that what it is: moral cowardliness, abdication of responsibility, voluntary myopia. And if we continue on this path we will continue to feel empty and devoid of meaning. (Keen 1991, 121)

Keen recognizes that Western culture is built on the notion of individual dignity, and the virtues of individualism were ratified by the American Revolution and by a frontier nation. Nevertheless, he expresses the fear that individualism is rapidly leading into anarchy. To Keen, the passive submission of anonymous masses in mindless conformity to competitive goals is the down side of individualism and weakens bonds to others and to nature.

Bly (1990) uses the Interior Warrior and the Wild Man to illustrate his lament for lack of rituals initiating boys into manhood. He distinguishes the Wild Man, who he likens to a Shaman or Zen priest, from the Savage Man, who does great damage to the soul, earth, and humankind. Indeed, in describing relationships of the Interior Warrior, Bly paraphrases Jung on the value of distinctiveness:

We note that the hawk always remains a hawk, even when the hawk is living among owls; an owl remains an owl, even when living among porcupines. But human beings are suggestible and can lose distinction. When they merge into 'the masses,' as in Fascism, they fall into indistinctiveness. The Gnostics imagine the place called Pleroma, which is an enormous abundance, but also an enormous indistinction. It is desirable, then, for men and women to aim for distinction consciously. It is dangerous if they do not do so. (Bly 1990, 166-167)

The aim is not to be the Wild Man, but to be in touch with him; the need is to delicately brush the Wild Man and Wild Woman with the wing tips of our minds. Nevertheless, Bly observes the propensity in American culture for people who do not make this subtle distinction and who want to be the Wild Man.

The failure of the Wildness metaphor is a need, not for a more atomistic conception of the individual that feeds our cultural weaknesses, but for a world view that defines self as a part of a greater whole, inextricably linked, in more than just economic or geopolitical terms, with all humanity. Bly recognizes this danger too by attaching the Wild Man to a community. In that community, he ascends and develops intellectually, step by step, until he is capable of recognizing the enormity of what he shares in common with others, especially women, the minutia of that which he does not, and the appropriate sacrifice that he owes to the community. Yet folklore is vivid with episodes in which the Wild Man is held in judgment and thrown into the fire by the community out of fear and anger over his distinctiveness and independence. The age old philosophical problem is to find a syncretic balance between the individual and the collective, the few and the many, the majority and the faction, the Wild Heart and the conformist. The authentic individualism paradigm developed in this paper is an attempt to find such a syncretic balance in a synthesis of the individual from Western philosophy and United States history.

Cosmos and Society

Thoughtful people are often fearful that problems have become too big to handle, human nature prevents us from dealing with them, and humanity has lost its way. At the end of the second millennium, Western society again stands at a crossroads and the future depends upon what people think and how they view the universe:

> Over the past few years hundreds of people have expressed the belief that humanity is at a crossroads, facing either collective annihilation or an evolutionary jump in consciousness of unprecedented proportions. It seems that we are all involved in a process that parallels the psychological death and rebirth that so many people have experienced individually in non-ordinary states of consciousness. If we continue to act out the destructive tendencies from our deep unconscious, we will undoubtedly destroy ourselves and all life on our planet. However, if we succeed in internalizing this process on a large enough scale, it might result in evolutionary progress that can take us as far beyond our present condition as we now are from the primates. (Grof 1992, 220)

Even as the Stalinist model in the former Soviet Union and Eastern Europe demonstrates its own inadequacy, it appears that Western society has begun to retreat as well. In the United States, Western Europe, and Japan, real wages are stagnant or falling. Average real wages in America have retreated to levels of the Fifties since their peak in 1973, and the median American family with two incomes earned less in 1989 than a single-income family did twenty years earlier.[2] As wages have fallen, leisure has dropped from twenty-six hours per week to sixteen, and two hundred billion dollars in profits per year is diverted to corporate takeovers. This reversal of social advance has become global and all encompassing. In Europe, unemployment has been at or near ten percent for a decade. Factories around the globe are shutting down, and steel production per capita dropped forty-four percent in the past fifteen years.[3]

Scientific thought and technology can greatly change the course of economic and social evolution. Science is inextricably tied to ideas about society, including religion; events on earth affect ideas about the universe; and social evolution and cosmology are closely intertwined, one affecting the other. Since the beginning of scientific inquiry, humanity has sought a Theory of Everything--a single set of equations, or first principles, that will explain all the phenomena of nature, including human behavior. In the late sixteenth and seventeenth centuries, European society reached its limits and was in deep crisis. Helped by science and resultant new thinking, the populace came to see that the old order was not divinely ordained. A new society of merchant, manufacturer, worker, and free peasant replaced the old order of lord and serf. Challenging authority, the scientific revolution offered in place of the finite, fixed, and limited medieval cosmos of the popes and kings an infinite universe and abolition of limits on mankind's achievements. In the seventeenth century, Thomas Hobbes applied the new science of his time to philosophy and politics by trying to explain humans as simple collections of discrete particles obeying the laws of physics. One hundred years ago Lord Kelvin stated that all the main problems of physics had been solved and only further accuracy "in the last decimal place" (Lerner 1991, 3) was needed. He and Hobbes were obviously wrong, yet today we again hear scientists such as Stephen Hawking claiming a Theory of Everything is within their grasp.

Cosmology studies how the universe as a whole--the entire physical world of space, time, and matter--came to exist, and how it will end. Conventional cosmology adds credibility to the counsels of despair today just as Augustine's cosmology did in fourth-century Rome, and it gives a scientific veneer and cosmic endorsement to the pessimism and despair in the prevailing ideas of leading thinkers today. The Big Bang of cosmology--the idea that the universe originated in a single cataclysmic explosion some ten or twenty billion years ago popularized in the pessimistic Fifties and Sixties--has become central to astronomy and all current theories of the basic structure of matter and energy. This old cosmology reinforces, and is reinforced by, society's dominate ideas, and the Existentialist ethos in which humans are alienated from the universe is the leitmotif of modern science.

Big Bang theorists see much the same universe as medieval scholars did--a finite cosmos created *ex nihilo*, from nothing, perfection of which is impossible, and which is degenerating to a final end. This modern cosmic myth arose in a period of social crisis and retreat, and it bred a fatalistic pessimism. St. Augustine included the doctrine of creation *ex nihilo* as part of a profoundly pessimistic and authoritarian world view denigrating all earthly endeavor and condemning material existence. He interpreted the fall of Rome to the Visigoths as a consequence of cosmic decline beginning out of nothing and returning to nothing. Similarly, by positing an end to all things, conventional cosmology implies one of two philosophical stances; a blind existential pessimism of humanity condemned to a meaningless existence, or a dualistic faith like the Middle Ages, finding meaning only in the world beyond. The social crisis of the present century gives credence to this old philosophical view.

Cosmologists are nearly unanimous in the belief that the universe originated in an immense explosion of an infinitely hot, point-like ball, or a *singularity*,[4] smaller than the tiniest atom. In one-trillionth of a second all space, matter, and energy was created as the singularity expanded a trillion-trillionfold. This undoubtedly fantastic and bizarre concept dooms human purposes to decay, and hostile, alien forces in a universe that is a one-way street from explosive start to ignominious end. In this model, the future of the universe is doomed either to an end in the Big Crunch, collapsing into a universal black hole from which not even light can escape, or to expand and decay into the entropic nothingness of eternal, cold darkness. Wound up twenty billion years ago, the universe is now running down as is human progress on earth, progress or evolution is at best an accident, and decay will finally triumph.

The principles governing such a universe are only known by pure reason, guided by authority. Soon scientists will have discovered a Theory of Everything which will mark the final chapter in the quest for knowledge. In order to do so, they will rely on extraordinarily complicated mathematical models that no lay person and few scientists will understand and that cannot be duplicated for empirical observation. When they arrive at such a theory, scientists will be the experts of existence--new High Priests of reality--science will be indistinguishable from mythology, authority will be back in vogue with a new kind of King on the throne, and the populace will receive the word to be taken on faith from scientific authority. Yet this cannot be considered an inevitable phenomenon or ultimate limit upon human achievement. New ideas of an emerging scientific revolution bring an entirely different outlook.

Changes in the fields of cosmology, particle physics, and thermal dynamics are molding a transformation of how science views the universe.[5] An opposing view to the Big Bang theory, plasma cosmology, sees an infinite universe evolving and changing over infinite time. In plasma cosmology there is no answer in science and no final authority, the universe is evolving from an infinite past to an infinite future, and human development is merely the latest stage of continual progress through unlimited time, so the very idea of an end to history is ludicrous. This new cosmology replaces Newton's universe with an open future that recognizes the creative and progressive nature of vast physical processes. No sharp division is drawn between living and non-living systems, and the origin of life is seen as one step along the path of organization of matter into ever more complex structures. This toward-the-future outlook encourages social progress, offers renewed hope, and provides the motivation human beings need to join together in collective efforts rather than to fragment into the anarchy of self-centered groups. The idea of an evolving universe, which includes humankind is a powerful concept for religion and science.

Some say the Big Bang is a scientific version of Genesis, a universe created in a instant; therefore, the work of a creator. For these advocates the new cosmology eliminates the moment of creation and they argue that a deity precludes the idea of a universe infinite in time and space. Like medieval orthodox, they believe an infinite universe challenges the authority and infinite perfection of the deity. On the other hand, their opponents believe only a universe without limits is worthy of an infinite God and human beings in search of infinite knowledge. For these advocates, the moment of creation was simply development of order, not out of nothing, but out of the formless void of preexistent chaos, the waters of Genesis. For them, the universe of plasma cosmology lacks not only a beginning, but an end as well. This view avoids an end in the scorching heat of the Big Crunch or the frozen expansion of entropy and replaces it with an optimistic view of continual evolution and development. It, therefore, seems much more consistent with the concept of a compassionate and loving God; certainly more so than one that envisions a moment in the remote future when the last living being in the universe goes up in flames or is frozen to death in lonely, dark silence.

CHAPTER NINE

Changing the Paradigm

Before development of Einstein's Theory of Relativity in 1905 and the rise of quantum physics, Western humanity believed the universe to be composed of solid objects occupying empty space. Newtonian-Cartesian science viewed the universe strictly as deterministic mechanical events, governed by cause and effect. This view led to mechanism as a belief system, which itself can be traced to Ancient Greece, but Sir Isaac Newton and his contemporaries of the seventeenth century gave it modern impetus. This Newtonian-Cartesian mechanistic paradigm, or conceptual scheme, interpreted the physical universe as merely a collection of material particles interacting in a gigantic purposeless machine, to which the human body and mind were insignificant.

The basic elements of this material universe were atoms, compelled to move in an orderly manner by fixed laws. Mankind exerted no influence and had only to discover the laws governing the machine. In this view, the notion of matter as inert substance, formed and shaped by external forces, became deeply ingrained in Western culture and often led to machine-mindedness, the tendency when looking for explanations to conceive of every situation by analogy to a machine. This image of the universe conceived of human beings and other life as accidental by-products that coalesced from a swirling, dazzling array of matter. Humans were no more than a collection of material particles, bounded by an outer surface--skin encapsulated objects. Consequently, Western populations inherited the tendency to think of themselves in everyday life as autonomous, individual physical bodies with fixed and absolute boundaries. Humans simply occupied space with no relationship to their surroundings in any transcendental manner, and the differences between self and others made each individual sovereign and singular.

Physicist Paul Teller (Cushing and McMullin, 1989) labels this *particularism*, which defines the world as composed of individuals that have non-relative properties. He believes *particularism* unreflectively conditions all thinking in Western culture without ever being explicitly stated in a conception of the world. Consequently, Western populations inherited the tendency to think of themselves in everyday life as autonomous, individual physical bodies with fixed and absolute boundaries. Until recently, this Newtonian science and Cartesian philosophy nurtured a very limited view of human beings.

Conceptual Framework for Change

Now an exciting new vision of the cosmos and human nature is emerging that has extraordinary meaning for individual and collective life. First, relativity theory exposed the universe to shifting and warping. In Einstein's Theory of Relativity, space is not three-dimensional, time is not linear, and space and time are not separate but are integrated into a four-dimensional continuum known as space-time. From this perspective, boundaries between objects and distinctions between matter and space are less obvious. Instead of objects simply occupying empty spaces, the complete universe is seen as one never-ending field of varying density. The universe is an infinitely complex system of vibratory phenomena rather than an agglomerate of Newtonian objects.[1]

Second, newly discovered subatomic particles exhibit strange behavior that defies Newtonian principles. In place of Newton's deterministic machine and rigid rules of causality, quantum theory substitutes an invisible and conflicting conjunction of waves and particles governed by the laws of chance. Called the *wave-particle paradox*, quantum particles behave in some experiments as material entities, and in others they appear with wave-like properties. In the so-called double-slit experiment, electrons pass through two slits in a wall simultaneously as if they are wavelike, but they strike a fluorescent screen in a single location as if they are particles. In fact, it even seems that the state in which these particles are observed and their location is not determined until the observation takes place.[2] The behavior of particles such as electrons seems to vary according to whether they are watched or not and, in this context, the observer plays an active role in creating the reality itself. Thus, quantum physics presents a picture of reality in which observer and observed are inextricably interwoven in an intimate way, and the effect of observation is fundamental to revealed reality. Quantum field theory reveals solid matter dissolving away to be replaced by weird excitations and vibrations of invisible field energy in which little difference remains between material substance and apparently empty space that itself "seethes with ephemeral quantum activity" (Davies 1992, 14). The extreme proponents of this phenomena have even developed an extremely individualistic participating universe philosophy in which observers are central to the nature of physical reality and matter is ultimately relegated to the mind.

The Quantum Universe

The quantum non-locality principle--in which all quantum particles exert influence on all other quantum particles--forbids one from considering even widely separated particles as independent entities. Instead, "[t]he universe is in reality an interconnected whole" (Davies and Gribbon 1992, 157). Physicist Jon Jarrett (Cushing and McMullin 1989, 79) says this new "world view challenges any straightforward notion of the individuation of physical objects." David Bohm, a leading quantum theorist agrees, echoing the words of Werner Heisenberg: "The common division of the world into subject and object, inner world and outer world, body and soul is no longer accurate" (Davies 1993, 112). Davies (1993) notes a strong holistic flavor here, an all-embracing wholeness, with interlocking levels of description and everything somehow made up of everything else.

Teller (Cushing and McMullen 1989) argues that *particularism* should be questioned because quantum mechanics itself proves *particularism* is wrong and provides very strong reasons for rejecting it. According to Folse (Cushing and McMullin, 266-267), the renowned physicist Niels Bohr is widely thought to have "banned an independent reality from physics" when he rejected the separability of Einstein's physical reality in favor of a "quantum postulate" that implied systems do not have separate states. Folse, however, explains that Bohr did not debate with Einstein from a phenomenological philosophical stance. Bohr did not see the truth of theoretical statements as being determined by whether they "correspond" to an ontologically dependent order--to which we can never have empirical access--existing behind the "phenomena" (Ibid., 267). Thus, Bohr did not "throw out reality," but he may have intended a new conception of physical reality; one in which considerable, even detailed, but not complete knowledge and understanding can ever be attained; an independent, objective reality which we can symbolize, because of our incomplete understanding, only by partially stated laws and idealized abstractions (Ibid., 269-271). This would be the same reality in which Bohr struggled to find and understand the existence and extent of the connections between individual physical states and systems.

The "indivisibility of interaction" embodied in the non-locality principle (Ibid., 261) at the quantum level required a "radical revision of the problem of physical reality" (Ibid., 264). As a result, Teller and Howard (Cushing and McMullin 1989) both espouse an ontological holism, or nonseparability based on quantum mechanics. Teller calls his theory *relational holism,* which takes into account the likelihood of a commonalty from the past that binds otherwise separate particles together. Howard's holism tries to reconcile the spatio-temporal separability principle that individuates physical states and systems in general relativity theory with the nonseparability of quantum mechanics that binds spatio-temporally separated particles together creating a kind of interconnected system. He entreats physicists to give up the separability principle associated with general relativity and accept a world view in which spatio-temporally separated but previously interacting physical systems lack separate states and perhaps separate physical identities. The authentic individualism paradigm that follows is an attempt to find--in a synthesis of individualist ideas from Western philosophy and United States history--a "quantum" connection, or nonseparability, between individuals based upon commonalty of origin.

Existential Phenomenology

Soren Kierkegaard, the founder of existentialism, conceived of human existence in relationship to God and as intensely personal, absolutely original and unique to the individual, without validity for others. Thus, say Luijpen and Koren (1960), his position was deliberately anti-scientific, or at least incapable of the dimension of universality claimed by science. It also tended toward spiritualistic monism by exalting the individual subject over the material thing until the latter evaporated into mere consciousness. On the other hand, Edmund Husserl launched phenomenology as the science of philosophy to investigate consciousness or knowledge, which he called *intentionality.* This theory tended toward materialism, or scientism, using the term to describe absolutism of the physical sciences. Materialism posits a human as a chain of processes or a moment in the endless evolution of the cosmos. It is itself a kind of monism in the way it disregards individual subjectivity, absolutizes objective things-in-themselves, and leaves room in reality for only the being of the material thing unconnected to any other thing and without subjective meaning.

These two philosophical streams merged, and existential phenomenology was born in Martin Heidegger's philosophy of Dasein, or existence. The latter was an intermediate view that took into account the valuable insights of both materialism and spiritualism, while avoiding the extremes of both and not lapsing into the illusions of either idealism or positivism. Existential phenomenology opposes objectivity as the brute reality of Descartes' embrace of physical science and divorce of the subject from the world. Instead, humans are viewed as conscious-being-in-the-world, or being-conscious-in-the-world. In other words, being-in means dwelling, being familiar with, being-present-to, or actively observing and participating and not simply existing or occupying (Luijpen and Koren 1969, 20, 27, 33-34).

Phenomenology is often accused of being subjective or relative by adhering to a subjectivistic concept of truth. However, this is inaccurate because phenomenology does not deliver truth to the individual subject's arbitrary choice. Rather, truth expresses objectivity-for-a-subject, or is absolute in relation to the subject. In this way, the subject originates truth by giving things meaning for that person. Indeed, being-in-the-world means being in it dynamically as a free subject, not merely the subject of processes and forces. Nevertheless, in doing so he cannot proceed arbitrarily, and he must respect that which shows itself and be guided by it. He is not lord of being, only shepherd and guardian.

For Sartre, another existential phenomenologist, absolute freedom was the universal norm. In absolute autonomy a person creates values, invents norms, and chooses his reality. Absolute freedom is depreciated by reliance on heavenly norms or pointing to passions as an excuse for deeds. At the same time, Sartre believed freedom imposed itself on everyone as a subjective as well as an objective universal. This subjectivity must not be compromised by another; no individual may destroy another's subjectivity.

The impetus to honor another's freedom does not come from the law, but one's personal conscience. The conscience arises above its primitive forms and its biological, sociological and psychological infrastructures to become an adult conscience. Though the individual is free to choose a life project, one is bound not to destroy another's subjectivity. This does not determine how to act in a concrete situation, since there are no norms-in-themselves for ethical conduct. Even universal moral norms would not guarantee a moral choice, because they express moral demands in minimal fashion. An authentic moral life implies on the part of the individual an ever-renewed application to a task that is never finished. A moral individual is always in progress, having to be, faithfully executing an ever more clear sighted conscience, rather than observing sharply but minimalistically defined laws. Moral life accomplishes more than the law and goes beyond automatic functioning under the law.

Being human is intersubjectivity, or being-through-others. Existence is co-existence; at no level is one absolutely alone. The presence of others makes being-through-others an absolute essential of humanity. The behavior and speech of others make an individual think, speak and act. This making-one-another-be is why existence is co-existence and is the indispensable condition for an authentic, personal existence. The discussion of authentic individualism that follows finds its philosophical foundation in the being-through-others of existential phenomenology.

A New Model--Authentic Individualism

Authentic individualism is not revolutionary, but reformist. It is not an ultimate truth, or a social and political theory of everything that will explain all human behavior. Authentic individualism is not a discovery of objective principles out there from which solutions will coalesce. It is a construct of abstract ideas, idealistic inspirations and realistic assumptions, rather than a product of inductive reasoning. Accordingly, the general organizing principles espoused here are only tentative approximations intended to guide and encourage the individual and practitioner through an indeterminate, non-linear, chaotic, dynamic, and unpredictable world incredibly sensitive to external environment. Since the universe is contingent and not fully defined, a complete explanation can only be found in something metaphysical, and authentic individualism can only offer partial answers and principles for action valid in the context of late twentieth century American culture.

Authentic individualism rejects the Newtonian-Cartesian mechanistic view of the universe and human existence as self-contained objects occupying empty space. In place of that limited outlook, it adopts a relativistic and quantum frame of reference that space and time--indeed all components of the universe--are interrelated and interdependent, not merely interacting, in a never-ending continuum of evolution and development. This evolution is the purpose for humankind's existence; conscious and conscientious development of humanity and the world is the reason for being; and no thing or no one is outside or without this other-interested purpose in life. Accordingly, authentic individualism is evolutionary--not in the sense of static activity or inert substance waiting for change to evolve--but in the sense of individual development and change on a daily basis. This is to say that self is not buried beneath the collective, subservient to group will, or mired in other-directed conformity. Rather, the highest expression of self is interest in and contribution to the flowering and unfolding of understanding, acceptance, and compassion in self and others.

Humans are more than mere parts of a machine, or even of a process; they are the process, the focus and the ends-in-themselves. Instead of collective skin-encapsulated objects--individual, inert, and ready formed--humanity is a sharing of commonalty across boundaries. Rather than accidental by-products of extra-terrestrial forces, humanity is a logical, ordered and important sub-system in an otherwise chaotic process of cosmic evolution from base substances, through life, and toward perfection. No part of humankind can be divorced from the rest, because the effects from that separated part reverberate through the remainder in a life version of quantum non-locality. Each individual plays a role in and has a responsibility to the whole, as each plays an active role in creating reality for all. Those who take this other-interested role seriously and practice it daily impart an invisible field energy to others as observer and observed become intimately interwoven one within the other. Those who do not accept other-interest, but embrace self-interest as the guiding principle for politics and society contribute to a society and political *wave-particle paradox* of subjectivity in which one's essential nature, momentum or position--in short, reality--can never be determined until it is observed.

Authentic individualism sheds the pessimism, finality and futility of conventional cosmology and existentialist philosophy in pursuit of a optimistic look toward-the-future view of humanity. It struggles to escape the restrictive effects of pure reason in scientific and economic approaches to problem-solving and decision-making by emphasizing qualitative and value-laden criteria. It abandons authority as the only source of truth and accepts intuition in its place, and it combats the harshness of extreme particularity with a balance of individual and group identity.

Authentic individualism implements the limits on autonomy and control offered by Camilla Stiver's Wild Patience. As she states, competition and particularity demand change rather than reverence; they are part of the problem, not the solution. Recognition of dependence on and responsibility for others replaces strident clutching of individual rights. Stiver's authentic self acts as a repository for legitimate self-interest in attaining the good life for all, rather than the few. Calling upon the transmoral conscience of Keen's Wild Man, authentic individualism trades autonomy of will for harmony of human interests. Individual identity is attained through commitment to and sacrifice for the moral dignity of human life. Devotion to *me* and to the economic order is exchanged for compassion and the sacred trust for the well-being of others. Authentic individualism borrows Hiskes' community as caring which construes the social fact of community as a special quality of individuals, not of the group, which exists within individuals, not between them.

Similar to Bly's Interior Warrior, authentic individualism keeps close at hand the vision of damaged soul, earth, and humankind perpetrated by Savage Man, who wants to be the Wild Man and Wild Woman and who carries distinction to an extreme. Authentic individualism holds close the enormity of what the Interior Warrior shares in common with the community and the minutia of the differences that exist. This viewpoint resists the notion that social, political, government, or business organizations should be inert substances reacting to forces from without, compelled by fixed conceptions along predetermined paths. Organizations and groups of people are seen within this framework as systems constructed by humans and guided by general organizing principles and encouragement of humans toward spontaneity, surprise, a sense of becoming, and moral meaning in life, work, politics, and government.

The philosophical base for authentic individualism comes from a synthesis of Western philosophy, but finds its place in the modern world under a phenomenological/noumenological philosophy label and interpretivist public administration theory. It begins by recognizing as Homer did the chaotic over the predictable, but refuses to adopt Homer's Warrior ethic and oppression of weak by the strong, or Thales' Monistic notion of a single unifying principle. Instead, it embraces Hesiod's concept of moral choice and dedication to humanity, the Milesian concept of process and ordered changed, and Heraclitus' absorption into a transcendent world process called *logos*.

Authentic individualism is opposed to the doctrine of materialism given life by Democritus, nurtured by the Pythogoreans, cared for during its adolescence by the Atomists, and molded into full adulthood by the Logical Positivists. Accordingly, authentic individualism adopts the necessity seen by Plato for reconciling a purposive and conceptual nature of humans with the universe in which they live, but it rejects the mechanistic universe of Newtonian-Cartesianism. Humanity is neither a special and unique form of life created by an omnipotent being as in other-worldly religious thought, nor the accidental combination of elements as in Pluralist thought. The universe is neither the chaotic hodgepodge of Homer nor the thoroughly ordered system intelligible through pure reason seen by Plato and Pythogoreans. Rather, humanity is an ordered consequence of the same indeterministic creative process guided by general unifying principles as all other life and substance in the universe.

Authentic individualism recognizes the good in Socrates' refusal to conform and the need for minority protections against the popular majority sentiment. It adopts the Sophistic teaching of mutual respect, but discards the practical concern for here and now that led Thrasymachus and other Sophists to define individuals as the measure of all things. In this way, the Socratic fulfillment of individual potential in accordance with humanity's real and essential nature--eudaemonia--replaces autonomy of will and self-interest. In this conception of eudaemonistic individualism as in authentic individualism, there is no place for Plato's Philosopher Kings, elite guardians of the state, or separation of thought and action. Rather, primacy is given to becoming over being, as thought and action are combined--that is, work and change are viewed as creative processes--and democratic, or group, interests are given primacy over the self-seeking individual.

The Socratic-Platonic plea for human renewal--a transcendent individual soul--was preserved in Aristotle's *polis*, where inter-related individuals developed and unfolded. Individuals shared the identity of the organic whole and had responsibility to it for exercising moral choice; a habit of virtue flowing from a disposition, attitude, or state of character. The same is true in authentic individualism which, like Socrates, awards collective interests primacy over the self-seeking individual, but retains primacy over the majority of the authentic individual, whom it teaches to become other-interested. These teachings adopt the notion of responsibility to the whole through Roman Stoic-like duties. However, instead of social duties owed to society, the obligations of freedom in this context--such as love, compassion, forgiveness, and ethical leadership--are more like

Thomism's natural virtues and are owed to one another out of respect for human life and individual worth.

The secular point of view that the essential human problem is how to get into a right relationship with one's self and one's fellow, and the interdependent nature of social relations of the Greeks is retained by authentic individualism. Augustine's pessimism, sinfulness, and depravity of humanity is rejected while his guilt, passed to us through Calvin and the Puritans, is embraced and ameliorated; guilt for the inequities and injustices of rich over poor, white over black, conqueror over native, and the strong over weak that still form the basis of America's national character today. The guilt for these horrific abuses is recognized, felt, and alleviated through daily teaching and practice of the obligations freedom places on each individual.

Jesus' love of neighbor, his democratic equality, and his individual responsibility are the essential principles of authentic individualism. These exalted and abstract concepts form the basis for a creative and generative force--John's *logos*, Augustine's bond of peace, or Camus' kingdom of the human heart--that formed and still molds the universe. Through this force the waters are calmed, and there is order in chaos, unity within diversity, moral will in politics, human dignity in life, and individual freedom. In place of pessimism and the human predicament as dominant paradigms, authentic individualism substitutes optimism and creative energies directed toward betterment of self and others. Failure is not a sin, but merely a lack of knowledge in an indeterminate world where knowledge is always imperfect. Though the single individual is the starting point of all humankind, that single individual is the result of a universal process and shares kinship with everything and everyone. As a result, one owes responsibility to others as to one's self for the common origin and dignity all inherit from nature.

Authentic individualism too accepts the existence of universal truths, although they may not always be fully understandable by reason alone. Rather, there are different degrees of truth, goodness, and reality as recognized by St. Thomas. A diversity and multiplicity of viewpoints results from these different realities lived by each individual. Each individual has the opportunity to exercise free will; to shape lived reality in a way that reflects one's own character and hopes. An individual can never be fully free of the effects of others on one's own development. What reality one perceives is so impacted by experience and action of others that all share responsibility for lack of development in one of their milieu.

Authentic individualism encourages a Thomistic state in which the ruler and ruled alike aim at cooperation with others and the common good of all rather than self-interest. Autonomous individuals are interdependent and liberty consists of honoring the human dignity found in each person. The Naturalism and power politics of Hobbes and Machiavelli gain no support and play no part in authentic individualism. The Renaissance sense of limitless possibilities is replaced, not by existential hopelessness, but a sense of limits to what humankind can and should do in a natural environment. Only within a framework of limits or moderation can one of the basic motifs of individualism from the Reformation--primacy of the immediate, felt-data of conscience--have legitimacy. Without limits, freedom and spontaneity have no balance and excess destroys civil liberty for the individual.

Though sympathetic to Descartes' efforts at blending the new physics with a world of value and rejecting Hobbesian amorality, authentic individualism does not accept the Cartesian Compromise. Rather, like Phenomenology, it recognizes the interconnection between mind and body, experience and thought, fact and value. Mind and body cannot be viewed as completely different kinds of things or separated into distinct substances. To the contrary, trends in modern medicine and psychology view the mind and body as interdependent, affecting one another in profound ways. Indeed, it is not difficult to accept the proposition that states of mind can affect physical health or vice versa. Therefore, it is now quite clear that Descartes' philosophical synthesis--like Locke's historical plain method--is not supported by subsequent developments in science that now demonstrate all the mind's ideas do not come from pure experience, and sense perception is influenced by both mind and body.

Locke's emphasis upon attainment of property and pleasure as the greatest good encouraged simple calculation of long-range advantage. Likewise, his reliance upon autonomy, independence, and alienable rights directed interest inward and separated individuals from one and another. Unlike Lockean philosophy, authentic individualism sees individual development through interest in community as the chief good. Fundamental rights do indeed flow from individual dignity as humans rather than as citizen, and with rights go the balancing obligations of freedom that require responsibility toward others, but rights do not belong to people because they are human. Rather, rights are concomitant; that is, they are bestowed on one another by individuals who respect their shared dignity and common origin. These rights and duties are universal within the community of shared values, but they are not true for all times and all places. Instead, they are guidelines for conduct that represent the most likely path towards authentic individualism until greater knowledge and experience demonstrate a better alternative. An individual's chief duty is not to serve oneself while avoiding interference with the rights of others, but to assure concomitant rights are respected by looking out for the well-being of others. Therefore, authentic individualism derides market-oriented, laissez-faire theory in favor of an active, positive, and compassionate state devoted to the well-being of its citizens rather than their economic status. This is Kant's universal imperative to treat humanity as having intrinsic value just because one is human and to respect shared humanity.

As did Hegel and Neitzsche, authentic individualism views thinking and perception as acts of interpretation in which desires, memory, and passions affect the object perceived or thought about. However, it does not reflect existential attention on the individual person and his needs and problems as did Neitzsche and Kirkegaard. Rather, Hegel's ideal of a greater whole transcending finite individuality appears in authentic individualism not as the state, but as human dignity and shared origin, as does his developmental view of mind and matter as changing, evolving, extending, and unfolding in experience. Existential rejection of the ethical, and concern with self and subjectivity is replaced in authentic individualism with Hegel's synthesis of morality and right into an ethical life. Existentialism's attention to individual problems is combined with an other-interested orientation and optimistic view of the universe in spite of people's demonstrated savagery.

Authentic individualism coincides in some respects with the thought of William James, whose vision was of an open, growing, and incomplete universe in which individuals need flexibility and readiness to live with insecurity. However, authentic individualism avoids the intense individuality and subjectivism of James pure experience where there are no moral absolutes. Authentic individualism takes Bergson's reliance on intuition as a form of knowledge necessary for use by an active self in continuous, unfolding, new experience. It also shares his belief in a necessity to counteract by other forces the tendency of individuals to think of themselves as separate from the community. Likewise, it adopts Kant's, Hegel's, and Dewey's belief that experience is a product in which the mind is active and directive; Dewey's view that no final absolute laws can be found but only more and more adequate instrumentalities for dealing with change; his conviction that freedom of mind and intelligence limits freedom of action; his recognition of uncertainty; his search for public rather than private ends;

and his acceptance of values as facts discoverable in nature. Like the Romantics, authentic individualism downgrades the importance of human uniqueness and reason, while elevating the view of humanity as a part of nature. Similarly, it accepts Whitehead's interfusion of all things and his process theory in which reality is manifested in the continual creative advance of nature's activity.

Authentic individualism follows Heidegger's phenomenological stance of being-in-the-world; a mode of being human in which concern for others dominates over a preoccupied, manipulative, and competitive they. Technik, what Heidegger saw as a scientific attitude of calculative thought, domination, role, manipulation, and control, is suborned to contemplative thinking and authenticity. Authenticity is an ability to live in a mode of being-with-others and to perceive others as having being. Sartre conceived of the authentic individual as one who experienced doubt, suffered anguish, and faced up to and made moral decisions. Authenticity was a category of acting, or becoming, a reconstituted social self with responsibility for choosing one's own project, or moral life. Authentic individualism affirms this phenomenological effort to repudiate Technik and seize authenticity.

It also welcomes Camus' philosophy of limits to human action grounded in a common human nature and his kingdom of the human heart, where reality is in the common life of the human community and the full humanness, dignity, and integrity of personhood. It is a philosophy of limits founded on the value of the individual and the finiteness and fallibility of human knowledge. It is an Other-world in which human conduct is governed not by expectations of others, but conduct is directed toward development of self and others. While authentic individualism espouses the developmental nature of ethical conscience, it discards Sartre's absolute freedom as the expression of human essence. Rather, it teaches human dignity as the moral norm and embraces the notion that law is only the minimal expression of one's obligations to others.

Authentic individualism repudiates the Gemeinschaft, or greedy institution as Coser calls it, in which members are cognitively and emotionally oriented toward one another. Perhaps this was the failure of Heidegger's philosophy of Dasein in National Socialism, where orientation toward self was also misplaced. Instead, people must be oriented toward the transcendent human soul and common origin that all share, within a group and outside that group. Complete devotion within the group must be broken and integrated with occurrences and influences outside the community. Particularism, whether oriented toward the individual or the group, has the same corrosive effects.

Authentic individualism claims existentialism's allowance that the individual is central for creating possibilities for one's own existence, and the Emersonian conclusion that people are not merely a product of social forces. Authentic individualism believes individuals are not merely carriers, but are generators of society, at the same time individuals are affected in important ways by society; there is synergystic relationship in which each affects the other, often without measurable cause and effect. It disavows Riesman's other-directed personality and Descartes' *cogito ergo sum*, which transformed the locus of meaning to the self. It supports Hegel's attempt to vest meaning outside the individual in a "quest for transpersonal meaning." But it renounces William Whyte's organization man and rejects the need for belongingness to a group in place of the need for moral purpose. Instead, moral purpose may be found in service to others.

Authentic individualism rebuffs the Lockean paradigm of absolute rights and state of nature depictions of natural humans as solitary creatures, and it denies Emersonian self-sufficiency, because they separate individuals from one another. It takes the view that freedom is realized by individual pursuits within a complex of groups and relationships: family, society, state, and world. Authentic individualism is social individualism--law, custom, and social constraints vary widely. It is collective in the ethical sense--the individual can be transcended and protection of nature and growth of science is important along with freedom, happiness, rights, and autonomy. A person's status as human makes one important. The individual is prior to society in the sense that attributes of humanity reside in each person.

Authentic individualism abandons survivalism, manifest destiny and the soldierly values of the rugged individualist, spurns the laissez-faire economic analysis of the Robber Barons and Spoilsman, and objects to the intensely competitive culture of control of modern corporate America. In place of these outmoded concepts it substitutes Native America's community of shared concerns, the Calvinist sense of responsibility and obligation, the social orientation of the Puritans, the dignity and humility of the civil rights movement, the perseverance of the American worker, and the individuality in thought of the Jeffersonians. Instead of Madisonian self-interest in the role of virtue, the moral sense of personal conscience must be nurtured and developed to understand and accept a world of common origin and shared human interests. The harsh, compassionless profit orientation of the business mind becomes the Other-world of human commonalty and public good. Separatist and divisive feelings are ameliorated by habituating a practice of exhibiting the concrete, authentic, caring individual soul in every-day face-to-face encounters.

CHAPTER TEN

Soul of the Third Administrative State

The restraints acquired on the exercise of our appetites are precarious, but not because they are rules imperfectly learned. Instead, they are not rules at all or even wholly learned. Indeed, they are not really the product of the higher regions of the brain (neocortex), but are products of the more primitive parts (the limbic system). Many self-seeking impulses can be kept in tow by more social ones as both are part of the primitive nervous system. Circumstances--the rewards, penalties and rituals of daily life--constrain or subvert these precarious sentiments of the moral sense that arise from the most primitive, intuitive, and unconscious sources. As a result, these moral sentiments are partial and incomplete guides to action. There is no single moral principle or trait on which to found moral philosophy or single good for political philosophy, only several partially consistent ones. Neither happiness nor virtue can be prescribed by rule.

Yet philosophers continue to search for principles that can account for the existence of social order. These principles fall into two categories. The first is rationalistic and individualistic. Hobbes' argument that government is needed because everyone is enemy to everyone falls here. Later individualistic thinkers dropped the emphasis on a powerful sovereign in favor of self-regulating systems occupied by self-interested individuals linked together by market transactions. The second is normative and communal: Here is Durkheim's thesis that order exists because a system of beliefs and sentiments held by members of society limit what those members can do, rather than government. In other words, social norms that are part of a collective consciousness induce people to live peaceably. Thus, for some the human is an animal, while for others humans are social. In its worst form, radical individualism is mere self-indulgence; in its best form, it is life governed by conscience and cosmopolitan awareness. In its worst form, extreme communalism is parochial prejudice; in its best form, it is life governed by honor and intimate commitments. For Wilson, as for Aristotle, humans are social animals; a balance of self-regarding motives with other-regarding ones. Moral life is senses in conflict and requires striking a delicate balance among the moral sense and prudent self-interest. A good life is not living according to a fixed rule, but by habitual behavior of a life in balance. One becomes virtuous by the repetition of many small acts practicing virtue and by acquiring virtues as one acquires crafts.

Normative Ethical Considerations of Authentic Individualism

Some ethical considerations flow from authentic individualism and related philosophies. One of these is expressed by James Q. Wilson (1993), Collins Professor of Management and Public Policy at UCLA, who adopts a profoundly hopeful view of human nature as fundamentally good and decent:

> If modern man had taken seriously the main intellectual currents of the last century or so, he would have found himself confronted by the need to make moral choices when the very possibility of making such choices had been denied. God is dead or silent, reason suspect or defective, nature meaningless or hostile. As a result, man is adrift on an uncharted sea, left to find his moral bearings with no compass and no pole star, and so able to do little more than utter personal preferences, bow to historical necessity, or accept social conventions. (Wilson 1993, 5)

Wilson also notes that, while some people are criminals, most people are not, and almost everybody acquires a conscience.

The Moral Sense

Despite the pessimistic pronouncements of philosophers, psychologists, economists, political scientists and other experts and the images of human immorality, corruption, and exploitation that appear in the news as constant reminders that human nature is greedy, selfish, neurotic, and cruel, Wilson presents evidence that humans have a moral sense which is biological and behavioral in origin. Contrary to the teachings of many social scientists and anthropologists that morality is entirely relative and cultural with no basis in science or logic, he believes most humans possess a moral nature that is part of a collective unconscious and aspects of which--sympathy, fairness, self-control and duty--are universal.

Wilson sees moral confusion in the populace, not from loss of either moral bearings or religious commitment, or their giving way to immediate impulse or self-interest, but because most people try to talk themselves out of having a moral sense. Ordinary men and women wish to make moral judgments, but their culture does not help them. The learned often teach cultural relativism; that moral philosophy has no factual basis. A cultural pressure exists to conform to the view that one must not judge others, that social problems are the result of social ills rather than individual responsibility, and that moral arguments are nothing more than expressions of feelings--the last vestige of stuffy, puritanical values--with no objective validity whatsoever. People are told that justice and morality are merely a matter of transient consensus about what attitudes are normal. As a result, many doubt they have a defensible philosophy or credible conviction.

By moral sense, Wilson means an intuitive or directly felt belief about how one is obliged to act when one is free to act voluntarily. Having such a moral sense is not the same as saying people are innately good, and its existence does not require universal moral rules. According to Wilson, the great errors in moral philosophy are the beliefs that truth can be known and that there is no truth to be known. The moral sense is no sure cause of moral action, because behavior is the product of our senses and dispositions interacting with our circumstances. The moral sense must compete with other senses, such as self-interest. How the struggle is resolved depends on one's character, circumstances, and culture.

The Communal "We"

The fundamental debate over the relationship of personal rights to social obligations is what moral development is about, and the highest form thereof is to maintain the balance, the tension, between rights and obligations. This antithesis rather than the synthesis is what justice is about and moral development is the wisdom to conduct justice. To resolve in some arbitrary way the argument over rights and obligations is to surrender society to the Anarch or the Behemoth at the price of democratic community.[1]

Accepting a communal *we* as a valid ethical consideration, authentic individualism defines organizational community as consisting of the following components:

1. Purposefulness: Organizational members share in the goals of the organization, working together to strengthen their own characters and the integrity of the organization.

2. Openness: Freedom of expression is uncompromisingly protected, and civility is uncompromisingly affirmed.

3. Justice: The sacredness of each person is honored, and empowering the weak is aggressively pursued.

4. Discipline: There is well defined governance that guides behavior for the common good.

5. Caring: The well being of each individual is sensitively supported, and service to others is encouraged.

6. Celebration: The heritage of the institution is remembered, and rituals affirming both tradition and change are widely used.

7. Inclusivity: Commitment to the proposition of coexistence is crucial. Recent computer studies of developing organisms disclose that only adaptive agents thrive. Communities with a subcritical or low diversity of organisms lack the momentum to develop explosively into a new breed.[2]

8. Individuality: The rugged individualism of historical America is traded for a new ethic of soft individualism. This is an understanding of individualism which teaches that one cannot be truly oneself until one is able to share freely the weaknesses that all humans have in common.

9. Leadership: Community includes the flow of leadership that comes from the complete decentralization of authority. It can be conceptualized as a group of all leaders which sets aside hierarchy and control by experts in favor of lay contributions.

10. Spirituality: The competitive spirit and jingoistic boosterism that takes pride in being better is replaced by a spirit of peace or grace.

It consists of the sense of cohesiveness and collective joy that each member experiences after shedding the selfish exterior and transcending the feeling of loss that follows it.

Erikson (1974) states there must be a network of direct personal and communal communication. He concludes:

> American democracy, if it is to survive within the superorganizations of government and commerce, of industry and labor, is predicated on personal contacts within groups of optimal size--optimal meaning the power to persuade each other in matters that influence the lives of each. (Erikson 1974, 123)

This concept of community, as it is described above, has its roots in pluralist theory. Its democratic notion of consensus building brings the decision-maker closer to the people from whom authority springs. The organizational leader's challenge is to foster this spirit in the organization; to answer the need for community while simultaneously allowing the fullest possible development of the individual's potential expertise and self-worth.

The Psychology of Moral Development

Morality is part of any reflective life, and ethical perspectives and deliberation shape culture and civic life. Moral reasoning is intrinsic to true humanity and unfolding patterns of moral perceptions can be seen in human persons and human communities.[3] Human life is a pilgrimage; perpetual movement without arrival interfused with other persons and the environment; a quest for meaning and *logos* inspired by the vision of who we are called to become.[4] Even Albert Einstein, scientist though he was, recognized that it was essential to acquire an understanding of and lively feeling for values, and a vivid sense of the beautiful and of the morally good: "Otherwise he--with his specialized knowledge--more closely resembles a well-trained dog than a harmoniously developed person."[5]

Developmental psychologists, such as Piaget, Kohlberg and Erikson reject the need, wants and passions approach to analyzing individual behavior. Instead, they describe individuals as passing through multiple, invariant, qualitative stages of moral development in which certain principles guide behavior. There are no disjunctive leaps in these stages, only an ascending journey, ebbing and flowing, upward to complexity and mature responses to life and experience. The Piaget-

Kohlberg contribution to understanding moral reasoning and motivation fixes moral responsibility with each person. Not only are humans capable of self-determination, each is morally accountable for how experience is processed and the consequences of actions and intentions. Individuals must make moral judgments, but they are not a sufficient basis for ethical action. Moral judgments require the reasoned assessment of the consequences of human actions for human beings.[6] Practitioners and scholars in public administration, as all organizational leaders, must take account of the necessity for moral judgment in individuals and adapt organizational goals, missions and decision-making processes to facilitate it.

Generally speaking, this developmental view of individuals is consistent with authentic individualism and calls the practitioner and scholar in public administration, as well as any organizational leader, to embrace moral development as one of the motivating forces in individual life. Yet moral development as derived from attitudes of order and civility is a handmaiden to many authoritarian ideologies, because moral development ultimately rests on imposition of behavior through methods of authority or divinity. At the same time, the notion of development of morals assumes a plurality of standards. Entering this conflict calls for a fusion of democratic temper and the scientific credo, so as to avoid the dangerous quest for certainty and the complete relativity of values. Such democratic moral development is not a claim for unlimited moral possibilities or the impossibility of assessing moral standards, but the simple recognition that moral choices are not revealed truths that deductively or cosmologically flow from nature.[7]

Bureaucracy is the antithesis of this, achieving efficiency through depersonalization and transformation of true individuals into tools of production. The consequent managerial philosophy flowing from bureaucracy can be summarized:

> Employees are being paid to produce, not to make themselves into better people. Corporations are purchasing employee time to make a return on it, not to invest in employees to enrich their lives. Employees are human capital, and when capital is hired or leased, the objective is not to embellish it for its own sake but to use it for financial advantage. (Norton 1991, 154)

This management theory totally robs individuals of their personhood and treats them no different--with no greater redeeming values--than money or private property. Research indicates that what today's workers see as normal has changed, and they are not willing to just take orders. Consequently, authentic individualism is an important component of enlightened organization theory.

Importance of Authentic Individualism for Group Theory

Members of today's organizations expect to be a part of decisions and to hold a more empowered job.[8] In contrast to the wide acceptance of conformity and social assimilation of the past, people celebrate their differences today. In place of theory that demeans the individual, organizational leaders need to substitute a framework of human dignity:

> Enhancing dignity is not about high silk hats and a string of pearls, but about being honorable and honoring others. It is about valuing the best efforts of another even if we could do better. . . . It is about challenging each other to do our best and being unwilling to accept shoddy work. It is about admitting another has hurt you by some action, forgiving that person, and trusting the one who caused your hurt to do better next time. It is about being unwilling to forgive the one who is unrepentant, knowing that accepting shallow apologies denigrates all involved in the interaction. Dignity is about honesty, integrity, and quality. By giving it to others, it is bestowed upon ourselves. . . . When we withhold it from others, we deprive ourselves of it. (Rice 1993, 1)

Lack of knowledge and skills for leading a diverse work force is a ticking time bomb for the insensitive organization. The challenge is to make room for differences, by fostering a work environment that naturally allows all organization members "to reach their potential in pursuit of organizational objectives" (Neely 1992, F9).

Mindfulness and Process Orientation

Lawler (1992) contrasts the old paradigm of control with an involvement approach in organizations. The involvement approach organizes work to be challenging, interesting, and motivating by viewing members of the organization as worthy and worthwhile. In contrast to the control approach which tries to program individuals with responses to all situations so that there is never any doubt about what they should do, Lawler recommends giving them general missions and philosophies as guides for their behavior and allowing them to respond to the client or customer as they see fit. They are also expected to improve the work system as time goes on so that it will operate at a high level of quality, solve problems on the job, and coordinate outcomes with others, without a controlling supervisor.

Langer (1989) contrasts the old outcome approach with mindfulness, where the former is controlled by rigid rules and the latter by a process orientation. Mindless individuals repeat tasks in predetermined uses of information and the individual parts of the task move out of consciousness as only minimal clues necessary to carry out the process scenario are noticed and other signals do not penetrate. In the process orientation, goals are subject to continual revision as awareness of new information requires change. Instead of moving along a predetermined path, mindful individuals see new choices and endpoints, and unexpected stumbling blocks become building blocks. A tolerance for uncertainty develops in the mindful manager, who sees problems as part of an ongoing process rather than disastrous deviations from the past. The office becomes a place where questions are encouraged, ideas are exchanged, and an error does not mean getting fired.

No entrepreneur, business manager, or government supervisor can claim to be a true individualist unless such a program is implemented as the life project of the organization. True individualism is impossible in organizations that demean the individual by treating humans as property:

> Normative individuation requires a supportive context. To reestablish the foundations of normative individuality in self-knowledge, self-identification, and self-responsibility, it is imperative to strengthen 'intermediate associations' that buffer individuals against the conditioning effects of impersonal associations-at-large. (Norton 1991, 155)

It therefore becomes the responsibility of organizations and managers to respect total personhood. They need not actively further it, but must define themselves and their functions in ways that do not obstruct, but facilitate worker's self-integrations. As Keen noted, management is a sacred trust for the well-being of others placed in one's care.

In a broader sense, people in organizations and leaders of organizations also need to change the way they think about their organizations and the role organizations play in daily life. Organizations need to become a part of society, to take a greater (not bigger) societal role, to show the same responsibilities toward others as an individual, and assume the same obligations. Since organizations are treated by the law as individuals, they must fulfill a more responsible social role, within their organizational boundaries and out.

Implications of Authentic Individualism for Leadership Theory

According to Harmon and Mayer (1986), Luther Gulick was one of the Neo-Classical organization theorists for whom instrumental rationality was the essence of that part of human organizing known as administration. His acronym POSDCORB was used to describe the primary activities of the executive as center of all authority and power in the organization. Harmon and Mayer believe there were three primary consequences to the outlook Gulick's theory encapsulated. First, was a Wilsonian emphasis on means of administration with little attention to government's purpose. Second, was to highlight the need for the division of work leading to scientific principles of management and reliance on a bureaucratic hierarchy. Third, was the centrality of efficiency as the premier value by which to judge government. Yet a fourth consequence might be a movement away from the profound moral leadership concerns of Chester Barnard (1938).

Return to Moral Leadership

Primacy of empirical and instrumental concerns seemed to dominate the organizational leadership scene until the late 1940s and 1950s. In 1957, Philip Selznick penned his tome on leadership called *Leadership in Administration*, which began to nudge leadership theory back toward the concerns of purpose and morality. Selznick (1957) begins his essay with a thesis statement about leadership: "The executive becomes a statesman as he makes the transition from administrative management to institutional leadership" (Selznick 1957, 4). This means the leader views the organization as an institution and has concern for its evolution as a whole. However, Selznick's theory is still very much related to structure and function of the organization as an entity without focusing much on the people that give it life.

Modern leadership theory has become much more personal, existential, and concerned with the human component than the organizational. DePree (1992), Torbert (1991), and Roestenbaum

(1992) all think it essential that leadership theory and leaders themselves return to an appreciation of the humanities and study of philosophy. This is particularly true in government, because its management, leadership and reform engages fundamental issues of political and social philosophy. Torbert believes organizations ought to exist in order to promote the development and self-realization of their members.

Max DePree, President and CEO of the Herman Miller corporation, says, "Leaders will plumb the depths of human authenticity, perhaps without ever reaching the bottom" (DePree 1992, 59). They need to commit themselves to individual authenticity "with openness and expectation, with grace and humor" (Ibid., 63). DePree recognizes that "[l]eaders must balance sensitively the needs of the people and of the institution" and leadership is a "posture of indebtedness" and the process of leading is the process of fulfilling commitments made to both persons and the organization (Ibid., 19).

Although leadership cannot be adequately summed up in a list of character traits, DePree offers the following statements to begin describing it:

1. Integrity is the linchpin of leadership.
2. Vulnerability permits those who follow the leader to do their best.
3. Discernment--the detection of nuance and the perception of changing realities--lies somewhere between wisdom and judgment.
4. All the qualities of a good leader stem from awareness of the human spirit.
5. Courage in relationships means leaders resolve conflict, define justice, and keep promises.
6. A passionate sense of humor requires a broad perspective on the human condition and is essential to living with ambiguity.
7. Leaders have the intellectual energy and curiosity to turn decision-making into a process of frantically learning from your followers.

Depree acknowledges the "sacred nature of personal dignity" and believes the need for dignity, opportunity, and reward must move beyond the requirements of law and regulation, which represent "only the most basic and generalized statement of fair behavior" (Ibid., 52, 56). According to DePree, leadership and ethics are inextricably woven together, because leaders learn how to make a commitment to individual freedom and the common good, neither of which work on trickle-down theory. "Above all, leadership is a position of servanthood" (Ibid., 220).

Depree also describes eleven promises that a leader makes to an organization and its members:

1. The organization expects the leader to define and express both in writing and, especially, through behavior the beliefs and values of the institution.

2. To carry out its work, the organization needs from the leader a clear statement of its vision and its strategy.

3. A leader is accountable for the design of the business.

4. A leader is responsible for lean and simple statements of policy consistent with beliefs and values, vision and strategy.

5. Equity is the special province of a leader.

6. A leader focuses not on the image of a leader, but on the tone of the body of the institution.

7. A leader ensures that priorities are set, and that they are steadfastly communicated and adhered to in practice.

8. A leader ensures that the planning for the organization at all levels receives the necessary direction and approvals.

9. A leader reviews and assesses results primarily in three areas: key appointments and promotions, results compared to the plan, and the connections to key publics.

10. Leaders are accountable for the continuous renewal of the organization.

11. A leader ought never to embarrass followers.

Similarly, Roestenbaum (1992) believes that work can be an opportunity for both personal and organizational greatness, and such a point of view ennobles human nature and strengthens society. This point of view involves refocusing the mind and achieving a mental transformation to the leadership way of thinking. The authentic leader does not accept the mind as he or she finds it, but chooses to construct or wake up to the leadership mind, providing an inner space for conflict, paradox, and contradiction.

When of the proper mind, a leader is concerned with matters of the heart--the importance of self-respect, feelings, sense of worth and destiny. These issues are of enduring concern and represent the conflict between values of love and survival, harshness and compassion. Leadership requires hard thoughts about soft subjects. To consider these issues is to go beyond questions of technique to fundamental dimensions of the human soul.

This amounts to simple recognition that organizations are people-driven. "They exist for people, are designed by people, and work through people. Leave people out, and you drain the blood right out of the body" (Roestenbaum 1992, 15). To do so, he thinks it necessary that middle management should devote one-third of its work time to leadership, and two-thirds to maintenance and managing. For upper management, the time devoted to leadership rises to fifty percent. He also believes one-third of the organization's resources (money, attention, emphasis, energy, and time) should also be devoted to leadership--not to production, administration, maintenance, or management. This training should be viewed as remedial work in the humanities. Ten years into the job, executives with a background of skills and no humanities will suffer, as will their followers, because the mindset or philosophy of the individuals and organization members determines the results achieved. As a result, Roestenbaum believes it is of the highest importance "to build cooperation on the common principles of humanity that bind us all" (Ibid., 309).

Conclusion of Part Three

Public life and the way it is viewed in the United States today is in desperate need of revamping. The purely mechanistic view of individuals as skin-encapsulated objects with no spiritual or moral bond between them is outmoded and dangerous in an interconnected world growing ever more complex and diverse, where the resources for progress are also more scarce. Instead of such a self-oriented view of reality and the self-interested pursuit of progress it engenders, progress itself must be reformulated. Who we are and what we pursue as good in life needs redefining. This can begin with change in the way we view the world and perceive the reality that surrounds us. Authentic individualism is an effort toward helping change the perception of our environment. Authentic individualism does not seek to make some political or ideological point, but seeks to lift up the human and ethical dimensions of public life. It asks three questions to be answered every day by institutions and individuals in their lives and work: What does this action do for people? What does it do to people? How may people participate in it?

Human dignity is the starting point for moral decision-making. Morality in turn is a growing appreciation for what enriches human dignity and what truly injures it. Every decision must be judged in light of whether it protects or undermines the dignity of the human person. If that happens, people and institutions will stop treating individuals as acquisitive, driven by wants, needs, and desires for goods. Business and government will stop treating each other as tools to create a business climate and both will put people first. Then each person will be treated as deserving of respect, driven by values, principles and the desire to do good.

Key parts of the foundation for authentic individualism can be summarized as follows:

1. Life is the organization of matter into growing and reproducing entities, and human life is simply more complex organization of matter into sentient and developmental entities. Dignity is present in all life and flows from the common origin of life and matter in the universe.

2. Being human is development of a moral sense that recognizes the dignity of life.

3. Each individual person possesses dignity that must be respected and enhanced by the government, employers and others; individual value is rooted in who we are, not what we do.

4.   Respect for human dignity is relational, reflexive and other-regarding; it requires individuals and institutions to govern their affairs according to the impact those affairs will have on humanity.

5.   Bestowing respect requires concomitant responsibilities; individuals and institutions are responsible for their own actions and have a duty to define and follow their life project with due regard to the life projects of others.

6.   The project of life is Authentic Individualism defined as independent, critical thought and compassionate devotion to development in self and others of human potential for good.

7.   An authentic individual has identity and worth apart from the community and has primacy over the majority, but human dignity can be fully realized and protected only in community.

8.   The will of the community may not be imposed arbitrarily upon the authentic individual, and the community works to develop individual human potential and enhance dignity.

9.   The community can expect in return a real commitment from each individual and institution to support community by completing a life project of developing the potential for good in self and others.

10. Good is held in common by all and present in all; it is dignity itself, but can only be maintained through completion of a life project devoted to the development of it in self and others.

These principles lead to the following paradox of perpetual renewal: Beginning with the dignity of life, if one cultivates respect for others and assumes responsibility to others, one embarks on a life project for good that leads to a community of individuals who value individual worth and exalt the dignity of life. In this way they may transcend the organization, give it a new paradigm, or vision, and in the process transform it into a place healthy for humans.

Linear systems are central to traditional scientific analysis-- understanding the parts of a complex system implies understanding the whole--but recent scientific work on chaos, self-organization, and nonlinear systems theory has forced scientists to think more about open systems.   Nonlinear systems must be understood in their totality-- which in practice means taking into account a variety of constraints and conditions.   Such systems are unpredictable and incredibly sensitive to influences by their external environments.   They display ordered and law-like behavior, yet they are indeterministic and subject to random outside perturbations.   These complex systems are more than the sum of their parts, and within a directed framework there remains an intimate amalgam of openness, freedom, chance, and choice.   General organizing principles supervise their behavior, but these principles are outside the laws of physics which operate at the bottom level of individual particles. The study of nonlinear systems shifts emphasis away from lumpen matter responding to impressed forces toward systems that contain elements of spontaneity and surprise.

A compromise between the changing and the eternal and a reconciliation of becoming and being can be found in *stochasticity* and chaos. A stochastic system is nonlinear and subject to random and unpredictable fluctuations, but stochasticity is not anarchy. The system is subject to general principles that guide and encourage, rather than compel development along certain predetermined pathways. Chaos is also a type of non-linear behavior, as are most natural systems. Though no one can ever predict exactly how a chaotic system will behave over long periods, chaos is manageable, exploitable and even invaluable. To the casual observer, chaotic systems appear to behave randomly, but upon close examination they have an underlying order. The disorderly behavior of a chaotic system is a collection of many orderly behaviors. By perturbing a chaotic system in the right way, the system can be encouraged to follow one of its many regular behaviors. Also, a non-linear system could be stable when driven with a chaotic signal. The process requires finding the sub-systems that react to a chaotic signal in a stable way. Moreover, two systems can be coaxed to operate in phase by changing the periodic driving signal. Then the trick is to find the right kind of chaotic signal for each system. (Ditto and Pecora 1993, 78.)

The philosophical thought that most closely accommodates these scientific views is process philosophy, which views the world as a process with definite directionality, rather than as a collection of objects or set of events. The flux of time places primacy on becoming over being and the Newtonian rigid mechanistic view of the universe is replaced by stress on the openness and indeterminism of nature. Process reality accepts the world as a community of interdependent beings rather than a collection of individual cogs in a machine. The vision of organizational leader that emerges from this process of becoming is the Steersman: guiding and encouraging public acceptance of right reason; always alert to random perturbations; piloting between Scylla and Charybdis, the dual perils of indeterminacy; constantly assessing available information to determine position; and continually making mid-course corrections for safe passage to the final destination; but open and flexible enough to take temporary shelter along the way if forced to do so by intelligible but unpredictable conditions. The steersman of an organization guides it like a pilot of a ship at sea. Many quantitative instruments at one's disposal produce data that are very useful during more-or-less routine situations. This methodology works very well so long as outside conditions remain within certain parameters. However, when conditions such as the weather begin to exceed normal, it is only the intuition and judgment of the pilot and crew that will steer a safe course.

The organizational steersman also tries to identify that part of the organization around which the remainder can come into synchronistic orbit, and the signal that will coax the various parts of the organization to synchronize. In today's American organizations the appropriate signal is one that respects and facilitates human dignity, one that offers the members of the organization the opportunity to make decisions according to general moral and organizational principles. Subtle acts downward offer a guiding hand to synchronize the diverse energies of the organization. The task is to monitor multiple streams of information flow at the same time, including those of destination and progress along the way, not as in Langer's mindlessness, but as in the Greek notion of a steersman in a cybernetic state of monitoring progress toward fulfillment of moral purpose and organizational goals.

Notes

Chapter One   Introduction to Individualism

1. One author who explicitly discusses individualism in a business context is Aram, J. D., 1993, *Presumed Superior: Individualism and American business*, Englewood Cliffs, New Jersey, Prentice Hall. Others who have recognized a need for ameliorating our intensely economic view of life are: Etzioni, A., 1988, *The Moral dimension: Toward a new economics*, New York, Free Press; Friedland, R., and Robertson, A. F., 1990, *Beyond the marketplace: Rethinking economy and society*, New York, Aldine de Gruyter; Hirschman, A. O., 1986, *Rival views of market society*, New York, Viking; and Koford, K. J., and Miller, J. B., 1991, *Social norms and economic institutions*, Ann Arbor, Michigan, University of Michigan Press.

2. Arieli, Y. 1964. *Individualism and materialism in American ideology.* Cambridge: Harvard University Press, p. 268.

3. Lukes, S. 1974. *Individualism.* Oxford: Blockwell, pp. 79-80.

4. Ibid., 158.

5. Hiskes, R. P. 1982. *Community without coercion: Getting along with the minimal state.* Newark: University of Delaware Press, pp. 13-14.

6.   Ibid., 15.

7.   Ibid., 17.

8.   Gilbert, A. 1990. *Democratic individuality*. New York: Cambridge University Press, pp. 1-12.

9.   Bellah, R. N., Masden, R., Sullivan, W. M., Swidler, A., and Tipton, S. M. (Eds.). 1987. *Individualism and commitment in American Life*. New York: Harper & Row, p. 12.

10.   The foregoing contrast of individualist and communitarian views is drawn from Avineri, S., and De-Shalit, A. 1992. *Communitarianism and individualism*. New York: Oxford University Press.

11.   Bettelheim, B. 1960. *The informed heart*. Glencoe, Illinois: The Free Press, pp. vii, 11, 47-48, 72-73, 96, 237.

Chapter Two   The Individual of the Ancients

1.   The principal sources of philosophical history used in this study are: Jones, W. T., 1970, *A history of western philosophy* , 2d ed., 5 Vols., San Diego, Harcourt Brace Jovanovich; and Tarnos, R., 1991, *The passion of the western mind*, New York, Harmony Books.

2.   Davies, P., and Gribbin, J. 1992. *The matter myth*. New York: Simon and Schuster, p. 10. Aristotle was largely responsible for pushing the notions of Democritus, but he did not even mention Anaxagoras, for which he has been criticized by other philosophers. Cf. Cleve, F. M. 1965. *Giants of pre-Sophistic Greek philosophy* (Vol 2). The Hague: M. Nijhoff. Yet, it appears that Anaxagoras, an older, pre-Sophist contemporary of Democritus, made a similar proposal earlier that nous (mind) enclosed all space, or atoms, and created, ordered and directed all--engendering the doctrine of spiritual consciousness embracing all, including the material. In Christian philosophy, Plotinus (125 A. D.) was the principal proponent of Anaxagorean views. Of course, the mystics of all time, both East and West, embrace the immanence view of the divine mind of all, uniting all.

3.   Other references used for explication of Plato's philosophy were: Plato, 1986, *The republic*, Buffalo, New York, Prometheus Books; and Rankin, H. D., 1964, *Plato and the individual*, New York, Barnes and Noble. Aristotle's views also came from Baker, E. (Ed.), 1958, *The politics of Aristotle,* London, Oxford University Press.

Chapter Three   The Individual of the Dark Ages

1.   This excessively pessimistic view of humanity probably stemmed from a profound brooding over his own life and agonizing inward conflict.

2.   The following description of Feudalism is from Ulmann, W., 1966, *The individual and society in the middle ages*, Baltimore, The John Hopkins Press. The earlier discussion of Augustine's work was also extracted from Saint Augustine, (1467)1984, *City of God*, London, Penguin Books

3.   The Holy Bible, First Corinthians, 15:10.

4.   Ulmann 1966, 68.

5.   Jones 1970, 2:189-190, 196.

6.   Ulmann 1966, 123, 129.

7.   Information about the Renaissance was likewise gleaned from Cassirer, E., 1963, *The individual and the cosmos in renaissance philosophy*, New York, Barnes and Noble.

8.   Machiavelli's politics were supplemented with Skinner, Q. and Price, R. (Eds.), 1990, *Machiavelli's: The prince*, Cambridge, Cambridge University Press.

9.   Tuck, R. (Ed.). 1991. *Hobbes: Leviathan.* Cambridge: Cambridge University Press.

10. The paradox is that Descartes reformed the entire structure of Western knowledge and provided the foundations for modern science

from insights that came to him in three dreams. The philosophical basis for rational, reductionist, positivist science--which rejects subjective knowledge--was conceived subjectively in an unconscious state.

Chapter Four   The Individual of Modernity

1. The ideas of Jean-Jacques Rousseau on the individual were obtained from Perkins, M. L., 1974, *Jean-Jacques Rousseau on the individual and society*, Lexington, University Press of Kentucky.

2. The following description of Dewey's philosophy is extracted from Dewey, J., 1927, *The public and its problems*, New York, Henry Holt.

3. These comments on Husserl's views on science came from Buckley, R. P., 1992, *Husserl, Heidegger and the crisis of philosophical responsibility*, Boston, Kluwer Academic.

4. Ibid.

5. Ellison, D. R. 1990. *Understanding Albert Camus*. Columbia, South Carolina: University of South Carolina Press, p. 1.

6. Woelfel, J. W. 1975. *Camus: A theological perspective*. New York: Abingdon Press, p. 117.

Chapter Five   Rugged Individualism of the Revolutionary U.S.

1. Zinn, H. 1980. *A people's history of the United States*. New York: Harper and Row, p. 12.

2. Roberts, D. 1992. Geronimo. *National Geographic*, October, 46-71.

3. Perry, R. B. 1944. *Puritanism and democracy*. New York: The Vanguard Press, pp. 193, 270, 275, 297.

4. *New York v. United States*, 505 U.S. 144; 120 L. Ed. 2d 120; 112 S. Ct. 2408; 60 L.W. 4603, 4608-4609 (1992).

5. Pessen, E. 1978. *Jacksonian America: Society, personality, and politics*. Homewood, Illinois: The Dorsey Press, pp. 10-30.

6. Berger, M. 1964. *The British traveller in America, 1836-1860*. Gloucester, Massachusetts: Peter Smith, pp. 42, 58, 61, 68, 74.

7. Joseph, F. M. (Ed.). 1959. *As others see us: the United States through foreign eyes*. Princeton, New Jersey: Princeton University Press, pp. 50, 58.

8. Staff. The wild wild west. 1993. *Life*, April(Special Issue), 10.

9. Ibid.

Chapter Six Rational Individualism After Romanticism and Reform

1. Joseph, F. M. 1959 *As others see us: the United States through foreign eyes*. Princeton, New Jersey: Princeton University Press, pp. 295-96, 318.

2. Ibid., 95.

3. Mead, M. 1967. *And keep your powder dry*. London: Ronald Whiting and Wheaton, pp. 202-03.

4. Berger, M. 1964. *The British Traveler in America, 1836-1860*. Gloucester Massachusetts: Peter Smith, p. 72.

5. Joseph, 59.

6. Lacour-Gayet, R. 1969. *Everyday life in the United States before the Civil War 1830-1860*. New York: Frederick Ungar, p. 276.

7. Bradley, P. 1945. *Democracy in America by Alexis de Tocqueville* . Vol. 1. New York: Alfred A. Knopf, pp. 260-61, 263, 265.

8.   Commager, H. S. 1950. *The American mind: An interpretation of American thought and character since the 1880's.* New Haven, Connecticut: Yale University Press, pp. 7-8.

9.   Morison, S. E. 1965. *The Oxford history of the American people.* New York: Oxford University Press, p. 945.

10. Gans, H. J., Glazer, N., Gusfield, J. R. and Jencks, C. (Eds.). 1979. *On the making of Americans: Essays in honor of David Riesman.* Camden, New Jersey: University of Pennsylvania Press, p. 6.

11. Ibid., 4, 5, 7, 9, 11, 12, 13, 19, 24, 26.

12. Hofstadter, R. 1973. *The American political tradition and the men who made it.* New York: Vintage Books, p. 410.

Chapter Seven Radical Individualism From Disillusionment and Loss of Faith

1.   Deshon, D. S., & Sweezey, C. 1990. [Summary Report on Survey of Undergraduate Culture]. School of Public Affairs and Administration, Western Michigan University. Unpublished raw data.

2.   Bensimkon, M. 1993. A working Teenager. *Life*, July, 76-82.

3.   Ibid., 80.

4.   Feinberg, B., and Kasrils, R. 1984. *Bertrand Russell's America* Vol. 2. London: George Allen & Unwin, pp. 336, 358.

5.   Huer, J. 1990. *The wages of sin: America's dilemma of profit against humanity.* New York: Praeger, p. 6.

6.   Ibid., pp. 4, 6, 7, 12, 246-247.

7.   Ibid., 18, 19, 23-24, 200, 235.

8. Boyd, R. 1992. Hard choices. *Detroit Free Press* (September 13), 1F.

9. Woodworth, F. L. 1991. President's page. *Michigan Bar Journal, 70,* 275-76.

10. Gilchrist, B. J., and Arellano, A. 1993. Pride and tension increase as students keep to their own. *Detroit Free Press*(May 16), 1F.

11. Cantor, G. 1993. Hostility 101. *The Detroit News* (December 12), 1B.

12. Gilchrist, B. J., and Arellano, A. 1993. Pride and tension increase as students keep to their own. *Detroit Free Press*(May 16), 5F.

Chapter Eight   Need for a New World View

1. Staff. 1993. Here ruining people is considered sport. *Detroit Free Press*(August 11), 1A.

2. Lerner E. J. 1991. *The big bang never happened.* New York: Times Books, pp. 407-408.

3. Ibid., 408.

4. Use of the term singularity to describe the origin of the Big Bang when compared to the modern emphasis on individuation is too powerful a metaphor to be mere coincidence.

5. Lerner 1991, 4.

Chapter Nine   Changing the Paradigm

1. Grof, S. 1992. *The holotropic mind.* San Francisco: HarperCollins, p. 7.

2. Lerner 1991, 351.

Chapter Ten   Soul of the Third
Administrative State

1.   Wilson R. W., and Schochet, G. J. 1980. *Moral development and politics*. New York: Praeger, p. 10.

2.   Staff. 1992. Science and the Citizen: The Edge of Chaos. *Scientific American*, October, p. 20.

3.   Joy, D. M. 1983. *Moral development foundations: Judeo-Christian alternatives to Piaget/Kohlberg*. Nashville: Abingdon Press, p 23.

4.   Ibid., 14, 34.

5.   Kalamazoo College. (1994, January). What can I do with a major in English? (Unpublished informational letter of the English Department).

6.   Wilson and Schochet, 138.

7.   Ibid., 17.

8.   Lam, T. 1993. Stifling military style lingers is the postal system. *Detroit Free Press*(May 11), B1.

Bibliography

Ackerman, B. 1991. *We the people.* Cambridge: The Belknap Press.

Adams, J. D. (Ed.). 1984. *Transforming Work.* Alexandria, Virginia: Miles River Press.

Aram, J. D. 1993. *Presumed superior: Individualism and American business.* Englewood Cliffs, New Jersey: Prentice Hall.

Arendt, H. 1958. *The human condition.* Chicago: University of Chicago Press.

Arieli, Y. 1964. *Individualism and nationalism in American ideology.* Cambridge: Harvard University Press.

Avineri, S., and De-Shalit, A. 1992. *Communitarianism and individualism.* New York: Oxford University Press.

Bailey, M. T., and Mayer, R. T. (Eds.). 1992. *Public management in an interconnected world: Essays in the Meadowbrook tradition.* New York: Greenwood Press.

Bailyn, B. 1967. *The ideological origins of the American revolution.* Cambridge: The Belknap Press.

Bailyn, B. 1990. *Faces of revolution: Personalities and themes in the struggle for American independence.* New York: Knopf.

Balkin, R. (Ed.). 1988. *Everyday people in America.* New York: Harper and Row.

Barker, E. (Ed.). 1958. *The politics of Aristotle.* London: Oxford University Press.

Barnard, C. I. 1938. *Functions of the executive.* Cambridge, Massachusetts: Harvard University Press.

Barrett, W. 1979. *The illusion of technique.* Garden City, New York: Anchor Press/Doubleday.

Bateson, M. C. 1989. *Composing a life*. New York: Penguin Group.

Bauman, Z. 1992. *Intimations of postmodernity*. London: Routledge.

Bellah, R. N., Masden, R., Sullivan, W. M., Swidler, A., and Tipton, S. M. 1985. *Habits of the heart*. Berkeley, California: University of California Press.

Bellah, R. N., Masden, R., Sullivan, W. M., Swidler, A., & Tipton, S. M. (Eds.). 1987. *Individualism and commitment in American life*. New York: Harper & Row.

Bennett, L., and Ourlian, R. 1990. Hidden interests. *The Detroit News and Free Press*(October 28), p. 1A.

Bennis, W. 1990. *Why leaders can't lead*. San Francisco: Josey-Bass.

Bensimkon, M. 1993. A working Teenager. *Life*, July, 74-83.

Berger, M. 1964. *The Brittish traveller in America, 1836-1860*. Gloucester, Massachusetts: Columbia University Press.

Berman, M. 1970. *The politics of authenticity: Radical individualism and the emergence of modern society*. New York: Atheneum.

Berting, J., Baehr, P. R., Burgers, J. H., Flinterman, C., de Klerk, B., Kroes, R., van Minnen, C. A., and VanderWal, K. 1990. *Human rights in a pluralist world*. London: Meckler.

Bettleheim, B. 1960. *The informed heart: Autonomy in a mass age*. Glencoe, Illinois: The Free Press of Glencoe.

Birnbaum, P. and Leca, J. (Eds.). 1990. *Individualism: Theories and methods*. New York: Oxford University Press.

Bivens, L. 1990. Rescuing an endangered generation. *The Detroit Free Press*(October 28), p. 1F.

Bly, R. 1990. *Iron John*. New York: Addison-Wesley.

Boslough, J. 1992. *Masters of time*. New York: Addison-Wesley.

Boulding, K. E. (1956, April). General systems theory: The skeleton of science. *Management Science, 2*, 197-208.

Boyd, R. 1992. Hard choices. *Detroit Free Press*(September 13), p. 1F.

Bradley, P. (Ed.). 1945a. *Democracy in America by Alexis de Tocqueville*. Vol. 1. New York: Knopf.

Bradley, P. (Ed.). 1945b. *Democracy in America by Alexis de Tocqueville*. Vol. 2. New York: Knopf.

Brush, S. 1992. How cosmology became a science. *Scientific American*, August, pp. 62-70.

Buckley, R. P. 1992. *Husserl, Heidegger and the crisis of philosophical responsibility*. London: Kluwer Academic.

Cantor, G. 1993. Hostility 101. *The Detroit News*(December 12), p. 1B.

Cassirer, E. 1963. *The individual and the cosmos in renaissance philosophy.* New York: Barnes & Noble.

Chandler, R. C. 1983. The problem of moral reasoning in American public administration: The case for a code of ethics. *PublicAdministration Review, 43*, 32-39.

------. 1984. The public administrator as representative citizen: A new role for the new century. *Public Administration Review, 44*, 196-206.

------. (Ed.). 1987a. *A centennial history of the American administrative state.* New York: Free Press.

------. 1987b. *Civic virtue in the American republic.* Kalamazoo, Michigan: The New Issues Press.

Cleve, F. M. 1965. *Giants of pre-Sophistic Greek philosophy: An attempt to reconstruct their thoughts .* Vol. 2. The Hague: M. Nijhoff.

Cohen, B. I. 1992. What Columbus "Saw" in 1492. *Scientific American*, December, pp. 100-106.

Cohen, J. L. 1992. *Civil society and political theory.* Cambridge: MIT Press.

Commager, H. S. 1950. *The American mind.* New Haven: Yale University Press.

------. 1985. *Individualism, virtue and the commonwealth.* Kent, Ohio: Kent State University Libraries.

Cooper, T. L. 1982. *The Responsible administrator: An approach to ethics for the administrative role.* Port Washington, N. Y.: Kennikat.

------. 1987. Hierarchy, virtue and the practice of public administration: A perspective for normative ethics. *Public Administration Review, 47*, 320-28.

Corcoran, E. (1992, October). The edge of chaos. *Scientific American*, pp. 17-22.

Coser, R. L. 1991. *In defense of modernity: Role complexity and individual autonomy.* Stanford, California: Stanford University Press.

Crick F., and Koch C. 1992. The problem of consciousness. *Scientific American*, September, pp. 154-59.

Damasio, A., and Damasio, H. 1992. Brain and language. *Scientific American*, September, pp. 88-95.

Davies, P. 1992. *The mind of God.* New York: Simon and Schuster.

Davies, P., and Gribbon, J. 1992. *The matter myth.* New York: Simon and Schuster.

Dawley, A. 1991. *Struggles for justice: Social responsibility and the liberal state.* Cambridge: Belknap Press.

Denhardt, K. G. 1989. The management of ideals: A political perspective on ethics. *Public Administration Review, 49,* 187-193.

Denhardt, R. B. 1981. *In the shadow of organization.* Lawrence, Kansas: University Press of Kansas.

Dennard, D. 1992. Unpublished manuscript, Western Michigan University, School of Public Affairs and Administration.

DePree, M. 1992. *Leadership jazz.* New York: Currency/Doubleday.

Deshon, D. S., and Sweezey, C. 1990. [Summary Report on Survey of Undergraduate Culture]. School of Public Affairs and Administration, Western Michigan University. Unpublished raw data.

Dewey, J. 1927. *The public and its problems.* New York: Henry Holt.

------. [1930]1962. *Individualism, old and new.* New York: Capricorn.

Ditto, W. L. (1993, August). *Mastering chaos.* Scientific American, pp. 78-84.

Donahue, W. A. 1990. *The new freedom: Individualism and collectivism in the lives of Americans.* New Brunswich, New Jersey: Transaction.

Douglas, M., and Wildavsky, A. 1982. *Risk and culture: An essay on the selection of technical and environmental dangers.* Berkeley: University of California Press.

Dumont, L. 1986. *Essays on individualism: Modern ideology in anthropological perspective.* Chicago: University of Chicago Press.

Ellison, D. R. 1990. *Understanding Albert Camus.* Columbia, South Carolina: University of South Carolina Press.

Erikson, E. H. 1974. *Dimensions of a new identity: The 1973 Jefferson lectures in the humanities.* New York: W. W. Norton

Estés, C. P. 1992. *Women who run with the wolves: Myths and stories of the wild woman archetype.* New York: Ballentine.

Etzioni, A. 1988. *The moral dimension: Toward a new economics.* New York: Fre Press.

Fairfield, R. P. 1981. *The federalist papers.* Baltimore: The Johns Hopkins University Press.

Fallows, J. M. 1989. *More like us.* Boston: Houghton Mifflin.

Feinberg, B., and Kasrils, R. 1973. *Bertrand Russell's America: His transatlantic travels and writings.* Vol. 1. London: George Allen and Unwin.

------. 1984. *Bertrand Russell's America: His transatlantic travels and writings.* Vol. 2. London: George Allen and Unwin.

Fischbach, G. 1992. Mind and brain. *Scientific American,* September, pp. 48-57.

Fleishman, J. L., Liebman, L. and Moore, M. H. 1981. *Public duties: The moral obligations of government officials.* Cambridge: Harvard University Press.

Fleishman, J. L., and Payne, B. L. 1980. *Ethical dilemmas and the education of policy makers.* Hastings on the Hudson: Hastings Center.

Frederickson, H. G. 1980. *The new public administration.* University of Alabama: University of Alabama Press.

Frederickson, H. G., and Chandler, R. C. (Eds.). 1984. Citizenship and public administration [Special Issue]. *Public Administration Review, 44,* 101-192.

Friedland, R., and Robertson, A. F. (Eds.). 1990. *Beyond the marketplace: Rethinking economy and society.* New York: Aldine de Gruyter.

Friedrich, C. J. (Ed.). 1967. *The public interest.* New York: Atherton Press.

Fromm, E. [1941]1969. *Escape from freedom.* New York: Avon.

------. 1976. *To have or to be?* New York: Bantam.

Gans, H. J. 1988. *Middle American individualism: The future of liberal democracy.* New York: Free Press.

Gans, H. J., Glazer, N., Gusfireld, J. R., and Jencks, C. (Eds.). 1979. *On the making of Americans: Essays in honor of David Riesman.* Philadelphia: University of Pennsylvania Press.

Gazzaniga, M. S. 1988. *Mind matters: How mind and brain interact to create our conscious lives.* Boston: Houghton Mifflin.

Gelpi, D. L. (Ed.). 1989 *Beyond individualism: Toward a retrieval of moral disclosure in America.* Notre Dame, Indiana: University of Notre Dame Press.

Gershon, E., and Rieder, R. 1992. Major disorders of mind and brain. *Scientific American,* September, pp. 126-33.

Giddens, A. 1991. *Modernity and self-Identity: Self and society in the late modern age.* Stanford, California: Stanford University Press.

Gilbert, A. 1990. *Democratic individuality.* New York: Cambridge University Press.

Gilchrist, B. J. and Arellano, A. 1993. Pride and tension increase as students keep to their own. *Detroit Free Press*(May 16), p. 1F.

Glendon, M. A. 1991. *Rights talk: The impoverishment of political discourse in America.* New York: Free Press.

Goldman-Rakic, P. 1992. Working memory and the mind. *Scientific American*, September, pp. 110-17.

Goleman, D. 1985. *Vital lies, simple truths.* New York: Simon and Schuster.

Greenway, H. D. S. 1993. Scientists: Xenophobia may be an inherited trait. *The Bradenton Herald*(January 1), p. 1A.

Grof, S. 1992. *The Holotropic Mind.* New York: HarperCollins.

Hanchette, J. 1993. U.S. and the world: Americans closing ranks poll shows. *Lansing State Journal*(November 2), p. 3A.

Handlin, O. 1964. *The American people in the twentieth century.* Boston: Beacon Press.

Harmon, M. M., and Mayer, R. T. 1986 *Organization theory for public administration.* London: Scott/Foresman.

Hawke, D. F. 1988. *Everyday life in early America.* New York: Harper and Row.

Held, V. 1970. *The public interest and individual interests.* New York: Basic.

Heller, T. C., Sosna, M., and Wellbery, D. E. (Eds.). 1986. *Reconstructing individualism: autonomy, individuality, and the self in western thought.* Stanford, California: Stanford University Press.

Himmelfarb, G. (Ed.). 1962. *Essays on freedom and power: Lord Acton.* New York: The World.

Hinton, G. 1992. How neural networks learn from experience. *Scientific American*, September, pp. 145-51.

Hirschman, A. O. 1986. *Rival views of market society.* New York: Viking.

Hiskes, R. P. 1982. *Community without coercion: Getting along in the minimal state.* Newark: University of Delaware Press.

Hocking, W. E. 1940. *The lasting elements of individualism.* New Haven: Yale University Press.

Hofstadter, R. 1973. *The American political tradition: And the men who made it.* New York: Vintage.

Homer, F. D. 1983. *Character: An individualistic theory of politics.* New York: University Press of America.

Hoover, H. 1929. *American individualism.* New York: Doubleday/Doran

Honneth, A. 1991. *The critique of power: Reflective stages in a critical social theory.* Cambridge: MIT Press.

Honneth, A., and Jonas, H. (Eds.). 1991. *Communicative action: Essays on Jurgen Habermas's 'The theory of communicative action'.* Cambridge, U.K.: Polity Press.

Hsu, F. L. K. 1983. *Rugged individualism reconsidered: Essays in psychological anthropology.* Knoxville: University of Tennessee Press.

Huer, J. 1990. *The wages of sin: America's dilemma of profit against humanity.* New York: Praeger.

Hummel, R. P. 1987. *The bureaucratic experience.* New York: St. Martins Press.

Jehlin, M. 1986. *American incarnation: The individual, the nation, and the continent.* Cambridge: Harvard University Press.

Jones, J., and Baron, J. 1993. Intolerance: One common thread connecting nations. *The Westerner,* May, Vol. 13, No. 3, p. 1.

Jones, W. T. 1970. *A History of western philosophy .* 2d ed. 6 Vols. San Diego: Harcourt Brace Jovanovich.

Joseph, F. M. (Ed.). 1959. *As others see us: The United States through foreign eyes.* Princeton, New Jersey: Princeton University Press.

Joy, D. M. 1983. *Moral development foundations: Judeo-Christian alternatives to Piaget/Kohlberg.* Nashville: Abingdon Press.

Kallen, H. M. 1933. *Individualism: An American way of life.* New York: Liveright.

Kandel, E., and Hawkins, R. 1992. The biological basis of learning and individuality. *Scientific American,* September, pp. 78-86.

Katz, D., and Kahn, R. L. 1978. *The social psychology of organizations.* 2d ed. New York: John Wiley and Sons.

Keen, S. 1991. *Fire in the belly: On being a man.* New York: Bantam.

Keller, J. E. 1974. *Jean-Jacques Rosseau on the individual and society.* Lexington, Kentucky: The University Press of Kentucky.

Kelly, G. A. 1955. *The psychology of personal constructs.* New York: W. W. Norton.

Kimura, D. 1992. Sex differences in the brain. *Scientific American,* September, pp. 118-125.

Koford, K. J., and Miller, J. B. 1991. *Social norms and economic institutions.* Ann Arbor, Michigan: University of Michigan Press.

Kolenda, K. (Ed.). 1988. *Organizations and ethical individualism.*
New York: Praeger.
Lacour-Gayet, R. 1969. *Everyday life in the United States before the
Civil War 1830-1860.* New York: Frederick Ungar.
Lam, T., 1993. Stifling military style lingers in postal system.
Detroit Free Press(May 11), p. B1.
Langer, E. J. 1989. *Mindfulness.* New York: Addison-Wesley.
Lasch, C. 1978. *The culture of narcissism.* New York: W. W.
Norton.
------. 1991. *The true and only heaven: Progress and its critics.* New
York: W. W. Norton.
Laszlo, E. 1963. *Individualism, collectivism and political power: A
relational analysis of ideological conflict.* The Hague: Martinus
Nijhoff.
Lawler, E. E. 1992. *The ultimate advantage: Creating the high
involvement organization.* San Francisco: Jossey-Bass.
Leinberger, P., and Tucker, B. 1991. *The new individualists: A
generation after the organization man.* New York:
HarperCollins.
Leonard, T. 1988. *Day by day: The seventies.* New York: Facts on
File.
Lerner, E. J. 1991. *The big bang never happened.* New York: Times.
Lilla, M. T. 1981. Ethos, 'ethics' and public service. *The Public
Interest, 63,* 3-17.
Lindblom, C. E. 1990. *Inquiry and change: The troubled attempt to
understand and shape society.* New York: Yale University
Press.
Locke, L. F., Spirduso, W. W., and Silverman, S. J. 1987. *Proposals
that work.* 2d ed.. London: Sage Publications.
Lodge, G. C. 1986. *The new American ideology.* New York: New
York University Press.
London, H. I. 1981. *Myths that rule America.* Washington, D.C.:
University Press of America.
Luijpen, W. A., and Koren, H. J. 1969. *A first introduction to
existential phenomenology.* Pittsburgh: Duquense University
Press.
Lukes, S. 1974. *Individualism.* Oxford: Blackwell.
Lyotard, J. F. 1991. *Phenomenology.* Albany: State University of
New York Press.
Machan, T. R. 1989. *Individuals and their rights.* Lasalle, Illinois:
Open Court.

MacIntyre, A. 1981. *After virtue.* Notre Dame: University of Notre Dame Press.

MacKinnon, C. A. 1989. *Toward a feminist theory of the state.* Cambridge, Massachusetts: Harvard University Press.

Macpherson, C. B. 1979. *The political theory of possessive individualism: Hobbes to Locke.* London: Oxford University Press.

Marshall, C., and Rossman, G. B. 1989. *Designing qualitative research.* London: Sage.

Martine, B. J. 1984. *Individuals and individuality.* Albany, New York: State University of New York Press.

Mason, C. 1953. *Socrates: The man who dared to ask.* Boston: Beacon Press.

May, R. 1981. *Freedom and destiny.* New York: W. W. Norton.

Mayer, R. T. 1990. *The tug of history: Two decades in the American administrative state.* Unpublished manuscript, Western Michigan University, School of public Affairs and Administration.

McCabe, M. M. 1994. *Plato's individuals.* Princeton, New Jersey: Princeton University Press.

McClay, W. M. 1994. *The masterless: Self and society in modern America.* Chapel Hill, North Carolina: University of North Carolina Press

McSwain, C. J., and White, O. F. 1987. The case for lying, cheating, and stealing--personal development as ethical guidance for managers. *Administration and Society, 18*, 411-432.

Mead, M. 1967. *And keep your powder dry: An anthropologist looks at American character.* London: Ronald, Whiting and Wheaton.

Merelman, R. M. 1989. On culture and politics in America: A perspective from cultural anthropology. *British Journal of Political Science, 19*, pp. 465-493.

Merritt, J. D. 1979. *Day by day: The fifties.* New York: Facts on File.

Meyers, C. 1988. *Discovering Eve.* New York: Oxford University Press.

Michigan Catholic Conference. 1989. *Action on behalf of justice, volume six: Religion and politics in the 1980s and 1990s.* Lansing, Michigan: Michigan Catholic Conference.

Miller, J. C. 1960. *The federalist era.* New York: Harper & Row.

Mills, G. H. 1965. *Innocence and power: Individualism in twentieth century America.* Austin: University of Texas Press.

Morison, S. E. 1965. *The oxford history of the American people.* New York: Oxford University Press.

Muller, H. J. 1985. *The uses of the past: profiles of former societies.* New York: Schoken.

Neely, A. 1992. A diverse work force builds on differences. *Detroit Free Press*(April 27), p. F9.

New York v United States, 505 US 144; 120 L Ed 2d 120; 112 S Ct 2408; 60 LW 4603, 4608-4609 (1992).

Norton, D. L. 1991. *Democracy and moral development: A politics of virtue.* Los Angeles: University of California Press.

O'Conner, J. 1984. *Accumulation crisis.* New York: B. Blackwell.

O'Neill, J. 1973. *Modes of individualism and collectivism.* London: Heinemann Educational.

O' Neill, W. L. 1971. *Coming apart: An informal history of the United States in the 1960s.* Chicago: Quadrangle.

Oakley, J. R. 1986. *God's country: America in the fifties.* New York: Dembner.

Oates, S. B. 1982. *Let the trumpet sound.* New York: Harper and Row.

Ogilvy, J. (Ed.). 1992. *Revisioning philosophy.* Albany, New York: State University of New York Press.

Onimus, J. 1970. *Albert Camus and Christianity.* Montgomery, Alabama: University of Alabama Press.

Oniski, N. 1993. Walled Lake factory moves jobs to Mexico. *Detroit Free Press*(June 4), p. 1E.

Pant, A. 1983. *The survival of the individual.* London: Sangam.

Parker, T. 1983. *Day by day: The sixties.* New York: Facts on File.

Patterson, O. 1991. *Freedom.* New York: Basic.

Peck, M. S. 1978. *The road less traveled.* New York: Simon and Schuster.

Peck, M. S. 1987. *The different drum: Community making and peace.* New York: Simon and Schuster.

Perkins, M. L. 1974. *Jean-Jacques Rousseau on the individual and society.* Lexington: The University Press of Kentucky.

Perry, R. B. 1944. *Puritanism and democracy.* New York: The Vanguard Press.

Pessen, E. 1978. *Jacksonian America.* Homewood, Illinois: Dorsey.

Piore, M. J. 1995. *Beyond individualism.* Cambridge, Masschusetts: Harvard University Press.

Plato. 1986. *The republic.* Buffalo, New York: Prometheus.

Porubcansky, M. J. 1993. Hatred is the kinship that binds. *The Detroit News*(April 18), p. 9A.

Powell, C. S. 1992. Born yesterday: A younger universe may spell
    trouble for cosmology. *Scientific American*, May, pp. 28-29.
------. 1992. The golden age of cosmology. *Scientific American*, July,
    pp. 17-22.
------. 1992. A matter of timing. *Scientific American*, October, pp.
    26-31.
Rankin, H. D. 1964. *Plato and the individual*. New York: Barnes &
    Noble.
Rawls, J. 1971. *A theory of justice*. Cambridge, Massachusetts:
    Belknap.
Reynolds, C. H., and Norman, R. V. (Eds.). 1988. *Community in
    America*. Berkeley, California: University of California Press.
Ricci, J. 1990. How fathers learn about being fathers. *The
    Detroit Free Press* (June 18), p 1E.
Rice, Rev. E. G. 1990. Pastoral letter. *All Saints Messenger*,
October, pp. 1-2.
------. 1993. Bestowing human dignity as Christ has restored us. *All
    Saints Messenger*, January, p. 1-2.
Richardson, W. D., and Nigro, L. G. 1987. Administration ethics and
    founding thought: Constitutional correctives, honor and
    education. *Public Administration Review, 47*, 367-376.
Roberts, D. 1992. Geronimo. *National Geographic*, October,
    pp. 46-71.
Rodgers, D. T. 1978. *The work ethic in America 1850-1920*.
    Chicago: University of Chicago Press.
Roestenbaum, P. (1992). *Leadership: The inner side of greatness*.
    San Francisco: Jossey-Bass.
Russell, B. 1949. *Authority and the individual*. London: Alan &
    Unwin.
Ruthen, R. 1992. The cosmic microwave mirage? *Scientific
    American*, October, pp. 30.
Sagan C., and Druyan, A. 1992. *Shadows of forgotten ancestors: A
    search for who we are*. New York: Random House.
Schlesinger, A. 1992. *The disuniting of America*. New York: W. W.
    Norton.
Schubert, G. 1960. *The public interest*. Glencoe: Free Press.
Selkoe, D. 1992. Aging brain, aging mind. *Scientific American*,
    September, pp. 135-42.
Selznick, P. [1957]1984. *Leadership in administration: A
    sociological interpretation*. Los Angeles: University of
    California Press.

Senge, P. 1990. *The fifth discipline: The art and practice of the learning organization*. New York: Doubleday/Dell.

Shafer, R. J. 1980. *A guide to historical method*. 3d ed. Homewood, Illinois: Dorsey Press.

Shatz, C. 1992. The developing brain. *Scientific American*, September, pp. 60-67.

Skinner, Q., and Price, R. (Eds.). 1990. *Machiavelli: The prince*. Cambridge: Cambridge University Press.

Smith, K. K., and Berg, D. N. 1987. *Paradoxes of group life: Understanding conflict, paralysis and movement in group dynamics*. San Francisco: Jossey-Bass.

Spitz, D. (Ed.). 1975. *John Stuart Mill: On liberty*. New York: W. W. Norton.

St. Augustine. [1467]1984. *City of God*. London: Penguin.

Staff. Science and the citizen. 1992. *Scientific American*, October, p. 20.

Staff. 1993. The wild wild west. *Life*, (Special Issue, April 5), p. 10.

Staff. 1993. Here ruining people is considered sport. *Detroit Free Press*(August 11), p. 1A.

Stratton, E. 1986. *Plymouth colony: Its history and people*. Salt Lake City, Utah: Ancestry.

Talbot, M. 1991. *The holographic universe*. New York: HarperCollins.

Tarnas, R. 1991. *The passion of the western mind: Understanding the ideas that have shaped our world view*. New York: Harmony.

Thurow, L. 1992. *Head to head*. New York: Warner.

Torbert, W. R. 1991. *The power of balance: Transforming self, society, and scientific inquiry*. Newbury Park, California: Sage.

Tuck, R. (Ed.). 1991. *Hobbes: Leviathan*. Cambridge: Cambridge University Press.

Tucker, D. F. B. 1980. *Marxism and individualism*. New York: St. Martin's Press.

Ullmann, W. 1966. *The individual and society in the middle ages*. Baltimore: Johns Hopkins Press.

Versenyi, L. 1963. *Socratic humanism*. New Haven: Yale University Press.

Wallach, M. A. 1990. *Rethinking goodness*. Albany, New York: State University of New York Press.

Walters, R. G. 1978. *American reformers*. New York: Hill and Wang.

Waterman, A. S. 1984. *The psychology of individualism*. New York: Praeger.

Weber, M. 1976. *The Protestant ethic and the spirit of capitalism.*
London: Allen and Unwin.

Westcott, M. R. 1988. *The psychology of human freedom. New York: Springer-Verlag.*

Wilson, J. Q. 1993. *The moral sense.* New York: Free Press.

Wilson, R. W., and Schochet, G. J. 1980. *Moral development and politics.* New York: Praeger.

Witcutt, W. P. 1958. *The rise and fall of the individual.* London: S.P.C.K.

Woelfel, J. W. 1975. *Camus: A theological perspective.* New York: Abingdon Press.

Wolin, R. 1990. *The politics of being: The political thought of Martin Heidegger.* New York: Columbia University Press.

------. 1991. *The Heidegger controversy: A critical reader.* New York: Columbia University Press.

Wolin, S. S. 1960. *Politics and vision: continuity and innovation in western political thought.* Berkeley: Little/Brown.

Wood, C. W. 1927. *The myth of the individual.* New York: John Day.

Wood, G. S. 1969. *The creation of the American republic, 1776-1781.* New York: W. W. Norton.

Woodworth, F. L. 1991. President's page. *Michigan Bar Journal, 70,* 1275-76.

Zeki, S. 1992. The visual image in mind and brain. *Scientific American,* September, pp. 68-76.

Zinn, H. 1980. *A people's history of the United States.* New York: Harper & Row.

------. 1990. *Declarations of independence: Cross-examining American ideology.* New York: HarperCollins.

Index

About the Author

R. Philip Brown is a baby-boomer, growing up in small-town America during the late Forties, Fifties, and early Sixties. His parents owned and operated the only movie theater in his home town of 1800 people. As he grew-up, Phil rode his bicycle, worked the theater, bailed hay for local farmers, and played high school sports. The only thing remarkable about this part of his life was the number of teachers in his family. His grandfather, grandmother, mother, and two of his mother's sisters were teachers, which meant he was always learning.

He married Nancy, a teacher, in 1969 and is the father of three children; Patricia Anne, Stephanie Janelle, and Arick Michael. Patricia and her husband, David, are teachers in northern Michigan; Stephanie is an Education sophomore in college; and Arick, also a sophomore iin college, studies Chemical Engineering. This means that Phil is still always learning.

As a defense lawyer for the Michigan Attorney General for twenty years, and as an Adjunct Assistant Professor for Western Michigan University and Central Michigan University, Phil spends his entire working life in service to the public. The position of Assistant Attorney General in the State of Michigan immerses him in government policy decision-making at both the state and federal levels. As a career public lawyer, he comes face-to-face with the issues of individualism on a daily basis, both in a constitutional law context and as a part of American social culture.

These experiences made him a student of political and social processes, and Phil earned the Doctor of Public Administration degree in 1994. He has published on legal and social issues before, but this is his first book. According to his observation, American politics and culture have come to revere a radical form of individualism and to adopt self-interest as their ethos. This work attempts to understand that phenomenon and to change it by offering citizens, managers, organizational leaders, and public administrators a new way to think about the social role organizations should play in our lives.